THE
THRU-HIKER'S
HANDBOOK

THE THRU-HIKER'S HANDBOOK

Dan "Wingfoot" Bruce

1992 Edition
Appalachian Trail Conference

The Appalachian Trail Conference
Washington & Jackson Streets
P.O. Box 807
Harpers Ferry, West Virginia 25425-0807

ISBN 0-917953-54-1

For additional information and a complete list of guidebooks and maps to the Appalachian Trail, contact the Appalachian Trail Conference at the above address, or call 304-535-6331, Monday through Friday, between 9 a.m. and 5 p.m., Eastern Time.

To Margaret Drummond,
ATC chair and friend of thru-hikers,
for her many years of service
to the Appalachian Trail.

Contents

Introduction

The Thru-hiker's Handbook is for people attempting to become Appalachian Trail "2,000-Milers," either by hiking the A.T. in one continuous end-to-end journey or in a series of long section hikes. It contains basic information about trip planning, traditions and practices of thru-hiking, things of interest on the Trail, and businesses and services in Trail towns. It has been written with one purpose in mind— to help you enjoy your time on the A.T. to the fullest.

The information contained here is the result of the best effort of the author, using information gathered in person or supplied by ATC staffers, A.T. club members, past thru-hikers, and other individuals interested in serving the hiking community of 1992. Reality will have changed since printing, however. Some businesses will have closed, reopened under new management, adjusted their prices and hours, or varied the services they offer to hikers. Hostels will have revised their policies. Trail relocations will have modified directions and distances to some facilities. In other words, the information provided here was the very latest available at publication date, but *you should expect surprises*. In a like manner, keep in mind that a listing in this handbook is not an endorsement or guarantee of businesses and services. Common sense should be exercised.

Invitation to Handbook Users

This publication depends on user feedback to keep it current and useful. Many users took the time to contribute information and ideas last year, and your hike will be easier and more enjoyable this year because they did. You can contribute to next year's edition by sending the following:

- *Corrections*, such as closed businesses, changed prices, changed post office hours, etc.
- *Omissions*, such as new businesses and services (with a mailing address, so that I can contact them for information), Trail relocations, etc.
- *Clarifications*, especially in reference to mileage figures, directions to and from the Trail, descriptions of services offered, etc.
- *Evaluations* of businesses and services (friendliness to hikers, quality of service, etc.)
- *Questions* about the Trail that occur to you as you hike (If you have a question, someone next year will probably wonder about the same thing, too).
- *Problems or helpful hints* about the Trail or thru-hiking that you feel should be passed along to the folks who hike next year.
- *Wildlife notes* (type of animal, where spotted, date sighted, time of day).
- *Wildflower notes* (type wildflower, location, date seen, number of plants).
- *History notes* (American, A.T., or native American) about sites on or near the Trail.
- *Quotes* (yours or other's, humorous or thoughtful) that capture the spirit of thru-hiking and the A.T. experience.

1

- *Artwork* depicting nature or Trail scenes (small black-and-white drawings only).
- *Photographs* that capture the thru-hiking experience (the best may possibly be used as the cover photo for the 1993 edition; black-and-white only, vertical scenes given preference).

As you hike along this year, write down information and questions in your copy of the handbook and send them to me at the end of your hike, or, if you prefer, send me cards and letters from time to time. I'll use your notes to provide next year's thru-hikers with the latest Trail information available, and you'll be listed as a contributor. Comments and suggestions for improving the usefulness of this book would also be appreciated. When you send me your ideas and information, feel free to include a Trail photo of yourself and a few personal comments about your thru-hike, because I really enjoy getting to know the people who use and contribute to this publication. I'll look forward to hearing from you.

Write to:

Dan "Wingfoot" Bruce
2520 Country Club Drive
Conyers, Georgia 30208

P.S. —I welcome telephone comments and inquiries during the following times: 7pm-10pm (Eastern time) on Wednesday, Saturday, and Sunday evenings. Call 404-922-1889.

How to Use This Handbook

This handbook is intended to be a general guide; it does not try to tell you how to hike the Trail. It assumes you are a person who wants to explore and evaluate things for yourself. Basic information is given— enough to point you in a particular direction, if you have an interest, with perhaps a comment from a past thru-hiker to add color. But, this publication does not recommend one facility, service, or Trail experience over another. It does encourage you to be adventurous, to use the information in this book as a springboard for a personal journey of exploration and discovery.

The entire book, except for the planning section, is intended to be carried with you during your hike. It is designed to be used with the *A.T. Data Book* and has ten chapter divisions that correspond, in reverse direction, to the main chapters in that publication. It is oriented primarily to the hiker going south to north, and all references to direction from the Trail, either to the right or left, are from the viewpoint of the northbounder.

Place names, directions, and mileage figures used in this publication are, with few exceptions, the same as those in the *Data Book*. A small diamond (♦) precedes information about places located more than 0.5 mile off the Trail. Town names are shown in bold print, with the most frequently used towns shown in capital letters as well.

The information in the ten chapters can be divided into two categories, Trail-related and town-related.

Trail-related information concerns things to be seen, heard, investigated, or considered as you hike along in the woods, such as shelters and their water sources, views and overlooks, sites important in American and/or A.T. history, places associated with native American activities, wildlife, wildflowers, and trees.
- Wildlife notes are placed in the text to indicate an area where past thru-hikers have often sighted the featured animal, although most animals can be assumed to range from Georgia to Maine unless noted otherwise.
- Wildflower notes are given for some of the more common varieties growing from Springer Mountain to Damascus, Virginia. Placement in the text is based on probable location of first sighting, and brief descriptions are included to help you identify the featured plant.

Town-related information deals primarily with businesses and services located near road crossings or in Trail towns (*i.e.*, towns either on the A.T. or within easy walking or hitching distance). Consistency has been attempted when describing Trail towns, but they vary considerably in the way they are used by thru-hikers, and so do the descriptions. Keep in mind that few towns have all services and that full information about some services is always lacking at time of publication. Except when clarity dictated otherwise, the following order has been followed when describing towns and services:

3

- *Town/state:* population, brief description of town.
- *Hostel:* mailing address (if it can be used as maildrop), telephone number, description of facilities and services, cost, special notes, and directions to hostel or street location.
- *Lodging:* rates (for single, double, each additional person), maximum number permitted to share a room, special features (air conditioning, television, cable, telephone in room, swimming pool, laundry, *etc.*), restrictions on pets, dates of operation (unless year-round), credit cards honored, and special notes.
- *Places to eat:* meals served (breakfast/lunch/dinner), type of eatery or description of food, menu items mentioned by past thru-hikers, AYCE specials and times, credit cards honored, dates of operation (unless year-round), business days and hours, and special notes. Fast-food outlets are listed without description unless they offer unusual services, such as AYCE specials.
- *Places to buy groceries:* rating as to suitability for resupplying (based on author's survey and hiker feedback), business days and hours, and special notes.
- *Laundromats:* availability of front-loading washers, business days and hours, and time for last load. Detergent and change can be assumed to be available on premises unless noted otherwise.
- *Stove fuels:* sources, types, and smallest quantity available for sale.
- *Outfitters:* brands of gear carried, special services, credit cards honored, business days and hours, and telephone number.
- *Cobblers:* notes on one-day service, special services, and business days and hours.
- *Other services:* bank, Western Union, ATM networks (Cirrus, Plus, *etc.*), pharmacy, drug store (mentioned only if town has no pharmacy), hardware store, department store, doctor, dentist, health clinic, hospital, veterinarian, movie theatre, UPS/FedEx pick-up, and special services not listed elsewhere.
- *Transportation services:* in-town shuttle, intracity bus service, Greyhound (or similar interstate) bus service, and taxi service.
- *Points of interest:* natural, historical, or unique features in or near the Trail town.
- *Special events:* festivals, parades, concerts, *etc.*
- *Friend(s) of hikers:* people who are usually available to help in an emergency, sometimes available to provide transportation and other kindnesses as their time and finances permit.
- *Post office and ZIP Code:* window hours, telephone number, special notes, and frequency of use (indicated by "LY-" followed by the number of hikers using the post office last year); information given only for locations used by 20 or more thru-hikers in 1991.
- *Nearby towns:* towns within easy hitching distance offering basic services, especially if services offered are not available in the Trail town.

The information in this handbook is organized to reflect the order in which places and things will be encountered on the Trail and contains details about far more things than you will have time or energy to sample on your trip. Since you won't be able to see or do everything, you should form the habit of reading several pages ahead so that you can anticipate and take advantage of the things that most interest or concern you. This is doubly important for southbounders, since information about regulations and permits is positioned in the text to alert the northbound hiker. Many past readers have found it useful to highlight or underline, beforehand, information that seems especially important or interesting.

Supplemental information also is included in this book:
- "Traditions and Practices" should be read before you start your hike and reviewed from time to time as you go along. Much of the material it contains will take on new meaning as you gain experience and perspective on the Trail.
- The telephone numbers for many equipment suppliers and manufacturers are listed and will be useful if you have problems with your gear.
- The hours and telephone numbers for the most frequently used post offices are listed for quick reference. This listing is especially useful for addressing maildrops and for changing plans during your hike.
- The glossary of Trail terms will help you quickly develop a new Trail vocabulary and contains both hiking and maintenance terms and abbreviations.
- "Planning Information" will help you before you begin your hike. This section is not needed during your hike and has been placed in the back so it can be easily removed before you head for the Trail.

Abbreviations

Lodging: S—single, D—double, S/D—single or double, DO—double occupancy, EAP—each additional person, # max—maximum number permitted in a room. *Places to eat:* B—breakfast, L—lunch, D—dinner, AYCE—all you can eat. *Laundromats:* FLW—front-loading washers. *Credit cards:* MC—MasterCard, Visa—Visa, Dis—Discover, AE—American Express, DC—Diners Club, CB—Carte Blanche. *Shipping services:* UPS—United Parcel Service, FedEx—Federal Express.

Traditions and Practices

The adventure of thru-hiking began in 1948, when Earl Shaffer became the first person to hike the entire Appalachian Trail in one continuous journey. Since then, thousands have followed in Earl's footsteps. One by one, over the years, they collectively have defined and established the traditions and practices of modern recreational thru-hiking. This section shares some of the cumulative knowledge and advice handed down by past thru-hikers. It also will acquaint you with customs and etiquette generally observed by A.T. thru-hikers today.

Safety Precautions

Personal safety is not a source of constant concern for most thru-hikers, for good reason. Statistically, the A.T. is one of the safest places in America. Few thru-hikers encounter challenges to their personal safety. However, you should keep in mind that the ills of society sometimes intrude on the normally idyllic Trail experience. Be aware that incidents of harassment can occur, especially in or near towns and along roads. Always be alert for trouble, and use common sense when approaching or being approached by strangers. Pay attention to the location, appearance, and behavior of strangers. Be friendly but cautious in your conversations, and avoid people who act strange, provocative, hostile, or drunk. Pack up and move on if you don't feel comfortable. Don't share your hiking plans with strangers, and don't provide information about the plans and whereabouts of other hikers, especially during town visits. If possible, travel with a hiking partner or as part of a small group. Avoid camping near roads or towns, or in areas with easy public access. Wear clothing that will not invite unwelcome attention. Refrain from carrying firearms, large knives, Mace, and other defensive weapons. They are unnecessary on the Trail and, in many areas, illegal. ATC has no law enforcement of its own but advises, "If you witness or are a victim of harassment or other crime, promptly report the incident to local law-enforcement authorities and also to the ATC at 304-535-6331, so that steps can be taken to enforce the law and prevent a recurrence."

Equipment safety is not a major concern for thru-hikers, either. Hikers generally observe a very strict code of honor when it comes to equipment, and few instances of tampering or theft are reported on the A.T. Nevertheless, you should avoid leaving your gear unguarded, especially in areas with easy access to the public, and you should *never* leave it unattended at road crossings or in towns. When you go into restaurants or other businesses, ask if they have a safe, out-of-the-way place to drop your gear inside or, if you must leave it outside, position it so that you can watch it from inside. Use your pack raincover to make zippers and pockets less accessible. Dirty socks hanging on your pack will also discourage interest. Theft should be reported as above.

Health Hazards

Blisters are preventable, so be alert for "hot spots." Apply moleskin at the first indication of tenderness, then tighten boots to prevent slippage. If a blister should develop, first wash the area, and apply antibiotic ointment. Sterilize a needle in a flame, and drain the swollen area from the edge. Try not to tear the distended skin. Apply more antibiotic ointment, cover with a sterile pad (or Second Skin by Spenco), then cover the pad with a larger piece of moleskin. If the distended skin is badly torn, treat as above but trim the torn skin before covering. In either case, change the dressing at least daily, to prevent infection.

Chafing is a very painful condition most often caused by the pressure of pack straps and waist belts against the skin or by skin rubbing against skin between the legs. It is usually aggravated by sweat. The best treatment for mild cases is the application of corn starch or medicated powder. If you are sweating profusely, an ointment or Vaseline may be more effective. At the end of the day, wash the chafed area, apply a light coating of antibiotic cream, and expose to air. Also, during the hottest months, you may want to carry a small tube of skin cream to alleviate rectal inflammation, a very painful condition encountered by many thru-hikers each year.

Athlete's foot can be neglected for a few hours back home, but, if left untreated even briefly while thru-hiking, it can cause major problems. Stop immediately, and wash the infected area before applying a fungicide. If possible, change to clean socks. Apply more medicine, and air your feet every time you take a rest break. Jock itch is another form of the same infection and is treated in a similar manner.

Poison ivy is an easily recognized plant ("leaves of three, let them be") abundant along the Trail. Any time you come into contact with the sap by bruising or brushing a plant in any season, you can have an allergic reaction. Symptoms are an itch and reddening skin, followed by seeping blisters. The problem can last for several days. When first exposed, wash the area with a non-oily soap. Treat with an over-the-counter lotion designed specifically for poison ivy. If these measures don't work in a few days, you should seek medical help, before the problem gets out of hand.

Ticks are bloodsuckers that usually get on you in high-grass areas. They don't attach immediately, so chances are you will be able to simply pick them off. If one does attach, however, you must gently extract the critter. Use care not to mash the tick's body fluids back into your bloodstream or break off its head under your skin. Try holding the glowing end of an extinguished match next to the tick, or try to suffocate it by covering its body with oil or insect repellent. If one of these measures doesn't make the tick release, you will need to use tweezers. After removal, wash and treat the bite as you would any puncture wound.

Lyme disease is caused by a bacterium transmitted by the painless bite of the deer tick, which is about the size of the letter "o" on this page. The tick must stay attached from 10 to 12 hours to pass on this still-rare infection. Shortly after infection, many folks seem to have flu-like symptoms such as headache, stiff neck, fever, muscle aches, fatigue, and vomiting. Sometimes a rash will appear days or even weeks later—often raised, red, and doughnut-shaped around the bite—or it can appear in various shapes anywhere on the body. Later symptoms include stiff joints and swollen glands. Your doctor may not immediately think to look for Lyme disease, so mention the possibility of exposure when you seek treatment for these or similar symptoms. No cases of Lyme disease were reported among thru-hikers last year.

Stings from insects (yellow jackets being the most common stingers on the A.T.) are normally a minor annoyance that varies widely in occurrences from year to year. Most folks hike the entire Trail without being stung once, and the few that are stung usually just say a few choice words and continue hiking. If you do get stung, move on quickly to avoid being stung again. It is also important to remove the stinger properly by scraping it off with a knife blade, taking care not to squeeze the poison sacks that are probably still attached. If you know you have a severe allergic reaction to insect stings, you should seek medical advice about field treatment before you begin your hike.

Snake bites are rare on the A.T. If you watch where you step, your chances of being bitten by a snake are very, very small. Your chances of being bitten by a poisonous snake are even smaller, and, even if poisonous, only about 50 percent inject venom. In the event venom is injected, you will have pain, redness, and swelling. The best course of action is to remain calm, tie a loose cord around your arm or leg, between the bite and your torso (don't cut off circulation!), and get to a doctor. If you can do so safely, kill the snake for later identification. As for the usefulness of snakebite kits, the experts are still divided. Should you decide to use one, follow its instructions precisely. Avoid the use of alcohol or stimulants. No snakebites were reported by thru-hikers last year.

Giardia lamblia enters your system when you drink water contaminated by infected animals (beavers being the most common culprit, hence the popular nickname, "beaver fever"). Early symptoms include gas, cramps, and diarrhea, and you may at first think you have a simple case of "the runs." *Giardia* is diarrhea that won't go away in a few days, and you will need to get prescription medication from a doctor to cure it. In the meantime, drink plenty of liquids to avoid dehydration. Several thru-hikers were treated for *giardia* last year.

Hypothermia results when the body's heat production cannot keep up with heat loss. It usually happens when the air temperature is between 25-50°F, aggravated by conditions of hunger, fatigue, wind, and wetness. Early indications are a general chill, tiredness, and irritability. Definite signs include slurred speech, loss of motor control and upper body strength, lethargy, and convulsive shivering. Rapid warming is the best treatment. Take shelter, remove wet clothes, get into dry clothes and a sleeping bag, and drink hot liquids.

Heat exhaustion occurs when the body's cooling system overloads. So much blood goes to the skin that internal organs are deprived. Early signs include faintness and nausea. You'll sweat profusely, your skin will feel strangely cool, and your face will be pale. Fortunately, you won't feel like hiking anymore, and that's good. Seek shade and lay down. Loosen or remove some clothing. Sip on lightly salted water or a Gatorade-type drink. In half-an-hour, you'll be able to resume your trek—at a more leisurely pace, of course.

Heat stroke is life-threatening, with symptoms that are very different from those of simple heat exhaustion. You will stop sweating and feel suffocatingly hot. Your skin will feel hot and be very dry to the touch, and you may be on the verge of losing consciousness.

Immediate cooling is the only treatment. If you can, lay down in a stream or lake, or pour water over your body. If you are with companions, ask them to massage your arms and legs to increase blood flow. Once you have recovered sufficiently, leave the Trail, and seek immediate medical treatment.

Lightning should be considered a real danger on the Trail. If you are caught in a thunderstorm on a mountaintop or ridge, get to a lower elevation if there is time, or take cover among same-sized boulders if not. If in an exposed meadow, take cover among the surrounding trees if there is time, or crouch down if not. If possible, insulate yourself with a sleeping pad or other nonconducting object, but don't lie flat. Get away from your pack and other metal objects. In general, avoid prominent rocks, cliffs, and the tallest trees. Try not to be, or be near, the highest point in your vicinity.

Trail Ethics

Low-impact hiking requires that you stay on the designated footpath and avoid taking shortcuts, especially at switchbacks, since the Trail route is selected and built to control erosion and minimize damage to the environment. Always walk single file and stay to the inside when slabbing around mountains. In camp, use established paths to the water source and privy.

Litter never occurs naturally—it's a people problem. Help keep the A.T. free of litter by not discarding candy wrappers, cigarette butts, orange peels, and other such nondegradable or slowly degrading items. You can be even more helpful if, each day, you will pick up a piece or two of litter carelessly left by someone else. In camp, don't leave unburned trash (especially foil food packaging) in the fireplace, even if it would make good firestarter for those coming in after you. Pack out everything you carry in.

Water quality depends on a little extra care on your part. Wash yourself, your clothes, or your dishes away from springs, streams, and lakes. Do your cleaning and empty the dirty water well away from water sources. Use care with soaps, since even biodegradable soaps can pollute. If you are traveling with a pet, keep it away from water sources. Other hikers will not appreciate your pet's walking around in their drinking water.

Sanitation in the woods is essential to the good health of all who venture outdoors. Use a privy or outhouse when one is available, instead of the woods (some areas request that hikers urinate in the woods). Privies are located to protect against contamination of nearby water sources. When you do use the woods, dig a shallow hole, and cover it thoroughly afterwards. Do this at least 50 feet from the Trail and 200 feet from water (even farther from shelters without a privy). If you are traveling with a pet, dispose of its droppings as you would your own.

Campsites are a luxury in today's woods. You should avoid camping in heavy-use or fragile areas, and observe local regulations that limit or prohibit camping. In general, camp only on public lands or at designated campsites. Try not to build new fire rings, and always restore your campsite to its original condition before moving on.

Campfires add much to the outdoor experience but place a great demand on limited forest resources. Use a stove for cooking instead of building a campfire. If you do build a fire, keep it small, and use only "down" wood (dead wood lying on the ground). Do not use the emergency wood supply left in and under shelters by thoughtful hikers, unless you have an emergency.

Living in harmony with nature should be your goal in the woods. As you move along the Trail, seek to be one with nature, and learn to appreciate the abundant life it contains. Realize that the A.T. serves as a protective corridor for many species of plants and animals, some of which are rare or endangered. Leave the wild foods for the animals. Leave the wildflowers for your fellow hikers to enjoy. Resist the novice's urge to conquer and destroy the outdoor environment.

Trail Etiquette

Private property still comprises about three percent of the Trail. Respect the privacy and rights of private landowners. Always close gates to pastures. Refrain from sampling apples, corn, and other tempting crops. Do not assume that, just because the Trail goes near or through private property, you have free run of the place.

Group travel should be limited to small groups. ATC requests that hikers travel in groups of ten or less. Thru-hikers rarely travel in groups as large as ten, since the dynamics of such groups tend to diminish the thru-hiking experience. Some do form into smaller informal groups, however, usually to the benefit of all concerned. If you are part of a group, resist the urge to be clique-ish with other hikers. Try not to exclude others from your activities, especially in shelters, and value diversity.

Pets impact on all Trail users. ATC recommends that you leave your pet at home. If you do decide to thru-hike with a pet, control it at all times while hiking, and consider leashing it in camp. Be careful your pet does not intimidate other hikers, and be doubly careful that it doesn't interfere with others while they are cooking, eating, and sleeping. Most hikers prefer not to sleep with animals, so keep your pet off the sleeping platform in shelters, even on rainy nights. Know that you are responsible for cleaning or repairing the equipment of others, to their satisfaction, should your pet soil or damage it.

Shelters and lean-tos are available to the public on a first-come, first-served basis. Thru-hikers have no special right to shelter space at the expense of others. If a shelter is full when you arrive, you should be prepared to camp elsewhere. When you are first into a shelter, don't occupy all the space. Leave room for those coming in after you, and make them feel welcome. If you are a late arriver or early riser, remember that quiet time is from dusk until dawn. If you choose to stay in a shelter a second night (unless you are sick or injured), fairness says that you should offer to set up your tent if the shelter begins to fill with newcomers. In bad or threatening weather, always make room for additional hikers seeking shelter. As "Spot" of '91 observed, "On a rainy night, the shelter is full when everyone is in it!"

Trail registers communicate with and entertain those who follow. They are used primarily by thru-hikers but are read by many others (including children and an occasional reporter). When you write something in a register, be sure the content of your entry reflects well on thru-hikers and on the Appalachian Trail. Be creative, but stay within the bounds of good taste. Avoid the use of profanity and vulgarisms. If you come to a shelter that has no register, or a full register, you are free to leave your own if you carry out and forward the old register to its owner, but under no circumstances should you leave a duplicate if the original register is still being used. Try not to have more than two registers active on the Trail at once.

Good manners are always in style during your hike. Be considerate and respectful of townspeople, and never forget that you are a guest in Trail towns. When using businesses, especially restaurants, remember that other patrons are not tuned in to sweaty bodies, dirty socks, and earthy language. In hostels, behave as you would at home with your own family. Don't make a mess bathing or cooking, and leave it for someone else to tidy up after you. Observe the house rules. Most hostels have them posted, so look for them when you arrive. Check with someone in authority about using alcohol and tobacco at hostels. If in doubt, refrain. Make sure that pets are welcomed by the hostel and other hikers before bringing them inside, and always keep your pet out of the cooking and sleeping areas.

Attitudes and Choices

Rules on the A.T. are relatively few and far between, and the ones that do exist are not meant to limit your freedom but have been designed to allow as much freedom to as many people as possible. For the most part, the rules you encounter have been written by dedicated conservationists and Trail workers who value personal freedom as much as you do. You will no doubt be tempted to ignore a seemingly pointless rule somewhere along the way. Before you do, however, ask yourself, "What would happen if a thousand other thru-hikers decide to do the same this year?" An honest answer often brings the value of a rule into its proper perspective.

The Golden Rule, "Do unto others as you would have them do unto you," is a good rule to live by on the A.T., and most of the problems that develop among thru-hikers could be eliminated if this simple rule were observed by everyone hiking the Trail. It requires that you value and respect your fellow hikers in the same way you expect them to value and respect you. It also requires you to consider the effect your actions will have on those around you and, equally important, on those behind you. Remember that "Trail magic" for you is usually the result of good impressions left by your hiking predecessors. Pass it on.

Generosity is often bestowed on thru-hikers by strangers. Some thru-hikers begin to take this generosity for granted. Some even come to expect or demand it. Remember, no one owes you special treatment because you are a thru-hiker. It was your choice to hike the Trail from end to end and submit yourself to the rigors involved in doing so. Nevertheless, many kind folks will rejoice in your trip and extend favors along the way. When this "Trail magic" happens, be thankful. Express your gratitude, and look for ways to include these new friends in your adventure. Also, get their names and addresses, so you can send them a note of thanks later.

Community spirit develops among thru-hikers as the miles go by. People really get to know, understand, and appreciate one another. You can seriously diminish this sense of community if you are openly judgmental or critical of others. Your critical attitude will create tensions and barriers that interrupt the feelings of good-will so valued by the thru-hiking community. If you have a gripe about another hiker, go to that individual, and discuss the matter face-to-face in friendship and in private. Don't involve others, and don't ever air your grievances in the Trail registers. Look for the good qualities in people, and value their uniqueness. Learn to do the same with yourself. That's what much of the Trail experience is all about.

Individualism and thru-hiking are synonymous, but every year there are people who seem to think that thru-hiking has well-defined rules and a correct way of doing things (usually their way!). Truth is, more than 2,400 people have hiked the entire Trail, and no two have done it exactly the same. There is no "ordained way" to hike the A.T., so develop a philosophy and style of thru-hiking that is satisfying to you, and allow others the freedom to do the same.

White blazes mark the official Appalachian Trail, and that raises a question. Must you hike every white blaze on your thru-hike? Only you can answer that question, and it's something you must decide early in your hike. Ask yourself, "Will it lessen my feeling of accomplishment at the end of my hike if I haven't walked every mile of the A.T. between Georgia and Maine?" Your answer will determine whether you should stick to the official white-blazed path or go your own way. Whichever you decide, don't try to impose your decision on anyone else. Be responsible for the way you do your hike, and let others be responsible for the way they do theirs. Realize that those who waste time and energy monitoring the manner in which others hike are probably not having a very rewarding experience themselves.

Competition and records have their place in the world of organized sports, but both are out of place on the A.T. Competitive activities and claims of superiority (fastest hike, most hikes, *etc.*) have been deemed from the earliest days of the Trail project to be a serious degradation of the equalitarian and recreational (some say *re-creational*) values of the Appalachian Trail, not in keeping with its primary purpose of allowing individuals to "seek fellowship with the wilderness." For this reason, ATC has never established competitive standards, sanctioned attempts to set records, or recognized records for thru-hiking the A.T., nor has any other responsible hiking organization.

Commercial ventures, including charity fund-raising hikes that attempt to solicit money or other services from Trail neighbors or those hiking the Trail, are contrary to the spirit of the A.T. and may violate federal laws against business activities on public lands. In a like manner, the Trail should not be used as a "soap box" for the promotion of personal crusades—political, religious, dietary, *etc.*—especially in captive-audience situations, such as occur in shelters and registers. Most thru-hikers come to the Trail to get away from such pressures.

Observations and Advice

The A.T. is not an updated version of an old Indian trail dating back to antiquity. Instead, it has been built entirely in this century by thousands of dedicated men and women and is maintained today by 5,000 selfless volunteers who donate their time, sweat, muscles, and money to keep it open and enjoyable. In a very real sense, the Appalachian Trail is a gift from these people to you. When you meet maintainers at work, let them know how much you appreciate the fine job they do. If they ask about Trail conditions, and they usually will, feel free to tell them about problems, but do so constructively, not critically. If it's convenient to them, you may want to join them for a few hours of Trail work and fellowship. You can also help the maintaining clubs by reporting Trail problems to the appropriate ATC regional representative. See page 158, *How to Report Trail Problems.*

Information sources vary in their reliability. The *Data Book* and this handbook are reliable sources of printed Trail information. Both are revised yearly in late fall. The guidebooks and maps are revised less frequently but are generally reliable for most thru-hiking purposes (if the white blazes contradict the guidebook, follow the blazes!). Hikers traveling in the opposite direction can be a valuable source of information about changes not listed in any publications. Form the habit of asking them about Trail conditions and water sources just ahead. Don't depend on neighbors for specific information about the A.T., no matter how friendly and well-meaning they seem. Most have never traveled very far on the Trail, and few know what it's all about.

Water sources are generally safe, but you must still be selective about the sources you choose. Rely on springs and small, fast-moving streams flowing from protected water-sheds. Avoid warm, shallow, or stagnant pools, and don't drink downstream from a campsite or Trail crossing. Exercise extra caution when the Trail goes through low areas or fields used by livestock. Since no water source along the A.T. can be guaranteed safe, purify all drinking water, including water used to wash dishes and brush teeth, to be absolutely safe.

Food protection is constantly required on the A.T. When camping away from a shelter in bear country, food should be hung from a tree—at least 15 feet above the ground and five feet away from both the trunk and the supporting limb. In shelters, bags should be protected from mice. Usually, hanging your food by a cord from a rafter nail is sufficient, but sometimes more elaborate measures are required. No food residue should be left in your pack, and pockets should be left unzipped to allow inspection without the mice having to gnaw through. Woolen items should be wrapped in a plastic bag to discourage mice from shredding them for nesting material. Never sleep with food in your tent. Skunks or bears prowling around outside can make for a very restless night, or worse.

Dogs and wildlife are not compatible. Traveling with a dog decreases the number of wildlife sightings you will have on the A.T. but increases the probability that you will have an encounter with a skunk or porcupine. If your dog gets sprayed, use "Skunk Off" or tomato juice to neutralize the odor. If your pet gets quilled, remove what quills you can with a pair of pliers, and get your dog to a vet for professional treatment.

Boot problems usually involve delamination of the Vibram or rubber sole. The best glue for repairing this problem, according to a thru-hiking cobbler, is "Barge Cement", sold by many hardware stores and some outfitters. Here's the procedure: Dry boots thoroughly (I can hear you laughing now!), roughen the surfaces with #40-grit sandpaper, then follow the gluing instructions found on the tube. Allow glue to set up overnight. If you have done a good repair job, your boots will wear well for perhaps hundreds of miles, or at least until you can visit a cobbler or get new boots.

Sleeping bags (both down and synthetic) can be washed successfully during your hike, but use only a front-loading machine to wash your bag. Agitator types will tear it apart. Pick the cycle for delicate fabrics, and use cold water for both wash and rinse. Add Woolite or Ivory Flakes little by little until the wash water is sudsy, but be careful not to use too much soap. Dry on the lowest dryer setting, and check often for overheating. Toss in a clean sneaker as a down bag is drying, to help restore loft. Airing your bag regularly in sunlight will help keep it fresh.

Hitchhiking may make you feel awkward at first, but hitching is the easiest way to get to towns near the Trail. Your pack will quickly identify you to townspeople as a Trail hiker instead of a transient, so keep it visible. Smile, and present a responsible appearance. In heavy-traffic areas, pick a spot with a wide shoulder or pull-off beyond you in the direction you are heading. When putting your pack in someone's trunk, mentally note their license number. Carry your wallet concealed on your person, so you won't lose it if the driver absconds with your pack. Pickup trucks make good rides, allowing you to stay in back with your pack, but watch for grease and chemicals that may soil or damage your gear. Never yell or signal insults at drivers that pass you by. Important: Decline a ride if you don't like the feel of things; trust your instincts.

Towns always will be eagerly anticipated after a week in the woods, but the abrupt return to civilization may disorient you somewhat. As a 1987 hiker observed, "Towns are intense!"—so much so that many thru-hikers complain they never seem to get anything done in town. Some have found that it helps to make a list of town chores the night before reaching a town, then do them as soon as they arrive. Go to the post office, do laundry, buy groceries (except last-minute perishables), find fuel, *etc.* Once these essential chores are out of the way, you can mentally relax and have truly leisure time for writing letters, catching up on your journal, mending equipment, visiting with friends, sleeping, and so on. After a day or so in town, you once again will be eager for the woods.

Partners are like packs. Having the right one makes a thru-hike just that much more enjoyable, but having the wrong one will be a constant irritation. If you and your partner are not getting along, try hiking separately for a few days. If you aren't looking forward to the reunion, then it's probably time to go it alone. Few partnerships last for the entire summer, usually because the partners have different hiking paces and develop dissimilar interests. Most thru-hikers prefer to hike without a permanent partner, instead enjoying the company of many short-term companions along the way.

Hiking Advice

Daily mileage should take a back seat to common sense at the start of your hike. Each day, go far enough to feel that you are making progress, but not so far as to cause major discomfort or injury. When other hikers are faster, don't chase them. You can't hike someone else's hike, so keep to the pace that is right for you. If you fall behind schedule in the early going, don't worry. You have all summer to make up the mileage, if necessary. As for the 20-mile days, you can have a perfectly wonderful trip even if you never do one, so let them come if they come.

Rest breaks add miles of enjoyment to your hike. Stop for a rest at least once an hour, especially until you get into condition. Drop your pack, and let your muscles relax. Use your rest breaks to check information about Trail sections just ahead, and eat a small snack. It's convenient to take breaks at water sources, although you must guard against getting chilled. Don't let muscles begin to stiffen by taking too long a break.

Pack weight should be kept to a minimum throughout your hike. Form the habit of reviewing your pack contents at each town stop, looking for items that you can do without. Except for a few luxury items and safety gear (Walkman, book, rainwear, first-aid kit, etc.), don't retain any item in your pack that you don't use every day. Send unused items ahead a few stops, or send them home.

Anticipation is the fuel that will keep your hike on course. Plan each day so that you have a carrot on the end of a stick, so to speak, some treat that you can eagerly anticipate. The treat can be a beautiful overlook, a grocery store and soda, a reunion with friends ahead, the best dinner in your food bag, or whatever turns you on. The important thing is to have something to look forward to every day. As someone observed in a Trail register, "It is usually better to travel hopefully than it is to arrive."

Discouragement hits most hikers right away. You will quickly learn that hiking the A.T. is a lot tougher than you thought it would be. Blisters, aching muscles, and frayed nerves can discourage even the most enthusiastic thru-hiker. If you will keep going through this early discouragement, your body will begin to adjust to the new demands. Before long, you will have a day without aches and pains. Soon, you will have two such days in a row, then three, and so on until your body is Trail-hardened and most of your days are very good indeed. This is when hiking the A.T. becomes a joy and you wake up eager for the day to begin. Just hang in there; the good days will come.

Despair probably will occur after you have been on the Trail for a while and the newness of your adventure has worn off. For many hikers, this period of gloom, which some claim is caused mainly by physiological factors, comes somewhere in middle Virginia (or Vermont for southbounders). Last year's thru-hikers dubbed this phenomenon "the Virginia blues," although "Broof" of '91, who survived a severe attack, insisted that it should really be called "Trailzilla!" When it happens, you will be tempted to give up, but don't. Even if you are bored silly and hate the thought of another climb or starchy dinner, keep making some miles. Your mood will usually change in a few days, and then you will be able to hike with zest once again.

Quitting is what we are all conditioned not to do, but sometimes it's the right course. If you come to the point where you know that the Trail is not for you and have absolutely no will to go on, head to the nearest town, and rest for a day or two. Pamper yourself with plenty of wholesome food and lots of sleep. Talk to the folks back home, and weigh their input. List the reasons for and against quitting. Ask yourself if you are missing the people and activities of the Trail. Try to imagine what it will be like back home. Then, decide what is right for you. If you do decide to leave the Trail, are you a failure? Of course not. There is more to life than the Appalachian Trail, and, if hiking it all summer is not for you, then it is best for you to move on to something that is.

Alternatives are offered by ATC and many local clubs, all of which have summer jobs that may interest you. Positions on Trail crews and as caretakers may suit your needs more than doing a thru-hike. Contact the following for information: Maine—Phil Pepin, Box 536, Stratton, Maine 04982; the White Mountains—Reuben Rajala, AMC Volunteer Trails Program, P.O. Box 298, Gorham, N.H. 03581; Vermont—Dennis Shaffer, Green Mountain Club, P.O. Box 899, Montpelier, Vt. 05602; ATC Crews—Mike Dawson, P.O. Box 10, Newport, Va. 24128.

Last-Minute Advice

A few last-minute things should be done before you leave home and while *en route* to the Trailhead to begin your adventure:

• Check your wallet to ensure that it contains an I.D. card, next-of-kin notification instructions, medical-insurance card, ATC membership card, driver's license (check expiration date and renew before leaving, if necessary), tickets for transportation to the Trailhead, traveler's checks, and a little cash.

• Check your gear to verify that you leave home with everything needed for beginning your hike. In the past, some over-excited thru-hikers have arrived at Amicalola Falls without such essentials as their boots. Fill your fuel bottle, unless your transportation to the Trailhead prohibits travel with fuel, and check the freshness of batteries in your flashlight, radio, and camera equipment.

• Leave a copy of your hiking schedule, maildrop posting schedule, and backup-gear list with the helper who will send packages and backup items to you during your hike.

• Take some simple precautions to ensure that your pack arrives with you. When traveling by air, have the airline put your pack in a protective box. You may have to ask for this service, but it is provided free on most airlines. When traveling by bus, pick a seat over the baggage doors, and watch that your pack is not removed when the bus makes stops. When changing from one bus to another, watch to ensure that your pack has been placed on the bus you are boarding. This is a slight hassle, but lost packs rarely are recovered. When traveling to Gainesville, Georgia, make sure that your pack is not tagged for Gainesville, Florida.

• Reread the "Traditions and Practices" sections while you are *en route* to the Trailhead. They contain important information and will help you anticipate life on the Trail.

Above all, accept the fact that everything won't go the way you've planned (real adventures never do!). Knowing this, be adaptable and be confident that you can handle the challenges that come your way. Welcome the surprises of the Trail as a chance to be creative and to grow. Resolve to make the most of every day, and...

HAVE A GREAT HIKE!

Travel to the Trailheads

To Springer Mountain

The easiest way to reach Springer Mountain is to have family and friends drive you to Georgia; go directly to Amicalola Falls State Park, then take the approach trail to the southern terminus. This personal mode isn't practical for most thru-hikers, so you will probably be relying on public conveyances. In that case, your transportation objective is still Amicalola Falls State Park. The typical air traveler flies to Atlanta, takes a bus or train to Gainesville, Ga., then heads from there to the park. Those traveling to Georgia by Amtrak train can go directly to Gainesville, Ga. Those traveling by bus may be able to do the same. Assuming that you choose to travel through Atlanta, here are the connections you make:

Airport to downtown Atlanta by rapid transit: MARTA (404-848-4711 for schedule information) is Atlanta's rapid-transit system. From your plane, follow the signs to baggage-claim by taking the "people mover" to the terminal baggage-claim area between the north and south terminals, where you will retrieve your pack. From baggage claim, follow "Ground Transportation/MARTA" signs to the MARTA station, which is inside the terminal. Pay $1 in coins (or purchase a token from token machines or MARTA information booth inside the station) as you go through the turnstiles, go up the escalator or stairs leading to the boarding platform. All trains head downtown (every 8-10 minutes, but not at all from about 1am to 5am), so any train you take is the right one. The ride downtown takes about 15 minutes, and trains are safe, clean, and easy to use with a pack. • If your destination is the bus station, get off at the Peachtree Center Station (#N1), exit on Peachtree Street West, turn right on International Boulevard, and walk two blocks to the Greyhound/Trailways station. • If your destination is the train station, get off at the Arts Center Station (#N5), ride the escalator to the bus boarding area, and take the #23 Lenox bus (no extra fare needed inside the MARTA station) to the Amtrak (Brookwood) station. Or, you can exit to West Peachtree Street, turn right, and walk north to where it merges with Peachtree Street, then continue north on Peachtree Street a few blocks to the station, which is a brick building on the left just beyond where Peachtree crosses Interstate 85.

Airport to downtown Atlanta by shuttle bus: The Atlanta Airport Shuttle (404-524-3400) is a private bus service (leaves every half hour, operates 7am-11pm). Go to the terminal baggage-claim area as above and from there to the ground-transportation area outside the terminal. Look for the Airport Shuttle ticket booth. • If your destination is the bus station, buy an $8 ticket to the Greyhound/Trailways station. • If your destination is the train station, buy an $8 ticket to the Travelodge Midtown, located 1/2 block south of the Amtrak (Brookwood) station.

Airport to downtown Atlanta by taxi: Go to the ground-transportation area outside the terminal as above, and flag a cab (several should be waiting). Rates from the airport to anywhere in the downtown area, including the bus station, are fixed by the city ($15 for one/$16 for two/$6 per person for three or more). The fare to the Amtrak (Brookwood) station is a metered fare, usually about $18. Verify the rate with your driver before leaving for downtown.

Atlanta to Gainesville by bus or train: Three buses leave Atlanta's Greyhound/Trailways station (404-522-6300) for Gainesville, Ga., each day at 8am, 11:45am, and 6pm. The trip costs $12.72, takes about eighty minutes. Southbounders can depart Gainesville for Atlanta at 9:45am, 3:30pm, and 7:25pm. Note: Bus schedules have been changing almost monthly, so call ahead to verify departure times. • One train leaves Atlanta's Amtrak station (404-881-3060) for Gainesville, Ga., each day at 7:40pm. The trip costs $11, takes about an hour. Southbounders can depart Gainesville for Atlanta at 7:25am, or Gainesville to points north at 8:30pm. Note: Trains are often full, so call ahead for reservations.

If you have to stay overnight in Gainesville, two motels are within walking distance of the stations: Gainesville Motel (404-532-6327): $30S $32D $2EAP, 4 max; a/c, cable, phone in room, pool, pets permitted (MC, Visa, AE, Dis, DC, CB) • Holiday Inn (404-536-4451): $39 per room (special rate for A.T. hikers and guests), 4max; a/c, cable, phone in room, pool, washer/dryer, pets welcome (MC, Visa, AE, Dis, DC, CB); Gertrude's Restaurant in motel; ask guest-service manager Chris Jones about shuttle to Springer or bus and train stations.

Gainesville to Amicalola Falls State Park: Cabs will usually greet you at the Gainesville bus or train stations. If not, call Gainesville Cab Co. (404-287-3221; open 7 days, 24 hours). Fare to Amicalola Falls State Park is $38 for one person, $5 for each additional person (maximum of four per trip). Verify fares before leaving for Amicalola. Note: Veteran's Taxicab, listed in many older guides, has gone out of business. • Appalachian Outfitters (P. O. Box 793, Dahlonega, Ga. 30533; 404-864-7117 office or 404-864-3982 home; owned by Ben and Dana LaChance) offers a shuttle service from Gainesville to the top of the falls, but you must call ahead to make arrangements. Rates: 1-3 persons, $50; 4-10 persons, $15 per person. They will shuttle to other locations in northern Georgia (paved roads only) on a per-mile basis. Coleman fuel is usually available from them at cost. • Amicalola River Home AYH Hostel (404-265-6892, located five miles from Dawsonville) will meet you in Gainesville, bring you back for overnight at the hostel, then take you to the park the following day. Shuttle fee is $35 for one person, $7 each additional person (up to 3); call ahead to make arrangements. Hostel is $8.50 per night for AYH or ATC members, $14 per night nonmembers; operated by Bill Dulaney. Coleman fuel is available.

Atlanta to Amicalola Falls State Park: Jim Miner, who lives in northern Georgia and works in Atlanta, will shuttle you to Amicalola Falls State Park, Nimblewill Gap, or Big Stamp Gap on his way home. Arrangements need to be made at least a day in advance. You can write Jim at Rt. 1, Box 30, Suches, Ga. 30572 (enclose SASE for full information) or call him (404-747-5434). Jim will meet you at the Chamblee MARTA Station (#N9, the northern end of the MARTA line). He doesn't charge for this service but will accept a donation to one of his favorite causes, either the Woody Gap School or the volunteer fire department. • Bill Porter, an ATC member who lives in Atlanta, is available for shuttles to Amicalola Falls, Nimblewill, or Big Stamp. Arrangements need to be made by calling him a few days in advance (404-233-8877 home or 404-329-0880 work). Bill will meet you at the Lindbergh MARTA Station (#N6). He also has a basement apartment near the Lindbergh Station that can be used overnight by those arriving too late to go directly to the park. Bill doesn't charge for this service but, like Jim, will accept donations to his favorite charity, Inner City Outings. • Tom Watson, a 1984 2,000-Miler, is available for shuttles to Amicalola Falls, Nimblewill, or Big Stamp. Pickup at airport is possible. You can reach Tom by phone to discuss arrangements and costs (404-889-2688 home or 404-393-1072 work). He is also available for shuttles to anywhere in northern Georgia or western North Carolina. • Appalachian Outfitters (see above) will shuttle you from the airport to the park, but you must call ahead for availability and reservations. Rates: 1-3 persons, $110; 4-10 persons, $30 per person.

Amicalola Falls State Park: The park derives its name from a Cherokee word meaning "tumbling waters." Its beautiful falls plunge 729 feet in seven cascades, the highest falls east of the Mississippi. The park office (open 7 days, Sun-Thur 8am-4pm and Fri 8am-10pm; 404-265-2885) has Coke and snack machines, restrooms, picnic tables/shelters, and a public telephone located nearby. You should sign the hikers' register at the office and check for thru-hikers who have signed in ahead of you. Ask the ranger for the famous "Amicalola scale" to weigh your pack (Is it accurate?). All vehicles entering the park must pay a $2 park-user fee (payable at self-pay machines in the park; have exact change ready) unless only dropping someone off. A new shelter, located 0.3 mile beyond the park office on the approach trail, is available to thru-hikers free of charge. Campsites are $10 per night, with shower and coin-operated laundry nearby. If you arrive after office hours, see the bulletin board for camping instructions. For information, call park naturalist and 2,000-Miler Sonie "Light Eagle" Shams (404-265-2015); in case of emergency, call superintendant Bob Bolz (404-265-2902). The park also has cottages, usually booked far in advance, and the Amicalola Falls Lodge ($55S through Mar 31, $65S after Apr 1; MC, Visa, AE; call for reservations) with The Maple Restaurant (B/L/D, regional food, $5 breakfast 7-10am, $6 lunch 11:30am-2pm, $8 dinner 5-9pm except Sun until 8pm), located in the lodge and open to the public. Kincaid Grocery (limited hiker supplies, snacks; open 7 days, 7am-9pm) is located on Ga. 52 at the park entrance.

Approaches to Springer Mountain: The 8.3-mile blue-blazed approach trail (East Ridge Trail in the park) starts just behind the park office building, passing the "Anniversary Maple" and the falls before heading toward Springer. You can also reach the approach trail by taking the paved road (the one that turns left off the park entrance road, opposite the park office) to the top of the falls. From the parking area at the top of the falls, take the road bearing off to the left (in direction indicated by sign pointing to cottages), turn right on the first side road (at sign-post with double blue blazes), and pass through the cottage area to intersect the approach trail on the left. The roadwalk involves a steep climb, so get a ride up if you can. Be sure to fill your water bottles at the park office, because the approach trail can be dry. It also has several difficult climbs. Once underway, don't get caught up in the initial enthusiasm of your trip and burn out on the way to Frosty Mountain, as have all too many eager hikers. Take it easy at first, and enjoy the walk to Springer, which can be delightful on a sunny spring day. • USFS Road 28 intersects the approach trail at Nimblewill Gap. From the gap, it is 2.5 miles north to Springer Mountain.

• USFS Road 42 intersects the A.T. at Big Stamp Gap (look for parking area), 0.9 mile north of Springer Mountain, which means you must hike south to get to the terminus.

Note: USFS roads in the Amicalola area may be impassable during wet weather. USFS Road 28 to Nimblewill Gap was impassable except to 4-wheel drive vehicles with high clearance in 1991 and may be closed to automobiles this spring. Check at the park office for condition of nearby roads. A map of the Chattahoochee National Forest, showing roads, is available for $2 (Georgia residents, $2.10) from the USFS, 601 Broad St., Gainesville, Ga. 30501 (404-536-0541).

To Katahdin

Southbounders starting at Katahdin have fewer travel options. If you are using public conveyances, you must first get to Bangor, Maine. From Bangor's Greyhound bus station, travel to Medway, Maine, via Cyr Bus Line (207-827-2335; one bus daily, leaves at 5:30pm, arrives Medway at 7pm, costs $10.50). You must hitch the 10 miles from Medway to Millinocket, Maine, on Maine 157, since there is no public transportation. From Millinocket, you'll also have to hitch to Baxter State Park, which opens officially on May 15. Before heading into the park, southbounders are advised to call ahead to check on regulations and conditions for climbing Katahdin. Baxter State Park headquarters (207-723-5140) is located at 64 Balsam Dr., Millinocket, Maine 04462 (visible from Maine 157, on the left as you head into town), not in the park itself. Motels and other services in Millinocket and Medway are listed at the end of the Maine chapter.

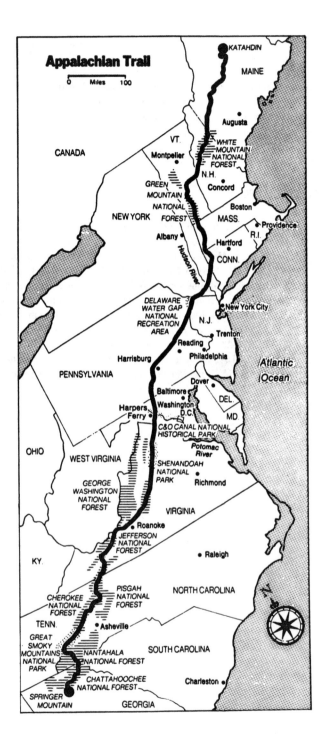

Georgia-North Carolina

This chapter takes you from Springer Mountain, Georgia, to Fontana Dam, North Carolina, and corresponds to *Data Book* chapter ten.

Springer Mountain: southernmost of the Blue Ridge Mountains and southern terminus of the Appalachian Trail since 1958. The Trail officially begins at the bronze Georgia A.T. Club (GATC) plaque mounted on a summit rock with a vista to the west. White blazes begin at the plaque and extend for more than two thousand miles to Katahdin. Nearby is a mailbox with the official GATC sign-in register, which will find its way to the club's archives at summer's end. In the early days, thru-hikers picked up a small pebble from Springer to be carried the distance and placed on the cairn atop Baxter Peak, a tradition that has been revived by many northbounders in recent years. (Do southbounders carry a Katahdin rock to Springer?)

Clubnote: The next 75 miles are maintained by GATC volunteers. Thru-hikers may meet members conducting the club's annual spring walk-through in March. More than 100 volunteers participate in this inspection trip, noting blowdowns, winter shelter damage, and other Trail defects on their maintenance section. Simpler problems will be fixed on the spot; the more difficult will be scheduled for prompt repair later.

> Trail Fact: *Five million steps are required to walk the A.T. from Georgia to Maine, assuming you have a 27-inch stride, on average, which is about right for someone 5'6" in height. If you are six feet tall, however, the trip can be done in only 4,583,000 steps, whereas a five-footer will use more than 5,500,000 steps. No matter how many steps you eventually take, congratulations for taking the first.*

Springer Mountain Shelter: usually crowded in early spring with eager thru-hikers grumbling about too much weight in their packs and trying to stay optimistic while operating cantankerous stoves for the first time. The reliable spring in front of the shelter can be easily contaminated, so use care when getting water. The privy was new last year. Level tentsites can be found on the A.T. near the shelter sign.

> Wildlife: *Chipmunks will be the first wild animals you encounter on your hike. As you pass, they will sound their high-pitched alarm and scurry into a nearby burrow, running with their tails held straight up. The burrow is 12 feet long, has side chambers for sleeping, food, garbage, and body wastes, and might hold up to half a bushel of seeds and nuts. (What! No raisins and M&Ms?)*

Wildflowers: From Springer Mountain to Neels Gap, you will probably have your first sighting of the following wildflower and tree varieties in bloom—
• *common blue violet:* five petals, purple to white, 3-8 inches high; white variety called Confederate violet.

23

- *downy yellow violet:* five petals, yellow, three lower ones veined with purple, hairy stem; 6-16 inches high.
- *bloodroot:* 8-12 oblong petals, white with golden center, 6-12 inches high; Indians used root sap as war paint.
- *buttercup:* five petals, bright yellow with yellow center; 2-3 feet high.
- *crested dwarf iris:* orchidlike petals, purple with orange and white crests; 3-5 inches high.
- *great chickweed:* five deeply cleft petals that look like ten, white flowers 1/2-inch across, stems sprawling and tangled; 6-16 inches high.
- *flowering dogwood tree:* four large petals, white with touch of rust on ends; tree 10-25 feet high.

Stover Creek Shelter: a good alternative if Springer Mountain Shelter is crowded. Bears have been reported in the area for the past two years but have caused no problems. Skunks make nightly visits.

Stover Creek: magnificent towering stand of virgin evergreens along the creek. Called Cathedral Hemlocks for obvious reasons, this is the only such timber stand you will see until you get to the Smokies.

Precolonial forests: Most forests along the Trail have been harvested at least two or three times and are but remnants of their former glory. To understand what the North American forest was like before the settlers came, double the height and triple the girth of every tree you see from Georgia to Maine, and imagine all the cleared areas filled with such trees.

Hawk Mountain Shelter: the site of many midnight visits by Army Rangers on training maneuvers and by a resident skunk. The Rangers can be noisy but have orders not to bother hikers. Be advised: The skunk has no such orders. If the shelter is full, a good meadow for camping is in the gap above the head of the spring, south of the shelter.

> Wildlife: *Spotted skunks are night feeders. If one visits your campsite, don't panic. Let the skunk sniff around and usually it will wander off, if you haven't been careless with food. If disturbed, it will arch its hindquarters over its head, take aim, and let loose with a noxious spray in your direction. The result won't make you happy. Spotted skunks have a white spot on the forehead and a white-tipped, bushy tail.*

Gooch Gap Shelter: reached after a steep, 0.2-mile blue-blazed climb from the Trail, so you may want to get water from the spring at the shelter sign before heading up. Privy new for 1992.

Gooch Gap (USFS Road 42): *Left 2.7m*—to the town of Suches (see below). *Right 0.2m*—to a small spring.

Woody Gap (Ga. 60): *On A.T.*—small picnic area with piped spring, tables, trash cans, and privy (usually locked). *Left 1.9m*—to "downtown" Suches.

- ◆ **SUCHES, GA.** (pop. 150): first convenient place for mailing excess gear home; supposedly got its name because someone years ago said, "It's our town, *such as* it is."

Services—Suches General Store: good for short-term resupply, open daily 8am-6pm, closed Wed afternoon and Sun • Tritts Grocery: limited hiker supplies; open most days 7am-7pm, closed Tues afternoon • Suches Medical Clinic: open weekdays except Wed, but call 1-800-521-7243 anytime • outside pay phone • Jim and Ruth Ann Miner (404-747-5434) are friends of hikers. *PO-ZIP 30572*: Mon-Fri 7:30am-noon and 1-4:30pm; Sat 7:30-11:30am; 404-747-2611; LY-75.

Slaughter Gap: site of the last water until Neels Gap. The spring, located on the A.T. just before you reach the gap, is the water source for northbounders staying at Blood Mountain Shelter. "Grandma" Gatewood, first woman to thru-hike the A.T. (in 1955 at age 67), was once frightened by a big rattlesnake coiled in the Trail near the spring.

> Wildlife: *Gray squirrels are taken for granted by most hikers but are possibly the most important animal in the forest. They probably planted most of the broad-leafed trees you see around you, by burying acorns and nuts in autumns past. Squirrels are very territorial and will greet you with a rapid tail-twitching and agitated "kuk-kuk-kuk" sound as you approach.*

Blood Mountain (4,461 feet): the highest point on the A.T. in Georgia and famous in Indian lore as the site of a battle 400 years ago between Creek and Cherokee warriors so fierce "the hills ran red with blood." Nearby Slaughter Mountain is reputed to be the cache of all the gold of the Cherokee nation, hidden when they were forced to leave Georgia in the early 1800s.

Blood Mountain Shelter: perched on the summit of Blood Mountain; no water but a new privy. The stone shelter was built by CCC workers in the 1930s and renovated several years ago by GATC, with help from the Army Rangers, who helicoptered materials donated by the Forest Service to the summit. Before renovation, a bear lived in the back room, which now has a sleeping platform and is occupied by numerous mice. (Is there also a woodrat in residence?) Rocks next to the shelter afford panoramic views. On a good day, you can see all the way back to Springer, and sunsets can be spectacular.

Neels Gap (U.S. 19): *On A.T.*—Walasi-Yi Center (see below). *Left 2m*—to Vogel State Park. *Left 4m*—to Goose Creek Cabins. *Left 14m*—to the town of Blairsville. *Right 17m*—to the town of Dahlonega.

♦ Vogel State Park: campsites on Lake Trahlyta $6-$10 per night with shower, camp store with limited hiker supplies, laundromat, public telephone, and showers ($1 per person if not camping).
♦ Goose Creek Cabins (404-745-5111): Cabins with kitchen and fireplace ($35D, $45 up to four persons), tentsites $10 with shower, lodge with telephone and game room, trout pond ($2.75 per pound), free shuttle to and from Neels Gap, shuttle to other points $1 per mile by arrangement; owned by Keith and Retter Bailey.
♦ Blairsville, Ga. (pop. 1,600): *Services*—motels • restaurants • Western Sizzler • McDonald's • Hardee's • KFC • supermarket • Alexander's Country store (described as "a mountain wonder") • laundromat • bank • pharmacy • doctor • dentist.

♦ **Dahlonega, Ga.** (pop. 2,844): pronounced "Duh'-lah-nah-guh" by residents, site of America's first gold rush and U.S. Mint in the early 1800s. *Services*—several motels and restaurants • The Smith House: L/D, family-style restaurant, world-famous for authentic Southern cooking • Red & White Supermarket: good for short-term resupply • Appalachian Outfitters (404-555-3958): mainly river rafting, some backpacking gear, Coleman by the pint • The Gold Museum, open year-round • Crisson Mines: pan for gold, open Apr-Nov. Also, North Georgia College, site chosen for the Appalachian Trail Conference biennial meeting in June 1993.

Walasi-Yi Center (Rt. 1, Box 1240, Blairsville, Ga. 30512; 404-745-6095): the only building the A.T. goes through, so you can't miss it. Center has hiker hostel and backpacking store with grocery section; open 7 days, 8am-6pm, Mar 3-May 31; remainder of year, Mon-Fri 9am-5pm, Sat-Sun 8:30am-6pm. Owned by Jeff and Dorothy Hansen, who live at the center with their two small children. *Hiker Hostel*—bunkroom with mattress bunks and shower $10; towel $1; open Mar 3-May 31 for long-distance hikers only, on first-come, first-served basis; maximum 16 hikers. Coin-operated laundromat for guests. Outside public telephone. No pets inside. Check-out time is 9am. Southbounders should call ahead to make arrangements for staying at the hostel after May 31. *Backpacking Store*—well-stocked with hiking gear, clothing, trail guides, Coleman by the pint, film, stamps, medical and first-aid supplies, repair items, *etc.* Repair services are also available. Many hikers have adjusted their gear and even reequipped here with help from the Hansens. Jeff has a background that includes NOLS, Outward Bound, and directorships of several wilderness schools. Dorothy is a 2,000-Miler. One appreciative thru-hiker summed it up when he said, "Jeff has seen a lot of thru-hikers. He gave me just the help I needed." If you need equipment advice, set up an appointment with Jeff when you arrive. *Grocery Section*—small, but targeted specifically for thru-hikers, so you should be able to resupply here. Items include standard backpacking staples (oatmeal, instant milk, peanut butter, mac and cheese, Lipton dinners, ramen noodles, granola, *etc.*), freeze-dried foods, and a wide selection of health foods. Also, fresh fruits, ice cream, and hot coffee. *Other services*—will hold some types of packages for hikers (you should call ahead to make arrangements for this service); shower $2.50; shower with towel $3.50; showers and coin-operated laundromat available to nonguests subject to sufficient well-water level; UPS pickup and delivery on weekdays. *Note*—The Hansens and their small staff really enjoy talking and visiting with thru-hikers but put in 14-hour days serving the 1,000 or so thru-hikers who come through each spring. Give them a break by making as few demands on their time as you can. If they look harassed once in a while, it's probably because they are.

Wildflowers: From Neels Gap to Unicoi Gap, you will probably have your first sighting of the following wildflower varieties in bloom—
• *pearly everlasting:* 1/2-inch flowers in clusters, pearly white with yellow tuft in center, stem and underside of leaves wooly-white; 1-3 feet high.
• *toadshade trillium:* three upright petals, maroon to brownish, in center of three broad leaves; 4-12 inches high.
• *toothwort:* four petals, white to pinkish, 1/2-inch flowers clustered atop slender stalk, three oval leaves bluntly toothed; 8-15 inches high.
• *robin's plantain:* violet or lilac with yellow center, 1.5-inch rayed flowers, dandelionlike; 6-16 inches high.
• *golden ragwort:* 8-15 narrow petals, flowers golden with yellow center in branched cluster; 1-3 feet high.

• *mayapples:* called "umbrella plants," white cup-shaped flower develops into a pale-colored, up to lemon-sized berry; plant 1-2 feet high.

Testnatee Gap: probable place where John Muir crossed the mountains on his now-famous 1,000-mile walk to the sea. The steep climb up Wildcat Mountain may be bypassed in foul weather by going right (uphill) on Ga. 348 to intersect the A.T. on the left at Hogpen Gap.

Wildlife: *Pileated woodpeckers, with their slow, rhythmic hammering, will make you think there is someone chopping down a tree with an ax. They hammer deep into old-growth trees for food and nesting, and the abandoned holes provide homes for many other animals. Their call sounds like something from a jungle movie. When you hear it, look for a very large black-and-white bird with a conspicuous red crest.*

Whitley Gap Shelter: the A.T. shelter located farthest from the Trail, with good piped spring, used by many Scout groups on spring school breaks.

Low Gap Shelter: similar to Springer Mountain Shelter, but built for folks with long legs. Numerous tentsites in area. Best water is up the creek, to the left as you look into the shelter.

Rocky Knob Shelter: demolished; area still usable as a campsite.

Blue Mountain Shelter: replaces the Rocky Knob Shelter. Can be wet on a rainy night, because of short overhang in front, but makes up for it by offering spectacular sunrises on clear mornings. Get water from the spring 300 yards before the shelter.

Unicoi Gap (Ga. 75): *Left 11m*—to the town of Hiawassee (see Dicks Creek Gap below). *Right 10m*—to the town of Helen.

♦ **Helen, Ga.** (pop. 353): alpine-theme tourist village located on the banks of the Chattahoochee River, Atlanta's water source. *Lodging*—Helendorf River Inn: $40-$60D $5EAP (discounts possible Sun-Thur); a/c, cable, phone in room, washer/dryer (MC, Visa, DC) • Chalet Kristy Motel: $45-$55D $5EAP, no pets (MC, Visa) • The Village Inn: $35-$55D $5EAP, 5 max; a/c, cable, no pets (MC, Visa, AE). *Places to eat*—Mountain Valley Kitchen: B/L/D, down-home cooking with soup-and-salad bar, country-fried steak and chicken, trout, AYCE breakfast buffet; closed Wed (MC, Visa, AE, Dis) • Paul's Restaurant: L/D, fine dining with prime rib, steaks, lobster; closed Sun • Wendy's. *Other services*— Betty's Country Store: limited hiker supplies, fresh produce, bulk and health foods, baked goods • convenience store • Soap Opera Laundromat: FLW, open 7 days, 8am-9pm • hardware store • pharmacy • bike rentals • tubing on the river.

Wildflowers: From Unicoi Gap to Dicks Creek Gap, you will probably have your first sighting of the following wildflower and tree varieties in bloom—
• *spring beauty:* five petals, pink to white with dark pink veins, leaves like blades of grass; 6-12 inches high.
• *wood vetch:* 1/2-inch pea-shaped flowers, white with bluish tip, oval leaves on vinelike stem ending in a curling tendril; a variety of wild pea.

- *large-flowered bellwort:* yellow to orange bell-shaped flowers hanging from tips of leafy branches, leaves oval with pointed tips, 1-2 feet high; also called merrybells.
- *daisy fleabane:* 1/2-inch daisylike flowers, white to pinkish with yellow central disk, leaves spatula-shaped and clustered at base; 1-5 feet high.
- *birdsfoot violet:* five lavender petals, upper two slanting backward and often darker, leaves on separate stem; 4-10 inches high.
- *serviceberry tree:* white flowers in drooping clusters, leaves elliptical and coarsely toothed; tree 30-40 feet high.
- *eastern redbud tree:* pink flowers in 4-8 clusters, leaves heart-shaped; tree 10-20 feet high.

Tray Mountain: panoramic views back to Blood Mountain and north to Standing Indian Mountain. On a very clear day, the Smokies are visible on the northern horizon.

Tray Mountain Shelter: excellent piped spring down blue-blazed trail behind shelter. Numerous grassy campsites in area, some with great views of distant valley. GATC dug a new privy pit and reroofed the shelter during the winter.

Wildlife: *Turkey vultures are the large black birds that you may have mistaken for eagles. Also called buzzards, they spend much of their time circling and soaring on outstretched wings held motionless in a shallow "V," searching for carrion. You will want to sit for hours admiring how efficient and graceful these birds are in the air. They are gosh-awful ugly on the ground, however.*

Addis Gap Shelter: demolished; area no longer used for camping.

Deep Gap Shelter: to the right at Deep Gap on a 0.25-mile blue-blazed trail. New this year, shelter is a cooperative effort of GATC, USFS, and a private company, UpperLoft Designs. Water source is the piped spring you pass on the side trail. Privy is on unmarked trail to the right as you look into the shelter.

Dicks Creek Gap (Ga. 76): *On A.T.*—picnic area with tables, trash cans, and small stream. *Left 11m*—to Hiawassee. *Right 18m*—to the town of Clayton.

♦ **Hiawassee, Ga.** (pop. 2,000): *Services*—Mull's Motel: $32S $37D $6EAP, 4 max; a/c, cable, phone in room, no pets (MC, Visa, AE); shuttle back to A.T. • Georgia Mountain Restaurant: reportedly has inexpensive, country-style meals • Waffle Shack • grocery store: good for short-term resupply • laundromat: FLW, open 7 days, 7:30am-9pm, last load 8:30pm • *Reach of Song:* an Appalachian summer drama, June and July. • country music festivals year-round • Georgia Mountain Fair: held in August. *PO-ZIP 30546:* Mon-Fri 8:30am-5pm, closed Sat; 404-896-3232; LY-24.

♦ **Clayton, Ga.** (pop. 1,613): Scenes from "Deliverance" were filmed nearby. Several cast members still live in the area, including the actor who appeared as an albino lad in the "dueling banjos" scene. *Services*—motel • Dillard Motor Lodge: B/L/D, country-casual, all meals served family-style and AYCE; open 7 days (MC, Visa, AE, Dis DC) • McDonald's • Hardee's • KFC • Pizza Hut • Dairy Queen • supermarket: good for short-term resupply • bakery • laundromat • bank • Western Union • pharmacy • hardware store with work boots • doctor • dentist • hospital • veterinarian • UPS/FedEx pick-up.

Wildflowers: From Dicks Creek Gap to Deep Gap, you will probably have your first sighting of the following wildflower varieties in bloom—

• *dandelion:* yellow composite ray flowers atop hollow stalks, seedhead fluffy white, sawtooth leaves clustered at base; 2-18 inches high.

• *sweet white violet:* five petals, white with maroon veins, two upper petals narrow and bent backwards, flower stalks reddish, leaves heart-shaped; 6-10 inches high.

• *wild strawberry:* five rounded white petals around yellow central disk, three oval hairy leaflets; 2-6 inches high.

• *squawroot:* yellow-brown "pine cones" standing in clusters; 3-10 inches high.

• *white baneberry:* 4-10 spoon-shaped 1/4-inch petals, white with hairy stamens and conspicuous purple eye, flowers in ball-shaped cluster on long stem; 1-2 feet high.

Plumorchard Gap Shelter: Best water is down 350 feet to the left at shelter sign; shelter is opposite way down old road to the right about the same distance. Small spring in front of shelter plays host to several eastern spotted newts. Bears were reported in this area early last year.

Bly Gap: noted for the gnarled oak tree that has been often photographed. You actually climb up to the gap, passing a small spring on the right, to the old tree and a vista looking north. For all practical purposes, the gap is the Georgia-North Carolina border, so celebrate the crossing of your first or last state line. You might also want to take a rest break, for the climb out of the gap up Sharp Top is steep.

Clubnote: The next 59 miles are maintained by Nantahala Hiking Club volunteers, who erected the new signs at the border but had nothing to do with the "Georiga-North Carolina" spelling.

Courthouse Bald: nice viewpoint constructed by the maintainer, who calls it "The Judge."

> Wildlife: *Rufous-sided towhees will make you think there is "something large out there" rustling in the leaves. They use both feet to scratch like chickens for seeds and insects. Males have black upper body, white under, with rust-colored flanks. Females are brown, instead of black. Their distinctive "to-whee" calls to each other are heard often on the Trail from Georgia to Massachusetts, their northern limit.*

Muskrat Creek Shelter: an A-frame shelter. Short, blue-blazed trail to the shelter goes off to the right immediately after the A.T. crosses a small creek with no footbridge. Anyone care to donate an umbrella for the privy?

Chunky Gal Trail: named derived from an old Cherokee fable about a very healthy Indian princess who was ridiculed by her beautiful and slender younger sister, to the point of fleeing into the woods on what became known as the . . . you guessed it!

Deep Gap (USFS Road 71): garbage can in gap parking area, picnic area down side road to the left. Blue-blazed Kimsey Creek Trail goes from the picnic area to Standing Indian Campground in the valley.

Wildflowers: From Deep Gap to Wallace Gap, you will probably have your first sighting of the following wildflower varieties in bloom—

• *bluets:* four petals, 1/4-inch flowers, pale blue with yellow centers; 2-8 inches high, also called Quaker ladies.

• *trailing arbutus:* five petals, white to light pink, flowers trumpet-shaped, large leathery leaves trailing on ground.

• *large white trillium:* three ruffed white petals, three leaves atop long stem; 6-20 inches high.

• *common wood sorrel:* five petals, pinkish with purplish stripes around star-shaped yellow center, leaves akin to three-leaf clover; 2-6 inches high.

• *red trillium:* three petals, red to maroon with foul smell, also called stinking benjamin.

• *squirrel corn:* heart-shaped flowers, white with yellow on bottom, nodding carrot-like leaves around stem; 6-8 inches high; roots have tubers resembling kernels of corn.

• *false Solomon's seal:* white starlike flowers in dense branching cluster at top of zigzag stem, leaves alternating; 2-3 feet high.

• *trout lily:* nodding orchidlike flowers, yellow with six upswept petals; 4-10 inches high.

Standing Indian Shelter: on stream unfortunately used for washing by many novice hikers, so go well upstream for drinking water. Yellow *trout lilies* grow along the banks of the creek. According to local folklore, trout season begins when these flowers start to bloom. Last year, the shelter was visited almost every night by skunks, but no one got sprayed.

Standing Indian Mountain (5,498 feet): the first time northbounders go above the 5,000-foot mark. The summit is not on the A.T. but well worth the short detour. Called "the grandstand of the southern Appalachians," it has magnificent views in all directions and a grassy area for camping. A small, variable spring is off the Trail to the left near the turn-off to the summit, but you may want to bring water up from the shelter.

Carter Gap Shelter: water source directly behind shelter, where you may find sodas left by caretaker if you're lucky.

Albert Mountain: infamous for its 0.2-mile rock scramble, which seems to go straight up at times. The summit is topped by a firetower, manned only during very dry periods, with excellent views of mountains in every direction. In foul weather, you may go left on the blue-blazed fire road at the base of Albert to avoid the exposed summit. Southbounders should turn right on the blue-blazed trail just before the summit.

Big Spring Shelter: numerous tentsites in area, used by large groups on weekends. Water from spring near shelter.

> Wildlife: *Golden eagles are being reestablished at several locations in the southern Appalachians with mixed results, so you could see one. Look for a large bird with up to a 7-foot wingspan, wings held straight out from a dark brown body, with golden-brown crown and nape.*

Rock Gap Shelter: near road, but no problems with vandalism or partying neighbors reported in recent years.

Rock Gap: a grassy area that looks as if loggers poached a few choice trees, but the NHC, ATC, and USFS allowed the cutting, and the Southern pine beetle was the reason. Years ago, the surrounding six acres were planted in white pine, which was not well-suited to this area and eventually succumbed to beetle attack. Half an acre was clear-cut to prevent dead trees from falling on the parking area and road; the remaining acreage was thinned of diseased trees. The A.T. skirts a paved road leading left to Standing Indian Campground. The blue-blazed trail down to the right leads to the Wasilik Poplar, said to be the second-largest yellow poplar in existence.

Wallace Gap (Old U.S. 64): *Left 0.8m*—to Chapel of the Ascension. *Left 1m*—to Rainbow Springs Campground.

♦ Chapel of the Ascension: outdoor pavilion where the Rev. A. Rufus Morgan, a Trail pioneer in North Carolina, preached every Sunday morning until his death in 1984 at age 97. Notice ages on headstones.

♦ Rainbow Springs Campground (1626 Old Murphy Road, Franklin, N.C. 28734; for questions and messages, 704-524-6376; for reservations only, 1-800-524-8293): a full-service campground with bunkhouse, cabins, campsites, camp store, volleyball, horse-shoes, trout fishing, public telephone, and coin-operated laundromat with detergent; open Mon-Sat 8:30am-7pm, Sunday 9am-6pm, Mar 1-Nov 30 (but have often accommodated early-season hikers). Owned by Buddy and Jensine Crossman, who live over the store and look forward to meeting A.T. thru-hikers each year (more than 400 stayed overnight last year). *Lodging*—bunkhouse with 12 mattress bunks, refrigerator, wood stove (wood provided), and hot shower, $10; cabins with stove, refrigerator, linens, private bath and hot shower, $25S $30D; campsites with hot shower, $5 per person; morning shuttle back to Trail (usually runs between 8:30-10:30am) free with overnight accommodations. *Camp store*—small, but geared for thru-hikers, good for short-term resupply; oven-baked pizza, milk, cheese, ice cream, fresh fruit, homemade chili and cinnamon rolls, homemade bread (yum!), microwave foods, Coleman in any quantity, other fuels, first-aid supplies, Spenco, small accessory items (water bottles, ditty bags, socks, *etc.*). *Other services*—shower without stay $3, with towel $4; laundromat $1.75. The Crossmans will hold equipment packages, special dietary-food packages, and medicines only (call ahead to make arrangements, don't just send them). *Note:* Many a thru-hiker has been driven to doctor, dentist, cobbler, and other "emergency" places by the Crossmans, but be considerate. They work long hours and can't always break away to cater to your immediate needs.

Winding Stair Gap (U.S. 64): *Right 10m*—to intersection with U.S. 441, on the way passing West Gate Plaza with Ingle's Supermarket (good for long-term resupply, open Mon-Fri 7:30am-midnight, Sat and Sun until 10pm), Burger King, K-Mart, pharmacy, and Books Unlimited (good bookstore with Western Union). At the U.S. 441 intersection, right (south) 0.2 mile on U.S. 441 to Pizza Hut, McDonald's, and Huddle House; left (north) one mile on Business 441 to the town of Franklin.

♦ FRANKLIN, N.C. (pop. 2,640): *Lodging*—Henry's Motel: $15 (1-2 persons, 1 bed) or $25 (1-4 persons, 2 beds), basic lodging managed by friendly Louise Gillespie, open Apr-Nov, possible shuttle back to Trail • Franklin Motel: $26S $32D ($39S $45D after May 1) $2EAP, 5 max; a/c, cable, phone in room, pool, no pets (MC, Visa, AE, Dis,

DC). *Places to eat*—B&D Restaurant: B/L/D, country-casual, daily luncheon special (three veggies and meat for $4), homemade pies, closed Tues • The Normandie Restaurant: B/L/D, casual home-style meals with vegetables, open Mon-Fri • Mi Casa Family Restaurant: L/D, Mexican-American, casual, extensive menu, weekly specials, open Mon-Sat 11:30am-11pm, closed Sun • Pizza Peddler: L/D, AYCE spaghetti specials for $4 (days vary), closed Sun • Top Shelf Pizza: Italian-American take-out • Western Sizzlin' with AYCE food bar • Hardee's • KFC • Subway • LJ Silver's. *Groceries*—Winn-Dixie Supermarket: good for long-term resupply, open Mon-Sat 8am-9pm, Sun 9am-8pm • bakery. *Laundromat*—Palmer St. Laundry: FLW, open 7 days, 7am-10pm, last load 9pm.
Cobbler—Franklin's Town Cobbler: same-day boot repairs, pack and zipper repairs, sells new and used boots, open Mon-Fri 8:30am-5pm, located on Fountain Square. *Other services*—bank • UPS/FedEx pick-up • pharmacy • doctor • dentist • hospital • veterinarian • hardware store • movie theatre • bus service to Asheville • taxi service • Jack Coriell (704-369-6820) of Nantahala Hiking Club is a friend of hikers who will shuttle you back to the A.T. for 25¢ per mile, to cover expenses. *PO-ZIP 28734*: Mon-Fri 8:30am-5pm, closed Sat; 704-524-3219; LY-70.

Siler Bald: being restored to its status as a grassy bald by the USFS, ATC, and NHC, causing a bit of a controversy with those who desire to see the forests left entirely alone. The bare summit offers an excellent view. Blue-blazed loop trail leads to the shelter.

Siler Bald Shelter: good piped spring, grassy field for tenting, and nice view of Franklin's lights at night. Reports of bear activity early last spring.

> *Wildlife: Owls are nocturnal birds, the nighttime equivalent of hawks. You will most often hear two types, the great horned owl (hoo, hoo-hoo, hooooo-hoo) and the barred owl (Who cooks for you? Who cooks for you-all?). Owls have excellent hearing and night vision, allowing them to swoop accurately and snatch prey in the dark. The victim is swallowed whole, digested, and discharged as a grayish pellet of hair and bones you will often see on rocks in the Trail. Owls eat large numbers of rodents, including shelter mice.*

Wildflowers: From Wayah Gap to the Nantahala River, you will probably have your first sighting of the following wildflower varieties in bloom—
• *Dutchman's breeches:* white with yellowish bottom, waxy flowers with two spurs pointing upward in shape of a "V" carrotlike leaves at base; 5-10 inches high.
• *wild geranium:* five petals, purple to rose, leaves deeply lobed and toothed; 1-3 feet high.
• *foamflower:* five petals, white with long stamens, flowers in clusters forming fuzzy cone-shaped spikes, leaves maplelike and hairy; 5-12 inches high.
• *hairy Solomon's seal:* greenish-ivory flowers, elongated and bell-shaped hanging on end of arching stem; 1-6 feet high.
• *rue anemone:* two or three 1/2-inch flowers, 5-10 white petals with reddish stamens, surrounded by whorl of leaves on wiry stem; 2-8 inches high.
• *jack-in-the-pulpit:* leaf stem 1-3 feet high with three pointed oval leaves, flower on separate stem (a greenish tube-like structure with maroonish inside and hood overhanging maroon, club-shaped spike).

Wayah Bald: pronounced "War-yuh" by nearby residents. The summit is topped by a stone observation tower with wonderful views; great place for a break on a sunny day. You pass the privy before you reach the tower. Water is available from a stream beyond the picnic/parking area. A camping area with spring is 0.5 mile north on the Trail.

Ramps: known locally as "mountain onions," can be found in abundance in this area. Be careful; several toxic plants look similar.

Licklog Gap: water 200 yards west on the road, past a meadow, then left 50-100 yards to a stream.

Cold Spring Shelter: small shelter constructed from remains of another shelter. No, George Washington didn't really leave his initials carved in that shelter log. Just a few feet beyond the shelter, a side trail leads to a ridge with a nice view and campsite.

A. Rufus Morgan Shelter: a good alternative to NOC on weekends, when whitewater rafters usually have all available lodging booked solid.

Nantahala River; Wesser, N.C. (U.S. 19): *On A.T.*—Nantahala Outdoor Center (see below). *Right 12m*—to the town of Bryson City. Note: There is no longer a Wesser post office, but the name is still used to denote the NOC area.

♦ **Bryson City, N.C.** (pop. 1,200): *Services*—Scenic View Motel: $20-$25 • Smoky Mountain Restaurant • Hardee's • Pizza Hut • Western Sizzler • A&P Supermarket: good for long-term resupply, Western Union office in store • Ingle's Supermarket: good for long-term resupply • health-food store • laundromat • bank • pharmacy • doctor • dentist • hospital • veterinarian • taxi service.

Nantahala Outdoor Center (U.S. 19W, Box 41, Bryson City, N.C. 28713; 704-488-2175): on the Nantahala River where the A.T. crosses, primarily a whitewater-rafting center with folks friendly to hikers. Facilities include a bunkroom, motel, outfitters store, three restaurants, public telephone, and laundromat, but no public showers. Store will ship parcels and may be used as a maildrop. All NOC facilities except Sloe Joe's take MC, Visa, AE, Dis. Rates from 1991, shown below, subject to increase. *Lodging*—Mattress bunk in motel room (6 bunks per room) with hot shower, no linens, $8; regular motel room with double beds, linens, private bath, $35 (2 beds, 4 max) or $45 (3 beds, 8 max); pets must stay outside. *Places to eat*—River's End Restaurant: B/L/D, home-style meals with NOC specialties (sandwiches, burgers, ice cream, yogurt and fruit), open mid-Mar thru Aug (7 days 7am-9pm), Sept-Oct (Sun-Thur 7am-7pm, Fri and Sat 7am-8pm), remainder of year (Mon-Fri 11am-2pm, Sat and Sun 7am-7pm); Rafter's Special (cheese, bread, soup) and the Veggie Hashbrown Delight (for breakfast) are hiker favorites. Also, across the river— Relia's Garden Restaurant: B/D, country-casual, regional and international specialties (trout, teriyaki chicken, shiskabob, garden fettucini), open Apr-Oct, 7-11am and 5-9pm • Sloe Joe's Cafe: B/L, take-out (sandwiches, nacho grande salad, burritos, and hot dogs), open Memorial Day-Labor Day and some weekends otherwise. *Outfitters store*—Backpacking clothing and gear (Camp Trails, Dana Designs, Sierra Designs, Eureka!, Moss, Nike, Merrell, MSR, Peak 1, Thermarest, ThorLo, Wigwam; possible 10% thru-hiker discount on major purchases), Coleman by the pint, butane cartridges, limited groceries, spare parts, stove and gear repair/warranty service on all major brands, laundry detergent by the cup, and Ben & Jerry's (but it goes fast!). *Rafting*—$22 weekdays, $26 weekends for a 3-hour ride, wet suit provided in off-season; raft rentals, $13-$20. Here's your first chance to go whitewater rafting during your hike.

Clubnote: The next 100 miles are maintained by Smoky Mountains Hiking Club volunteers.

Wildflowers: From the Nantahala River to Fontana Dam, you will probably have your first sighting of the following wildflower varieties in bloom—
• *fire pink:* five slender notched petals, red with yellow stamens, hairy leaves; 1-2 feet high.
• *cinquefoil:* five rounded yellow petals, toothed leaves in groups of five, crawling runners 6-20 inches long.
• *nodding trillium:* solitary flower, white with three backswept petals, nodding from three leaves; 10-18 inches high.
• *wood anemone:* solitary 1/2-inch starlike flower, white with yellow center on three-leaved stem, leaves divided into three or five leaflets; 4-12 inches high.

Sassafras Gap Shelter: small shelter with good piped spring, privy. Relocation in 1989 eliminated arduous climb immediately north of shelter. You can now slab around the steepest part on graded treadway, the new route creating a much more enjoyable hike (an on-going goal of ATC and many clubs).

Cheoah Bald: two beautiful vistas overlooking the Smokies and Cheoah-Stecoah ranges, with level tentsites on the ridge and on a grassy area just below the ridge. No water is available, so you'll have to tote it up from the Sassafras Gap Shelter. A thru-hiker said last year, "One of the finest sunsets on my hike."

Stecoah Gap (Sweetwater Creek Road): *On A.T.*—picnic table with trash can, water from nearby piped spring. Directions to the spring: From picnic table, go left 250 feet on the paved road, turn left on an old logging road, and continue for a short distance to the piped spring on the left. *Left 7m*—to the town of Robbinsville.

♦ **Robbinsville, N.C.** (pop. 800): *Services*—Phillip's Motel: $25S $35D (no charge for EAP), 4 max; a/c, cable, phone in room, no pets (MC, Visa); restaurant in motel (B/L) • San Ran Motel • Joyce Kilmer Restaurant • Papa's Pizza • Hardee's • Ingle's Supermarket: good for long-term resupply, open 7 days, 8am-10pm • bakery • laundromat • pharmacy • hardware store • UPS/FedEx pick-up • dentist • Tallulah Health Center • taxi service.

Brown Fork Gap: water to the right about 75 yards; possible site of shelter to be built by Smoky Mountains Hiking Club.

Cable Gap Shelter: once known as the "Ghetto Gap Shelter" because of abuse by neighbors and generally run-down condition. Renovated by Smoky Mountains Hiking Club, USFS, and Appalachian Long Distance Hikers Association. The shelter is about one mile past Yellow Creek Gap Road (some guides incorrectly indicate a shorter distance).

Wildlife: *Flying squirrels cannot really fly but glide 20-30 feet from treetop to tree trunk, using folds of skin between the front and hind legs as a parachute to slow and control their descent. They are the only nocturnal American squirrel. If you are lucky enough to see one gliding, watch as it lands. It will instinctively scramble to the far side of the tree to avoid any owl in pursuit.*

Walker Gap: Follow Yellow Creek Trail approximately 1.25 miles to Green Gap, and then go right on trail that descends steeply to Fontana Village. Last year, several thru-hikers reported that the route was confusing and wished they had stayed on the A.T.

N.C. 28: Left 2m—to the village of Fontana Dam. To reach Fontana Dam Shelter, cross the highway, and continue one mile on the A.T. until it comes out on paved Dam Road, turn right, and follow the road (also the A.T.) toward the dam.

♦ **FONTANA DAM, N.C.** (pop. 50): A resort community, not a true town, managed by Fontana Village Resorts. The resort offers cottages with kitchen and bath for $40-$125 (some cottages can be shared by as many as eight hikers) and rooms at the Fontana Inn for $46-$125. Meals are available at a cafeteria, open 7 days, 7am-8:30pm (breakfast $3-$5, lunch $4-$6, dinner $5-$7), and at the inn's Peppercorn Dining Room (dinner $9-$14). The resort's small shopping area has a laundromat (open 7 days, 7am-11pm, change and detergent available at store), grocery store (good for short-term resupply, Coleman fuel by the pint, generally open 9am-7pm but hours vary with the season), and an ice-cream parlor. A recent expansion added a recreation building with indoor pool and grill (burgers, pizza, open until 10pm). The village is a popular rendezvous point for thru-hikers and their families, with many recreational facilities available on a day-use basis. For reservations, call 1-800-438-8080. All major credit cards are honored for accommodations and meals. *PO-ZIP 28733:* Mon-Fri 8:30am-noon and 1-5pm, Sat 10am-noon; 704-498-2315; LY-215.

Fontana Dam Shelter: known as the "Fontana Hilton," easy to miss. Shelter is to the right, just before a parking area, down a paved driveway leading to a picnic area and restrooms. If you can see the dam, you've gone too far. The shelter, built by TVA, overlooks the lake and is one of the nicest on the Trail. Water spigots and picnic tables surround the building. An information board at the shelter has self-registration instructions and permits for entering the Great Smoky Mountains National Park. Resident skunks visit at night, so hang your food bag, but no bear raids have been reported here in recent years. Path behind the shelter leads down to the lake. "Not much beach, but great swimming," according to "Captain Noah" of '90. Free hot showers are available atop the dam (adjacent to dam restrooms).

Fontana Dam (480 feet high): the cornerstone in the network of dams built by the Tennessee Valley Authority in the first half of this century and the highest dam east of the Mississippi. A visitors center is open daily atop the dam, offering sodas, candy, souvenirs, and film. Tours of the dam are available.

Pets in the Smokies: No pets are allowed in the Great Smoky Mountains National Park, which you are now entering. You can have your animal picked up at one end of the park, boarded, and delivered to the other end by using a kennel/shuttle service. Two kennels have been used by thru-hikers in recent years: Loving Care Kennels (615-453-2028) in Pigeon Forge, Tenn.; Lida O'Neill, owner. One dog $200, two dogs $250. Lida says she will hold and deliver maildrops with your dog(s) at no charge and help with shopping for supplies. • The Mist Kennels (615-453-6369) in Sevierville, Tenn.; Mary Frasier, owner (licensed). Mary will pick up, bathe, board seven days, and deliver your dog for $200. She will also hold and deliver maildrops with your dog at no additional charge.

North Carolina-Tennessee

This chapter takes you from Fontana Dam, North Carolina, to Damascus, Virginia, and corresponds to *Data Book* chapter nine.

Great Smoky Mountains National Park (GSMNP): the most visited park in America but not overrun. The Trail climbs from Fontana Dam to the ridgeline and follows it for 70.5 miles to Davenport Gap. You will need to self-register before entering the park, and the GSMNP permit slip should be displayed on your pack at all times. As a thru-hiker, you are required to stay on the A.T. during your time in the park. In addition, you are required to use only the shelter system for camping. Shelters are constructed of stone, with wooden sleeping platforms. Sleeping spaces in shelters are allocated by reservation, with two spaces in each shelter being reserved for thru-hikers on a first-come, first-served basis from March 15-June 30. This arrangement is not generally known by other shelter users, so you should use tact if someone has usurped your "thru-hiker" space. If a shelter is full when you arrive, you must tent. Park regulations require that you set up your tent close to the shelter and hang your food bag inside the shelter. Shelters have chain-link fencing across the front to keep bears outside. Be sure to close the gate when leaving a shelter, even if only for a few minutes, so that you won't return to find a bear inside and yourself outside, looking in, as it riddles your pack or food bag. Because of the heavy use the park receives, you should exercise extra care at water sources and use only designated areas for sanitation. Good news: Privies are being installed at many locations. For additional information about GSMNP, call the backcountry ranger (615-436-1267).

Wildflowers: From Fontana Dam to Newfound Gap, you will probably have your first sighting of the following wildflower and shrub varieties in bloom—
• *dogtooth violet:* white flowers with six upswept petals, mottled leathery leaves at base of stalk; 6-12 inches high, also called white trout lily.
• *showy orchis:* purple to pink helmetlike flowers with white spur underneath the helmet, leaves shiny; 5-12 inches high.
• *yellow stargrass:* 6 petals, yellow star-shaped flower at top of long spike stem, leaves lance-shaped and clustered at base; 3-7 inches high.
• *white fringed phacelia:* white bell-like flowers with white fringe on edge of petals, grows in masses resembling patches of snow; 6 inches high.
• *flame azalea:* flowers orange with reddish veins, trumpetlike; shrub 4-10 feet high.

Shuckstack: a long climb up from Fontana Dam but graded, so take your time, and enjoy being in the park. The firetower atop Shuckstack requires a detour up a short side trail, offering in return inspiring views in all directions.

> Wildlife: *Wild boars often root near the Trail, leaving an area that you may think has been plowed or tilled by man. They were introduced from Europe for hunting and have thrived here, usurping the food of many native species. An extensive control program of trapping and*

shooting is underway in the park, where boars are a major threat to habitat. Do not approach these animals. They are unpredictable and can be dangerous, especially the females with piglets. Along the A.T., wild boars are found only in Georgia, North Carolina, and Tennessee.

Birch Spring Shelter: much improved by the addition of wooden bunks and gravel on the floor. The area is still muddy in front, however, with few camping sites in the immediate vicinity. Get water at the head of the spring, since the lower reaches are abused by boars from time to time.

Trees and shrubs: The GSMNP has more varieties of trees and shrubs within its boundaries than can be found in all of Europe: a truly magnificent forest environment that is protected from logging and other commercial uses forever. Unfortunately, fire and disease still take their toll, and no one yet knows the effects of global warming, acid rain, nonnative insects, and other factors. Studies are underway to determine why so many fir and spruce trees are dying in these mountains, especially around the Mt. Collins and Tri-Corner Knob areas.

Mollies Ridge Shelter: visited by numerous deer from late afternoon until dusk. A fox reportedly makes daily rounds, and bears make frequent appearances, especially early in the morning when hikers are cooking breakfast.

Spence Field Shelter: near a grassy field that attracts large numbers of deer in the evening. The field, with its view of Thunderhead, makes an excellent lunch spot on a sunny day. New privy in 1991.

> Wildlife: *Black bears are probably the animals you fear the most, yet the ones you most want to see close-up in the wild. You can often tell if bears are in the area by the presence of large black scat and untrampled (recent) paw prints in the footpath. Bears can be dangerous but rarely are unless provoked. Most will run from you, and usually all you see is a black rump charging into the woods. In the park, bears may be less likely to run. Give them room, especially females with cubs, and don't attempt to feed them. They won't settle for part of your food and are easily trained to expect hikers to provide hand-outs, possibly turning surly if food is denied (like some thru-hikers I've known!).*

Double Spring Gap Shelter: where a 1990 thru-hiker hung his food in a tree while he explored a side trail. A bear climbed the tree and started rocking it until the food bag swung close enough to be snared. The bear enjoyed five days of hiker food, the *piece de resistance* being a can of pressurized cheese that exploded in the bear's mouth. The hiker's comment, "It was a damn hungry bear." No comment from the bear.

Treeline: assumed to occur at 7,200 feet in the South, well above the highest summits in the Smokies, so it's impossible to go above treeline in this park. The evergreen line is quite evident, however. As you gain altitude through this section, notice the quick change from deciduous to mixed forest to totally evergreen forest above 5,800 feet.

Clingmans Dome (6,643 feet): the highest point on the A.T. The summit is 0.1 mile off the Trail, topped by an observation deck with photos identifying the distant peaks and sights in all directions. Sightseers in city dress come up from a parking area with restrooms 0.5 mile below the summit on a paved walkway. Most are unaware of the nearby A.T. and will often show real interest when they discover that you are hiking the entire Trail. Some will probably ask permission to take your picture.

Mt. Collins Shelter: on side trail (Sugarland Mountain Trail) to the left; water available on this side trail (about 100 yards past the shelter) from a small spring on the right. A blue-blazed trail leads from the shelter to another water source, but this one is down a steep, obstacle-ridden trail.

Wildlife: *Red wolves are being returned to GSMNP after an absence of nearly a century. Two pairs (four of only 135 genetically pure individuals alive) were released by the Fish and Wildlife Service near Cades Cove last spring and should be running free with pups this year. Red wolves, which have tawny, cinnamon-colored fur, are extremely shy creatures that hunt for small mammals, such as piglets, usually alone and at night. It is hoped that 50 to 75 of these predators will inhabit the park and surrounding national forests by the end of the decade.*

Newfound Gap (U.S. 441): *On A.T.*—parking area with restrooms and the Rockefeller Memorial where President Franklin D. Roosevelt dedicated the park. *Left 14m*—to Great Smoky Mountain National Park HQ (704-498-2327); one mile farther to the town of Gatlinburg. *Right 21m*—to the town of Cherokee.

♦ **GATLINBURG, TENN.** (pop. 3,500): a full-fledged tourist town (with many motels and restaurants) that overwhelms the senses, especially after a few weeks in the woods. A 25¢ shuttle bus runs continually during the day to all points mentioned below (places on U.S. 321 are on the "orange" trolley route). *Lodging*—Willow Motel: $14S $20-$25 (2-4 persons), 4 max; a/c, cable, pool, pets allowed, located on U.S. 321 (MC, Visa); owner Dennis Reagan welcomes hikers • Grand Prix Motel: $22.50 (1-2 persons, 1 bed), $28.50 (3-4 persons, 2 beds), rates higher on weekends, 4 max; a/c, cable, phone in room, use of refrigerator, pool, no pets (MC, Visa, AE, Dis). *Places to eat*—Ruby Tuesday: L/D, some of the best food in town, according to residents • Copper Kettle: B/L/D, casual, American fare, house specialty is prime rib; also fried chicken, country ham, steaks, seafood, salads, sandwiches; open 7 days, 7am-9pm • Anthony's Pizza (615-430-3865): Italian specialties, pizza, late-night delivery; open 7 days, 10am-midnight • McDonald's • KFC • Pizza Hut • Subway • Shoney's • LJ Silver's • Western Sizzler. *Groceries*—Battle's Supermarket: good for long-term resupply; open Mon-Sat 7am-11pm, Sun 8am-11pm; located on U.S. 321 • Mountain Market: good for short-term resupply. *Laundromat*—The Wash Tub: 24-hour laundromat, located on U.S. 321. *Outfitter/laundry*—The Happy Hiker (615-436-5632): backpacking gear (JanSport, Kelty, Mountainsmith, Lowe, The North Face, Sierra Designs, Hi-Tec Sports, Tecnica, Danner, Merrell, Vasque, One Sport, MSR, Camping Gaz, Peak 1, Thermarest, ThorLo, Wigwam), very expensive Coleman by the quart, 5% thru-hiker discount, shower for $2 and coin-operated laundromat next door, $30 for shuttle back to A.T. with one-day notice (up to 5 persons); open 7 days, 8am-7pm (MC, Visa, AE). *Other services*—bank • Plus • Western Union • UPS/FedEx pick-up • hardware store • pharmacy • doctor • dentist • health clinic

• veterinarian • movie theatre • *PO-ZIP 37738*: Mon-Fri 9am-5pm, closed Sat; 615-436-5464; LY-45. Nearby community of Pigeon Forge has an Elvis museum (control yourself!), hundreds of factory outlets, and Dollywood amusement park.

♦ **Cherokee, N.C.** (pop. 1,200): the center of activity for the eastern Cherokee Nation, catering primarily to tourists. *Services*—motels • restaurants • McDonald's • KFC • Burger King • Dairy Queen • LJ Silver's • Western Sizzler • Pizza Inn • Ponderosa • supermarket • laundromat • Plus, Relay, Affinity • outfitter: Venture Out (704-586-1464), with good selection of backpacking equipment, located 8 miles away in Dillsboro, N.C.

Wildflowers: From Newfound Gap to Davenport Gap, you will probably have your first sighting of the following wildflower and shrub varieties in bloom—
• *sand myrtle:* white flowers on rocks at Charlies Bunion.
• *painted trillium:* three white petals with reddish-purple stripes at base; 5-20 inches high.
• *Carolina silverbell:* white bell-shaped flowers; shrub 10-30 feet high.
• *red elderberry:* creamy-white flowers in clusters; shrub 3-10 feet high.

Icewater Spring Shelter: notorious for its resident skunks, which hikers have nicknamed Elvis and Priscilla. Both are friendly with hikers but occasionally have raucous disagreements with each other, sometimes spraying indiscriminately during the melees. New privy in 1991, one of the first on the A.T. in the Smokies.

Icewater Spring to Tri-Corner Knob: a spectacular section of Trail that sometimes goes above 6,000 feet and provides great views off to both sides as you walk for miles above the clouds (unless you're in them!). There is no water along the ridge, except at Pecks Corner Shelter.

> Wildlife: *Ruffed grouse males will be the first to get your attention. Early in spring, you will hear them drumming in the distance (thummmmp-thummmp-thummp-thump-thump-ump-ump-prrr), a strange auditory sensation that has convinced many over-exerting thru-hikers that they were having blood-pressure problems. Farther up the Trail, the hens sitting on eggs will startle you out of your boots. They fly up in your face when you get too near. Once the eggs have hatched, the hen will switch to the broken-wing-and-whining act to fend off predators.*

Charlies Bunion: an exposed rocky knob with a very narrow footpath, located on short loop trail to the left, offering wonderful photo opportunities that will awe the folks back home. Be careful on the rocks: A young man fell to his death here in 1990. The A.T. bypasses the Bunion, providing a foul-weather route around the exposed portion.

Pecks Corner Shelter: off the A.T. down a 0.4-mile side trail to the right, with good spring.

Tri-Corner Knob Shelter: marginal water source in dry years. When you venture past the big blowdown, be glad that no one uses camouflage toilet paper!

Cosby Knob Shelter: another shelter with acrobatic skunks. Hikers in the lower bunks have occasionally been used as runways. Best advice from a skunk-trampled thru-hiker:

"Hunker down in your bag, and let the rascals play!" Bears were reported almost nightly last year.

Mt. Cammerer: about 0.5 mile off the A.T. on fairly level side trail; one of the best views in the park. On a clear day, you actually can see forever.

Davenport Gap Shelter: the last shelter in the park, meaning no more "hemmed in" feeling after a night in this one. Water source is small spring in front of shelter.

Davenport Gap (Tenn. 32/N.C. 17): *Right 2.5m*—to Leatherwood Grocery. *Right 2.5m*— to Big Creek Ranger Station.

♦ Leatherwood Grocery: limited hiker supplies (but "enough to get you to Hot Springs," according to "Beastmaster" of '91), deli with subs, sandwiches, burgers, ice cream; open 7 days, 8am-7pm. Directions: After descending from the gap, go straight ahead at intersection, cross bridge, pass old store on left, and continue up hill on dirt road for several switchbacks to house on left with sign.

♦ Big Creek Ranger Station: public telephone and campground with tentsites, water, restrooms, no showers; ranger hours variable. Turn right at intersection mentioned above. Note: Southbounders should get park permit here at the self-registration board. The Chestnut Branch Trail from the campground intersects the A.T. one mile south of the Davenport Gap Shelter.

Clubnote: The next 91 miles are maintained by Carolina Mountain Club volunteers.

Wildflowers: From Davenport Gap to Hot Springs, you will probably have your first sighting of the following wildflower and tree varieties in bloom—
• *rattlesnake weed:* yellow dandelion-like flowers on stalk, maroon-veined spatula-shaped leaves hug ground; 1-2 feet high.
• *pink lady's-slipper:* nodding pink pouch-like structure with veined lip and purplish-brown twisted side petals; 6-14 inches high.
• *Indian cucumber root:* stem with two whorls of leaves, usually three at top and five below, yellow flowers with six upswept petals, reddish-brown stigma; 1-3 feet high.
• *wild lily-of-the-valley:* white flowers with four petals in dense spike atop stem; 2-6 inches high; red berries later in year.
• *tulip trees:* flowers tuliplike, green and orange; tree grows to 120 feet high.

Interstate 40: On A.T.—entrance and exit ramps where Trail goes under I-40, a good place to have your pet picked up or delivered. *Left 15m*—to the city of Newport. (Don't forget: Hitching on the interstate system is illegal.)

♦ Newport, Tenn. (pop. 7,580): *Services*—motel • Fox & Hounds Supper Club on Knoxville Hwy. • McDonald's • Hardee's • KFC • Burger King • Pizza Hut • Dairy Queen • Subway • Shoney's • LJ Silver's • Western Sizzler • Arby's • Cajun Joe's • supermarket good for long-term resupply • bakery • laundromat • bank • pharmacy • hardware store • Wal-Mart • doctor • dentist • hospital • veterinarian • Greyhound service • taxi service.

Snowbird Mountain: unique for its hum, and eerie in the fog. Your chances of getting hit by an airplane are probably better here than anywhere else on the A.T. Why? Strange-looking "spaceship" on summit is a FAA omnidirectional homing transmitter, one of hundreds in an overlapping network nationwide. The long climb up will be made refreshing by the scent of *sweet cicely,* which many have likened to licorice.

Groundhog Creek Shelter: called Deep Gap Shelter on some maps and signs. This is the shelter generally considered to have the most active mice on the A.T. In 1987, a thru-hiker claimed to have seen 13 mice playfully scurrying around the rafters at one time. Last year, a black snake took up residence in the area, so maybe nature has solved the problem for us. (Take note, trap-setters.)

> Wildlife: *Mice are most frequently seen by hikers at shelters but inhabit all parts of the woods. All varieties are nocturnal and eat primarily seeds and grains. The deer mouse and the harvest mouse are native species, while the house mouse is an Asian import that has flourished. The latter are the mice that most often visit your food bag, and they will make a nest of almost any material they can shred. Mice can produce up to eight litters a year, with up to 12 babies per litter.*

Max Patch: a high, grassy bald with magnificent views in all directions. The A.T. used to follow the gravel road you see below, but land was purchased in 1982 by the USFS, allowing the Trail to traverse the summit. Camping is permitted on top, but the summit is dry, so fill up at the creek before you start up. Refrain from building a fire. Warning: Expect very high winds in a storm.

Roaring Fork Shelter: replacement for the Walnut Mountain Shelter, which was to be demolished, but is now being rebuilt by the Carolina Mountain Club and should be "like new" for 1992 hikers.

Deer Park Mountain Shelter: water source is creek 100 feet to the left at the shelter sign. A small, usually slow-flowing spring is located to the right on the side trail to the shelter.

HOT SPRINGS, N.C. (pop. 678): a perennial favorite with thru-hikers because the community is friendly and everything is within easy walking distance—a true Trail town. The town has been known for its therapeutic mineral springs since the 1800s. Two resort hotels were built around the springs and operated until they burned, the first in the 1920s, the second in the 1970s. The springs lay dormant until 1990, when the property was sold to a developer. A new spa has been built, and change is on the way. Hopefully, the town will retain its charm for thru-hikers. ATC is working with the town toward that end. *Hostel*—The A.T. Hiker's Hostel, established in the 1960s and sponsored by the Jesuit Fathers; the first place you pass when coming into town. Overnight accommodations include a mattress bunk, hot shower, clean towel, kitchen privileges, and common room for relaxation; requested donation $9 per night (or work by arrangement). No dogs are permitted inside. No alcohol may be used on the premises. If no one is around when you arrive, sign in, and make yourself at home. A caretaker is usually on duty at night to check you in officially. *Other lodging*—The Inn at Hot Springs (P.O. Box 233, Hot Springs, N.C. 28743; 704-622-7206): a unique experience on the A.T. Innkeeper Elmer Hall, who thru-hiked most of the Trail in 1975-76, and his staff of former thru-hikers attract an eclectic mixture of interesting visitors to his white Victorian house (the one across from the BP station, marked by an historical marker that says "Balladry"). The inn has an extensive record and video collection and an excellent library. Meals are gourmet vegetarian ("Speaking as a diehard carnivore, the food was superb," was the reaction of one nonvegetarian guest) and served family-style; not AYCE, but few can handle more than is served. Rooms are entertainingly furnished. Upstairs baths have some of the most luxurious tubs you will ever see. A shower is also available. Rates for thru-hikers: bed with bath and towel $10, dinner $7, breakfast $3; labor (usually yard work or painting) can often be exchanged as payment. No smoking and no dogs. Space is usually available for hikers on weekdays, but weekends are often crowded with other guests. Can be used as maildrop. Note: The Inn is Elmer's home and very much an expression of himself. That's what makes it such a wonderful experience. When you check in, read the very simple house rules, a copy of which is laid on your bed, and observe them. Enjoy fitting into the ambiance of this very mellow place. • Duckett House Inn (P.O. Box 441, Hot Springs, N.C. 28743; 704-622-7621): the large white folk-Victorian house with the red roof, 200 yards from the A.T. (to the right after descending steps to Hwy. 209). Former thru-hikers Brian Baker and Frank Matula opened the inn in 1991 and are working hard to create an atmosphere of friendliness to thru-hikers. Most thru-hikers last year felt they had succeeded. Rates: $17.50 with full breakfast, dinner $12; reservations a must for breakfast and dinner if not staying at inn; can often exchange labor for stay. Meals are fine vegetarian served family-style, with produce from adjacent organic garden. No smoking or pets. Tentsites available on creek. Shower $2. Shuttle service 75¢ per mile. • Alpine Court Motel: $35D • KLR Rental Apartments: Each apartment has 2 bedrooms with complete kitchen for $60 per night; no limit on number of people who stay overnight (check at Ramsey's for details). *Places to eat*—The inns (see above) • Smoky Mountain Restaurant: B/L/D, diner-style meals, lunch and dinner buffets, located across from the Inn; open Mon-Sat 6am-9pm, Sun 7am-9pm • Kay's Trail Cafe: B/L/D, home-style cooking, burgers, fries, pies, Traveler's Special (breakfast with 2 eggs, hash browns or grits, sausage or bacon, 3 pancakes) a favorite, located near the PO; open 7 days, 6am-8pm. *Groceries*—Ricker's Grocery: good for short-term resupply; open Mon-Sat 8am-6pm, closed Sun • Carolina Grocery: good for short-term resupply; open Mon-Sat 7am-6pm, closed Sun. *Laundromat*—Bridge Street Laundry: open 7 days, 8am-10pm, get change and detergent at Ramsey's. *Stove fuel*—Gentry's Hardware: Coleman by the pint, post cards, film, boot glue, batteries, package wrapping; open Mon-Sat 8am-5pm, closes noon Wed; owned by nice folks who have gone out of their way to serve hikers for many years. *Other services*—Wachovia Bank • Ramsey's Amusements: game room, some hiker food supplies, pizza, and snack foods; open Mon-Fri 8am-10pm, Sat until 11pm, Sun 9am-9pm • USFS district office • Hot Springs Health Clinic: doctor, dentist, pharmacy • Hot Springs Animal Clinic • Carolina Wilderness: whitewater trips • NOC French Broad Outpost (704-622-7260): river trips, limited hiking gear and clothing (but they can usually get items not in stock and forward them to your next stop), showers for $1, shuttles (MC, Visa, AE, Dis); open Mar-Oct, 7 days, 8am-5pm • public telephones: two in town, one next to Kay's Trail Cafe and the other near the Jesuit hostel. *Point of Interest*—The springs are being redeveloped, with a new bath house already open for this year's hikers. A 30-minute soaking in the mineral baths costs about $10. *PO-ZIP 28743:* Mon-Fri 8:30-11:30am and 12:30-4:15pm, Sat 8:45-11:45am; 704-622-3242; LY-285.

Relocation: A new route takes you out of Hot Springs. At the northern (eastern) end of the bridge over the French Broad River, take a sharp right to Silvermine Creek Road below. Go through the NOC outpost, then bear right on new Trail (old Drovers Road), which follows the river. About 0.5 mile upstream, the A.T. turns away from the river and ascends. The old A.T. is yellow-blazed as a high-water loop.

Wildflowers: From Hot Springs to Erwin, you will probably have your first sighting of the following wildflower varieties in bloom—
• *rattlesnake plantain:* greenish-white flowers clustered on downy spike, hairy leaves with white markings, leaves at base; 6-18 inches high.
• *dwarf larkspur:* five petals, flower somewhat trumpet-shaped, purple or blue with white in center, flowers clustered along stem top, divided leaves scattered on stem; 1-2 feet high.
• *Virginia waterleaf:* densely clustered bell-shaped flowers, white to purple with long hairlike stamens; 1-3 feet high.
• *fringed polygala:* three petals, two wing-like, rose-purple with fringe at tip, shiny oval leaves; 3-6 inches high.
• *white clintonia:* creamy white bell-shaped flowers clustered atop stem, three shiny oval-shaped leaves at base; 8-16 inches high.

Pond and dam: on the Trail 4.8 miles north of town, frequently used by local anglers. Level tentsites can be found on the USFS fire road up the embankment 100 feet to the left, above the pond. Water is available from the spring that feeds the pond.

Rich Mountain firetower: on a side trail, usually locked and unstaffed, with road access, often frequented by amorous couples after dark. Water available from spring on A.T. just beyond side-trail junction.

Rex Pulford memorial: in memory of Dorothy Hansen's father, who died of a heart attack on this spot during his 1983 thru-hike.

Spring Mountain Shelter: small, with good piped spring down blue-blazed trail in front of shelter. Heavy growth of *wild (red) bergamot mint* around spring. Open-air privy.

Allen Gap (N.C. 208/Tenn. 70): *Right 0.1m*—to State Line Gas with ice cream, snack foods, candy, and tobacco products in abundance; no water or public telephone, but often a hot stove on a cold day; open Mon-Sat 9am-7pm, Sun 1-7pm. On weekends, this store is sometimes a hangout for a rough-talking "good-old-boy" crowd, so be cautious.

> *Wildlife: Bobcats are nocturnal and solitary, so you may not see this shy creature unless you are hiking at dawn or dusk. They eat mainly rabbits and hares but will eat other small mammals, birds, and carrion on occasion. Caves, rocky ledges, and hollow logs make good denning sites. Bobcats are two to three feet long, somewhat spotted, and have a distinctive 5-inch tail that is black on top.*

Little Laurel Shelter: good piped spring, 200 feet down blue-blazed trail across A.T. just beyond shelter. Several flat areas for tenting are nearby.

Camp Creek Bald: muddy, boggy area on summit, but it's ideal habitat for painted trillium. Great views into Tennessee.

Jerry Cabin: maintained by Sam Waddle (615-257-2586), a friend of hikers who mows the lawn but can't seem to remember to pay the light and phone bills for the shelter!

Bassett memorial: 1.5 miles north of Jerry Cabin; marks the place where Sam Waddle scattered the ashes of 1968 thru-hiker Howard Bassett, one of the first 50 people to thru-hike the Trail and a fine gentleman to all who knew him. Howie's hike was chronicled in Rodale's classic *Hiking the Appalachian Trail.*

Shelton graves: three graves with two headstones, 20 feet to the right in a clearing off the Trail. Markers were placed here in 1915 to honor the Shelton brothers, Union soldiers from Tennessee who were ambushed by Confederates as they returned to visit their families. A 15-year-old relative was also killed and is buried nearby in an unmarked grave. "Spring Chicken" of '91 saw a she-bear and two cubs near here last year.

Flint Mountain Shelter: one of the more unusual shelter designs, typical of the newer shelters being built by the Carolina Mountain Club in recent years.

Devil Fork Gap (N.C. 212): rumors for past few years of a new hostel to be opened by Eddie Ray, who lives down the road to the left. Look for notices.

Trail Fact: *The forest floor is covered with leaves, and one square yard of this leaf litter may be home to as many as 100,000 small creatures. On your trek from Georgia to Maine this year, you will probably pass within a hundred feet of 70 trillion living things*, not counting trees and plants!

Hogback Ridge Shelter: water a long way down, but what a great privy!

Sams Gap (U.S. 23): *On A.T.*—Empty buildings at the gap are marked "No Trespassing," definitely off-limits to hikers. *Right 3m*—to Little Creek Cafe.

♦ Little Creek Cafe: B/L/D, home-style meals, burgers, cornbread and honey, and "Grannie Boone's" delicious homemade pies; open Mon-Sat 5am-5pm, may close earlier on occasion.

Big Bald: a spectacular bald, with view of Mt. Mitchell (6,684 feet, highest peak east of the Mississippi), and hacking site for peregrine falcons. Four falconets were released successfully in 1989. You will see notices before you reach the nesting area if raptors are using the mountain. Read carefully, since the Trail may be rerouted temporarily, and be sure to observe to the letter any regulations. Masses of *fringed phacelia* can be seen just before you reach the open bald. Wolf Laurel Restaurant, mentioned in some older guides, closed last year.

*Wildlife: Peregrine falcons have been clocked at 275 mph in a dive.
These speedy birds of prey, a worldwide species, had been virtually
eliminated from the eastern United States by pesticides and human
encroachment. Peregrines are being reestablished, partly through ATC
programs, and hikers have reported seeing them in several locations
along the A.T. in recent years.*

Bald Mountain Shelter: the "Carolina Condo," home in 1990-91 to a stray cat, named "I-i-i-ick" for the pitiful sound it made. Be warned: The cat is an expert at yogi-ing tuna from thru-hikers.

High Rocks: excellent view of surrounding mountains, worth a few minutes' delay.

Clubnote: The next 126 miles are maintained by Tennessee Eastman Hiking Club volunteers, who work hard to keep the A.T. open through one of the more difficult sections to maintain. Past ATC Chair Ray Hunt, who compiled the first *A.T. Data Book* in 1977, is a member of this club.

No Business Knob Shelter: water from creek several hundred yards before shelter. Look for a blue-blaze to the left, soon after the A.T. crosses a creek and bears sharply left up a ravine.

Nolichucky River: flowing from the slopes of Mt. Mitchell. The river was frequently used by Davy Crockett when he was a young man, and much of the surrounding area has a Crockett flavor. A young Andrew Jackson also came to frontier gatherings (the forerunners of country fairs) near where the A.T. crosses the river.

Chestoa Bridge: rebuilt in 1991, eliminating a detour through the town of Erwin. The river is again crossed where the Trail comes out of the woods. After crossing the bridge, a reroute takes the Trail off the gravel road to the right, which leads directly to the NGC hostel, but the A.T. still passes within a few hundred feet of the hostel before turning away from the river (about 1.5 miles beyond the bridge on the Trail, look for hostel/campground signs pointing to the right). If you want to go into town, follow the road across the bridge, then bear left on the paved road 3.8 miles to the city of Erwin.

♦ **ERWIN, TENN.** (pop. 4,739): an increasingly friendly town but spread out, so getting around on foot can be a bit of a chore. The town satisfies most hiker needs. *Lodging*—Brotherton's Family Inn: $25S $35D $10EAP, 4 max; a/c, cable, phone in room, use of refrigerator; prefers no pets. *Places to eat*—Elm's Restaurant: B/L/D, country-casual dining and take-out, home-cooked meats and vegetables, salad bar; open 7 days, 6am-9pm • McDonald's • Hardee's • KFC • Pizza Hut • Little Caesar's • Western Sizzlin' AYCE (closed in 1989; too many thru-hikers ate there?). *Groceries*—White's Supermarket (2 locations): good for long-term resupply, open 7 days, 8am-10pm • Food Lion Supermarket: good for long-term resupply; open Mon-Sat 8am-10pm, Sun 9am-9pm. *Laundromat*—Maytag Laundry: FLW, open 7 days, 8am-10pm, last load 9pm; owned by friendly Jean Wright, who has coffee and snacks available while you wait. *Cobbler*—Baker's Harness & Shoe Repair: one-day service for thru-hikers, sells insoles and arch supports; open daily 8am-5pm, Wed and Sat 8am-2:30pm, closed Sun. *Other services*—bank • Western Union • pharmacy •

hardware store • Family Dollar Discount Store • doctor • dentist • health clinic • hospital • veterinarian • UPS/FedEx pick-up • showers no longer available at the YMCA • Worley Edwards (615-743-5617) runs a shuttle to town for $1 per person, minimum $4 per trip • Kent Garland (615-743-5585) is a friend of hikers, as are Beau and Betty Hardy (615-743-7685). *PO-ZIP 37650:* Mon-Fri 8am-5pm, closed Sat; 615-743-4811; anyone working will answer the buzzer at the back door after hours; LY-86.

Wildlife: *Elephants have been told for years to avoid Erwin, and the warning seems to have worked. You won't see any elephants hanging around town.*

Nolichucky Expeditions/USA Raft: a white-water rafting business on the river near the Trail. The office personnel are friendly to hikers and often offer rides to and from town. Lodging is usually available in two authentic 1800s cabins, one bunk-house style, the other with private rooms. Lodging and river trips can be arranged at the office (work exchange possible). An outside telephone and drink machine are located on the front porch. The staff warns: Beware of gravity surge at this beautiful place; allow a couple of days.

NGC Hostel: operated as part of Nolichucky Gorge Campground (615-743-8876), located on the A.T. next to Nolichucky Expeditions, across the small creek to the left as you come down the entrance drive; open Mar-Nov. The campground has a bunkhouse, tentsites, and showers. Bunkhouse has 12 bunks, wood stove, picnic tables, sofa, and electric lights, with hot shower and water next door. Rates: bunk with shower (no towel), $8 per person; tentsite with shower, $4 per person. No reservations accepted for bunkhouse or tentsites. The following was overheard being sung around a campfire here: "Slabbing the 'Chucky deep in the night, coal trains rumble and squeal with delight." Note: A camp store was located near the bunkhouse last year and carried A.T. essentials, Coleman by the pint, butane canisters, water filters, stoves, film, pack covers, blister aids, and stamps, plus "some unique stuff for the Trail." No information was available about availability of this store for the 1992 season at time of publication. If the store is not operating, Coleman fuel by the pint may not be available in the Erwin area, so watch for notices.

Wildflowers: From Erwin to Damascus, you will probably have your first sighting of the following wildflower and shrub varieties in bloom—
• *wild columbine:* five red tubular sepals with knobs, yellow cathedral-like petals inside, nodding, leaves fernlike; 1-4 feet high.
• *mountain laurel:* flowers delicate, white with pink edge in clusters; shrub 10-20 feet high.
• *rosebay rhododendron:* white to pink flowers in large clusters; shrub 10-20 feethigh.
• *purple rhododendron:* lavender flowers in large clusters; shrub 10-20 feet high.

Curley Maple Gap Shelter: concrete block structure with small spring to the right as you look into the shelter.

Beauty Spot: And, it is! On a sunny day, plan to take a rest break or have lunch at this place. Unfortunately, the summit is dry, the nearest water being a spring 0.5 mile north on the A.T., on a short blue-blazed side trail across the gravel road to the summit.

Unaka Mountain: "extensive stand of red spruce, rare south of New England," says "The Dharma Bum" of '90.

Cherry Gap Shelter: good piped spring, flat tentsites nearby across the A.T.

Iron Mountain Gap (Tenn. 107/N.C. 226): *Right 0.5m*—to Moffits Grocery with limited hiker supplies, ice cream, and snacks; no public telephone; open Mon-Sat 7am-7pm, closed Sun.

> Wildlife: *Shrews are the world's smallest mammals, and you will see them as they dash across the Trail, or at least think that you have seen them. Some can weigh as little as a dime. They have remarkable digestive systems, passing insects in less than 90 minutes. Most eat their weight in food every day (and you think you have a big appetite!). Shrews are active day and night. They look like mice (but are not rodents), with pointed noses, small eyes, and almost nonexistent ears. Their bite is venomous, similar to that of a cobra.*

Clyde Smith Shelter: not visible from the A.T., and the sign is a hard-to-see metal marker high on a tree. Watch for a blue-blazed trail to the left, and look carefully for the sign. Water is quite a way down from the shelter, but cold and dependable. If you've read Ed Garvey's book, you'll understand the graffiti on the right wall.

Roan High Bluff: parking area, tables, restrooms, and vistas on the summit just off the Trail. Cloudland Trail, originating at the far end of the parking lot, leads through the large, natural *rhododendron* gardens. Peak blooming season is in early June, when the Roan rhododendrons are said to be among the most beautiful sights in nature.

Roan High Knob Shelter (6,285 feet): a cabin formerly used by the fire warden and the highest shelter on the A.T. Two mattresses on the bottom floor are usable for sleeping. The loft is breezy on a cold night. Water is from a piped spring 100 feet down a path to the right of the cabin as you face it. Roots from a large blowdown somewhat hide the spring's rusty outlet pipe.

Carvers Gap: water fountain and privy off to the left, beyond the parking area. *Left 8.7m*—to Roan Mountain State Park.

♦ Roan Mountain State Park: tentsites $8.50 per night (Apr 15-Nov 15), hot showers, restaurant, laundromat, and public telephone.

Southern balds: still a mystery, with treeless summits below treeline. They have been studied extensively, but the reason for their baldness still eludes investigators. Some guesses: Indians cleared them, too much wind, bedrock too close to the surface, overgrazing by settlers' livestock, and lightning. A few folks have even resorted to blaming UFOs. Perhaps it's hereditary.

Roan Highlands Shelter: likened to a bus stop beside the Trail. Good piped spring down path in front.

Yellow Mountain Gap: historically important (see marker). The A.T. intersects the Overmountain Victory National Historic Trail here. A blue-blazed trail to the right leads to the Overmountain Shelter.

Overmountain Shelter: a renovated red barn with sleeping loft and great view of the beautiful valley. Water is available from a spring between the shelter and Trail. "Winter People," a 1988 movie starring Kurt Russell, Kelly McGillis, and Lloyd Bridges, was filmed on this site. The set, which has since been removed, featured a facade cabin and Hollywood-style plaster-of-Paris boulders out front.

Hump Mountains: spectacular balds, with great views off to either side. Hump was the focus of a successful $1 million "Save the Hump" fundraising campaign several years ago, led by former ATC Chairman Stan Murray. Today, the Humps are mostly protected from development, the only intruders being horses from farms in the valley that sometimes wander up to mooch treats from thru-hikers. If you're tempted, remember that pack animals are not allowed on the Trail. Northbounders should note that the Trail bears left after descending from the summit of Hump Mountain. Southbounders should note that the Trail turns left in Bradley Gap.

The Greenway Concept: Stan Murray was also responsible for developing "the Appalachian Greenway" concept, which seeks to protect the environs of the Trail beyond the treadway and corridor. Stan felt that we should have not only a footpath, but a footpath through associated lands that preserve the values of wilderness so vital to the Trail experience. Stan passed away in 1990, after 40 years of service to the Trail community.

> Wildlife: *Woodchucks are the groundhogs of legend, but you won't see them emerging from their burrows on February 2 to look for their shadow, since they hibernate until late winter. Woodchucks feed during the day, eating tender, succulent plants, especially clover and alfalfa, and are most often seen by hikers along the edges of fields and at road crossings. They are beaver-like animals with short legs and a short, bushy tail.*

Apple House Shelter: airy but said to be watertight on the stormiest nights. Water source is creek behind shelter. You may want to pick up water from one of the creeks you pass at higher elevation as you descend to the shelter.

U.S. 19E: Right 1.3m—to J's Market. *Left 4m*—to the town of Roan Mountain. *Right 2.5m*—to the town of Elk Park.

♦ J's Market: good for short-term resupply, ice cream, fresh fruit, outside soda machine, and public telephone out front; open Mon-Sat 7am-7:30pm.
♦ ROAN MOUNTAIN, TENN. (pop. 850): *Lodging*—Stack's Roan Mountain Motel (P.O. Box 7, Roan Mountain, Tenn. 37687; 615-772-3432) with motel rooms, hostel, and restaurant; owned by friendly and personable "Jersey John" and Carmen Stack. Motel room with double beds, bath, air conditioning, and cable, $32D $10EAP. Hostel is a no-frills bunk and shower for $10. Shuttle back and forth to the A.T. is free with room or hostel. Tentsites are $2 with shower. The restaurant caters to hikers by serving large portions, and offers two hiker specials: a $4 breakfast and a $5 Italian dinner (lasagna, ziti,

spaghetti), both served family-style; vegetarian meals available. John makes an ice-cream run to Knoxville once a month to get Ben & Jerry's, just for hikers! Gear for sale includes fuel (Coleman by the pint), socks, and underwear. John and Carmen have a nephew who thru-hiked the Trail and both relate well to hikers. They will accept UPS or mail packages if addressed c/o Stack's Roan Mountain Motel. Shuttles can be arranged within a 100-mile radius. MC and Visa cards are honored. *Services*—Roan Mountain Supermarket: good for short-term resupply, open 7 days, 8am-9pm • Cloudland Food Market: good for short-term resupply • laundromat: FLW, open 7 days, 5am-midnight • bank • Cirrus • doctor • dentist • health clinic • veterinarian. *Point of Interest*—Room #7 in the motel! *PO-ZIP 37687:* Mon-Fri 8-11:30am and 12:30-4:30pm, Sat 8-11am; 615-772-3661; LY-50.

♦ **ELK PARK, N.C.** (pop. 200): *Services*—Times Square Motel (about 1.4 miles beyond PO): $30D, motel restaurant with AYCE breakfast, open Mon-Fri 6am-9pm, Sat and Sun 7am-9pm (no reports in 1991) • Country House Restaurant (between A.T. and town): "liar's table" and country breakfast with saucer-sized biscuits • grocery store: limited hiker supplies • hardware store • Elk River Campground: tentsite and shower $5 per person, shower $2 if not camping, sink to wash clothes, recreation pavilion, possible shuttle back to Trail. *PO-ZIP 28622:* Mon-Fri 7:30am-noon and 1:15-4:30pm, Sat 7:30-10:30am; 704-733-5711; LY-40+.

Notice: The five-mile section just north of U.S. 19E was the scene of vandalism near and on the Trail in 1990. The Don Nelan Shelter was burned early that year, and fish-hooks were strung across the footpath at eye level. Forest Service personnel were confronted on several occasions. No hikers were challenged or harassed in 1990 or last year; nevertheless, hikers are advised to be cautious. Stay on the A.T., and go through this section in groups, if possible. Keep a low profile. Do not linger or camp in the section from U.S. 19E to Moreland Gap Shelter. Look for notices posted by ATC and TEHC that may have further information about this, hopefully, temporary situation.

Elk Park to Hampton: Many of the water sources in this section flow out of inhabited areas and may be polluted by people or animals upstream.

> Wildlife: *Slate-colored juncos are the little gray-and-white sparrows that build their nests on low banks along the footpath and suddenly fly out at your feet as you pass by. Don't follow the bird. Instead, look back to where it flew out, and you will find a cuplike nest hidden under a tuft of grass, usually with 3 or 4 eggs, perhaps with several tiny chicks. Be careful not to disturb eggs or chicks. The junco, also known as the eastern snowbird, is the most frequently seen bird on the A.T.*

Moreland Gap Shelter: good piped spring in front of shelter, quite a way down.

Laurel Fork Shelter: on blue-blazed side trail that continues straight ahead where the A.T. takes a sharp left and descends into the gorge. Water source is a creek beyond shelter that flows from the Pond Mountain Wilderness.

Laurel Fork Gorge: a deep, rhododendron-rimmed gorge with a big, beautiful waterfall, one of those "magic places" that you imagined when you dreamed of hiking the A.T. The Trail down is steep, but the views are worth the torture. Swimming is possible at the base of the falls, and the area is usually crowded on weekends. Level tentsites can be found all along the creek until you begin to climb out of the gorge. The blue-blazed trail before Pond Mountain leads to U.S. 321. Note: The first bridge you come to in the gorge, built in 1990 by Tennessee Eastman Hiking Club (TEHC) volunteers and ATC's Konnarock Trail crew, using no power tools or metal hardware, won a USFS National Primitive Skills Award.

Pond Mountain: to be tamed by the end of 1992. Reroutes will take some of the severity out of the climb and possibly shorten the distance over the mountain by three miles. Look for notices.

U.S. 321: On A.T.—Rat Branch Store and Motel: very limited hiker supplies, drinks, snacks, grill with sandwiches, burgers; open 7 days, 8am-10pm, grill until 8pm (operation sporadic, depending on availability of cook). Next door, Rat Branch Motel, $25S $30 (2-4 persons), 4 max; no pets inside (outside on leash); camping with shower for $8; outside telephone. *Left 2.8m*—to Brown's Grocery, Braemar Castle Hostel and Guest House. *Left 3.6m*—to the town of Hampton.

♦ Brown's Grocery & Hardware: good for long-term resupply, Coleman by the pint, open Mon-Sat 8am-7pm (will open Sun for hikers on request). Public telephone outside.

♦ Braemar Castle Hostel and Guest House: bunkroom, kitchen facilities, and reading room. Bunk with shower $10 per person, shower only for $2, private rooms and apartments $20-$30S $25-$35D; located across the road from Brown's. Shuttle back to A.T. by grocery/hostel owner Sutton Brown (615-725-2411 or 2262), a friend of hikers. Check in at grocery store.

♦ Hampton, Tenn. (pop. 1,000): *Services*—Big B Restaurant: B/L/D, country cooking, specials every day; open 7 days, 7am-9pm • diner • bank • pharmacy • taxi (615-725-2262). Farther out on the 4-lane highway, almost to Elizabethton: Comfort Inn and supermarket. *PO-ZIP 37658:* Mon-Fri 7:30-10am and 11am-4:30pm, Sat 8-10am; 615-725-3703; LY-25.

Shook Branch Picnic Area: picnic tables, water, and restrooms. If you don't want to purify stream water at the Watauga Lake Shelter, get water here. The Trail north of this picnic area may be partially submerged in very wet years, in which case you can follow the road that parallels the A.T. on the left.

Watauga Dam: first large earth-filled hydroelectric dam built in the United States, dedicated in 1949.

Watauga Lake Shelter: water from creek adjacent to shelter; no good tenting sites nearby.

Vandeventer Shelter: excellent view overlooking Watauga Lake from the rocks behind the shelter. Water for this shelter is a long way down on the side trail you pass on the left 500 feet south of the shelter. Instead, you may want to get water from the spring on the A.T. 1.7 miles south of the shelter.

> Wildlife: *Whip-poor-wills are rarely sighted, but you will hear them often. Your best chance of seeing this bird is when one flies down to sound its three-part call in front of shelters, perhaps to enjoy the echo*

effect. The call may be repeated up to a thousand times or more (but who's counting?) before the whip-poor-will stops to catch its breath and begin the series again. It is a mottled-brown color, nine inches long, with a large head and eyes that reflect red in the dark.

Iron Mountain Shelter: water from small stream you cross about 0.2 mile before shelter; flat areas for tenting in front.

Grindstaff Monument: off the A.T. about 100 feet to the left; looks like a chimney from an old cabin, and that's exactly what it is. "Uncle Nick" Grindstaff reportedly lived here as a hermit for 46 years, his only friend a pet rattlesnake that was eventually killed by visitors. In 1988, a blowdown almost demolished the memorial. Nick's sad epitaph is on the side away from the Trail.

Double Springs Shelter: actually has two good springs, both piped. No flat tentsites near shelter, but some beyond on the hill about 0.1 mile north on the A.T.

Low Gap (U.S. 421): *Right 3m*—to the community of Shady Valley, Tenn. (pop. 100) with small grocery store, no other services.

Firewarden's cabin: dubbed the "holiday inn," rebuilt in fall of 1991, but usable only as an emergency shelter.

Abingdon Gap Shelter: water source is spring about 300 feet behind shelter; numerous flat tentsites nearby.

Tennessee-Virginia line: marked by sign that welcomes you to the Mt. Rogers National Recreation Area. You aren't far from Damascus, now!

Southwest and Central Virginia

This chapter takes you from Damascus, Virginia, to Rockfish Gap, Virginia, and corresponds to *Data Book* chapter eight.

DAMASCUS, VA. (pop. 1,200): known far and wide as "the friendliest town on the Appalachian Trail." The Trail goes through the center of town, and residents eagerly anticipate the arrival of thru-hikers each spring, as they have for more than four decades. Highlight of the Damascus social year is the "Appalachian Trail Days" festival in May. Thousands of visitors converge on the town to take part in this event, and usually more than 200 thru-hikers attend. As a hiker, you will feel a town-wide welcome here that is unmatched anywhere else on the A.T. *Hostel*—"The Place," an old house behind the Methodist church that serves as home and headquarters for hikers in town. It has seven rooms with bunks and foam pads on the floor for sleeping, a common room with picnic table and sofa for lounging, limited kitchen facilities (sink and refrigerator, but no stove), two bathrooms with hot showers, a screened back porch for cooking (no cooking inside building), a front porch with swing, and grassy yard for pitching tents. The telephone, located inside the hostel, is a courtesy of the local telephone company. The hostel is for overnight use only by thru-hikers (no family or friends) and cyclists on the Transcontinental Bike Trail that also comes through town. A donation of $2 per night is requested, with a two-night limit on stay unless you are sick or injured. All donations are used by the church to keep the hostel open and operating, but they never collect enough to cover expenses, so give a little extra if you can. Several things should be noted: No alcohol is permitted on the property (remember, this is part of the Methodist church!); the hostel is located in a residential neighborhood, so keep noise to a minimum, especially after dark; and, much of the maintenance on this hostel is done by thru-hikers, so, if you have a few spare hours, pitch in and do some cleaning or light repair. *Other lodging*—Nannie Wright, in the white house across from the Methodist Church, sometimes takes in hikers overnight, usually charging about $20D. *Places to eat*—Quincy's Pizza & Subs: L/D, pizza, assorted pasta dishes, "Philly steaks," open 7 days • Cowboy's: B/L/D, fast-food and deli, eat-in or take-out, fried chicken, potato wedges, burgers, subs, country-style breakfast, salads, open 7 days • Dairy King: L/D, burgers, hot dogs, frozen custard, pies, carrot cake, open 7 days • Dot's Inn & Cafe: B/L/D, short-orders, biscuits and gravy, burgers and fries anytime, flounder, daily luncheon special (meat and 2 veggies), live music on weekends; open Mon-Sat 7am-midnight, closed Sun. *Groceries*—Minute-Ette Food Market: good for long-term resupply, open Mon-Sat 8:30am-9pm • CJ's Grocery & Deli: good for long-term resupply, deli take-out; open Mon-Sat 8am-10pm, Sun 8am-9pm. *Laundromat*—Damascus Laundry: detergent and change available next door at CJ's. *Stove fuel*—Damascus Video: Coleman by the pint • Town & Country Hardware: Coleman by the pint. *Outfitter*—Mt. Rogers Outfitters (703-475-5416): backpacking gear and clothing (JanSport, Kelty, Sierra Designs, Eureka!, Hi-Tec Sports, Merrell, MSR, Optimus/Svea, Trangia, Caribou, Thermarest, ThorLo, Wigwam, Nalgene, Equinox), stove and pack repairs, butane fuels, UPS pickup service (MC, Visa); open Mon-Fri 9am-5:30pm, Sat 9am-1pm, closed Sun (after hours, call 703-475-3751); operated by thru-hiker "Damascus Dave" of '90. *Cobbler*—City Shoe Shop: overnight service if boots dry, open Mon-Sat 9am-5pm, a friend to hiker boots for 59 years. *Other services*—bank • pharmacy • library. *Special event*—Appalachian Trail Days: an annual festival started in 1987 as part of the national celebration of the A.T.'s golden anniversary. The 1992 festival will be held during the third week of May, with most activities scheduled for the weekend of May 15-17. Events that were special favorites of thru-hikers last year included sidewalk chalk-art, fish fry, rubber-duck race, spaghetti dinner, pizza-eating contest, children's talent show, pancake break-fast, arts and crafts, fireman's barbecue, backpackers' parade, clogging and street dance, chili cook-off, hikers' reunion, and the hikers' talent show on Sunday afternoon at the gazebo. During "Trail Days," newly arriving hikers should check in at the city-hall welcome center for information, sodas, cookies, and smiles. *Points of interest*—Virginia Creeper Trail: built on an old rail bed as part of the rails-to-trails system; for horse, bike, and foot travel; runs from Virginia to North Carolina • Daniel Boone Heritage Trail: proposed to run from North Carolina to Kentucky • Backbone Rock: unique rock formation and tunnel 4 miles south of town on Va. 91. *PO-ZIP 24236*: Mon-Fri 8:30am-12:30pm and 1:30-4:30pm, Sat 8:30-11am; 703-475-3411; LY-500+. *Nearby towns*—Abingdon (14 miles west on U.S. 58) and Bristol (25 miles west).

♦ **Abingdon, Va.** (pop. 4,000): *Services*—several motels • McDonald's • Pizza Hut • Wolf Creek Plaza with large supermarket, drug store, and discount department store.
♦ **Bristol, Va.** (pop. 19,000): *Services*—wide variety of services, including an outfitter, Mountain Sports Ltd. (703-466-8988) with clothing and gear (Kelty, Camp Trails, Mountainsmith, Diamond Brand, Lowe, The North Face, Sierra Designs, Asolo, Danner, Merrell, Vasque, MSR, Optimus/Svea, Trangia, Marmot, Moonstone, Thermarest, ThorLo, Wigwam); open Mon-Fri 10am-7pm, Sat 9am-5:30pm, Sun 1-5pm (MC, Visa).

Leaving Damascus: The A.T. doesn't leave town at the Dairy King, as old blazing still indicates, but follows the highway past Dot's Inn to a stairway on the left side of the road about 0.5 mile out of town, where it enters the woods.

Clubnote: The next 64 miles are maintained by Mt. Rogers A.T. Club volunteers.

> Wildlife: *Blacksnakes are frequently encountered stretched across the Trail. They usually stay motionless as you step over or around but do vibrate their tails, and, in dry leaves, this may make you think you've come across a rattlesnake in disguise. Blacksnakes are not poisonous, but they do have nasty dispositions and will bite if handled. They are also known as rat snakes by farmers, who value them as "rodent ridders."*

Saunders Shelter: blue-blazed side trail to shelter actually a loop trail. Piped spring easy to miss if you don't go far enough down the water trail, which bears left off an old road.

Trailside pond: on A.T. 11.7 miles north of Damascus, with level tentsites covered by pine straw. The stream feeding the pond is the water source. This pond is always cold, but refreshing.

Whitetop Mountain: site of the Whitetop Ramp Festival, which is held around the time of "Trail Days." The big event of this music-filled weekend is the ramp-eating contest, won by "Scarecrow" in '88. He ate 53 ramps in three minutes, a truly remarkable (f)eat. The following year, "Andrew of Scotland" took second place. For the past two years, no thru-hikers placed in the contest.

Elk Garden (Va. 600): *Right 3.4m*—to the community of **Whitetop, Va.** (pop. 600) with small convenience store, no other services.

Deep Gap Shelter: accessible to horses, good piped spring, lots of ramps in the area. Scheduled for demolition in June or July.

Briar Ridge: meadow in the saddle one of the nicest spots in Virginia, can be accessed by a stile where the A.T. makes a sharp reverse to the left. "Great spot to hang out," say the ATC regional reps.

Mt. Rogers (5,729 feet): the highest mountain in Virginia. The summit is on a 0.4-mile side trail to the left. It has no views but holds a beautiful park-like area with rocks, mosses, ferns, and the northernmost Fraser firs on the Trail: an ideal place for lunch. Originally named Balsam Mountain, the name was changed to honor William Rogers, Virginia's first state geologist, and later, first president of MIT.

Thomas Knob Shelter: new in late 1991, located 0.1 mile north of Mt. Rogers summit side trail. Water source is spring near shelter. If spring is dry, you can pick up water from the dependable stream 0.5 mile south of shelter.

Rhododendron Gap: Blue-blazed short cut from here leads to Old Orchard Shelter, but at dubious savings. You'll miss Wilburn Ridge, with some of the most beautiful scenery to be seen on the southern A.T.

Grayson Highlands State Park: likened to the grasslands of Montana by some, speckled with magnificent rock outcroppings and blessed with plenty of sky. Sunrise over the highlands can be awesome. As soon as you enter the park, you will probably see several herds of feral ponies. Many of the females will have foals. These animals are wild but will come up to you for a handout. A dirt road to the right at Massie Gap leads off the ridge to a parking area. Water can be obtained by following this road to a rail fence, turning right at the fence, then going several hundred feet to a small spring. A campstore at the park campground is more than two miles from the A.T., rarely open for those who make the trek. Park closed to overnight use except at campground.

Old Orchard Shelter: piped spring, many good tentsites in shelter area.

Hurricane Campground (USFS): 0.5 mile off Trail to the left at sign; free hot showers (use a piece of wire to hold shower button in) and campsites with picnic tables along a fine trout stream; $5 self-registration for overnight stay.

> Wildlife: *Muskrats may make you think you've seen a beaver. They are aquatic mammals and build similar but smaller lodges, made of grasses*

and sedges. Muskrats eat mainly aquatic plants, supplemented with snails, crayfish, and frogs. They are 15" in length, reddish-brown with black, scaly, rat-like tails.

Dickey Gap (Va. 16): automobile entrance to Hurricane Campground. *Right 2.6m*—to the town of Troutdale. Warning: Don't confuse the similarly named towns of Trout*dale* and Trout*ville*, Va., when addressing maildrops.

♦ TROUTDALE, VA. (pop. 500): *Services*—The Trading Post Grocery (P.O. Box 132, Troutdale, Va. 24378): good for short-term resupply; open Mon-Sat 8:30am-8pm, Sun until 7pm; owned by friendly Terry and Diane Ransome, who will usually give customers a ride back to the A.T. Store may be used as a maildrop if packages addressed c/o The Trading Post • Danny's Country Store & Deli: good for short-term resupply, deli, restaurant (B/L/D, eat-in or take-out, country-style breakfast, burgers, sandwiches, flounder, fried chicken, *etc.*), store open Mon-Sat 5:30am-9pm, restaurant until 7pm, both closed Sun • bank. *PO-ZIP 24378:* Mon-Fri 8am-noon and 1-5pm, Sat 8-11am; 703-677-3221; LY-75.

Raccoon Branch Shelter: water source intermittent in dry years.

Trimpi Shelter: twin of the Pine Swamp Branch Shelter north of Pearisburg, both built as a memorial to a young student, Robert Trimpi. A new roof was added in 1990 by the Mt. Rogers A.T. Club and Konnarock crew, with funds provided by the Trimpi family.

Mt. Rogers National Recreation Area HQ: lobby area with wildlife exhibits, maps and books for sale; open all week Memorial Day-Labor Day (Mon-Thur 8am-5:30pm, Fri 8am-7pm, Sat 9:30am-6pm, Sun 10:30am-6pm), weekdays remainder of year (Mon-Fri 8am-4:30pm). Restrooms and drink machine (takes $1 bills or coins) are located in the hallway to the right just before the front entrance. Water is available from a spigot across the driveway opposite the front entrance. No public telephone is available. An exhibit showing Civil War iron-furnace operations and lumbering done in the Mt. Rogers area earlier this century is adjacent to the lobby (note size of the virgin trees in the photos). Sleeping on the covered porch may be allowed after hours, but ask first and leave the place clean if you are granted this courtesy.

Va. 16: Right 3.2m—to the town of Sugar Grove.

♦ Sugar Grove, Va. (pop. 800): *Services*—diner and small grocery store. *PO-ZIP 24375:* Mon-Fri 8am-noon and 1:15-5pm, Sat 8-11am; 703-677-3200; LY-25. The ATC regional reps say, "Any thru-hiker who wanders into Sugar Grove during June-August can come to the Konnarock base camp, which is a bit more than a mile along Route 601 (across from the PO, follow the signs). In return for a day's work, ATC will provide a tent site, shower, meals, and laundry, if there are spaces available on a crew. Shuttle back to the A.T. is a possibility. Thru-hikers are urged to contact ATC's Newport office in advance to include a week's crew work in their A.T. experience." Said a 1991 thru-hiker: "Anyone who complains about the Trail should work one day with the crews for an attitude adjustment."

Clubnote: The next 42 miles are maintained by Piedmont A.T. Hikers volunteers.

Chatfield Shelter: creek you just sloshed through is the water source; privy adjacent to shelter. No level tentsites are available near the shelter.

Settler's Museum: in old school building, 100 feet to the left where Trail crosses Va. 615.

Cows: usually oblivious to the A.T. route, and you will encounter many as the Trail winds through farmlands from Virginia to New Hampshire. A good technique for making your way past cows is to keep walking slowly and steadily, looking them straight in the eye. Even if they wait until the last second, they will move! Thanks for the hint, Geoff and Jodie.

U.S. 11/Interstate 81: On A.T.—Village Motel: $20-$23S $29-$35D $2EAP, 5 max; a/c, cable, washer/dryer, pets allowed with $2 deposit (MC, Visa, AE); desk clerk may arrange shuttle to PO and laundromat • Village Restaurant: B/L/D, home-cooked meals, two daily specials, steaks, country ham, turkey, seafood (MC, Visa, Dis); open 7 days, 5am-11pm, breakfast 'til 11am • Cumbow's Country Store: limited hiker supplies, restaurant (B/L, country-style breakfast, daily lunch specials); open Mon-Sat 6am-4:30pm (MC, Visa, Dis). • Texaco Truckstop & Deli: limited hiker supplies, possible new deli, open 24 hours • Mt. Empire Exxon: snack foods, drinks, open 7 days, 24 hours • outside public telephones. *Left 3.5m*—to the town of Atkins.

♦ **ATKINS, VA.** (pop. 500): *Services*—Atkins Grocery: good for long-term resupply, deli; open Mon-Sat 5:30am-9pm, closed Sun • laundromat: get detergent and change at grocery store next door • hardware store. *PO-ZIP 24311:* Mon-Fri 8am-noon and 1-5pm, Sat 8-11am; 703-783-5551; LY-40+. Note: Many hikers commented on the friendliness of the postmaster last year.

Davis Valley: relo eliminates the obstacle course of multiple stiles that once greeted thru-hikers. The old route used to be a mess, with "cow plops" almost solid for hundreds of feet. The new treadway is part of ATC's land-management focus, ensuring a pastoral landscape in the Davis Valley.

Davis Path Shelter: No water at shelter, so take water from town, or get water two miles north of town from piped spring, beyond pond on a blue-blazed side trail.

Va. 42: Right 5.2m—to the community of **Ceres, Va.** (pop. 100); no services.

O'Lystery Community Pavilion: private picnic pavilion with tables, fireplace, and privy, can be used overnight by thru-hikers. Do not drink from the adjacent stream. Water is available down the road 300 feet to the right, at the home of Fire Warden Wayne Bruce. A faucet on the left side of his house can be used even if no one is home. If Wayne is in, ask him about the Indian relics he finds in his fields. Over the years, he has found many arrowheads and pieces of pottery. In 1990, he found a stone hoe. Obviously, a large Indian settlement once graced this beautiful little valley.

Knot Maul Branch Shelter: Recently officially changed to Knot Maul from "Knot Mole," based on the fact that local settlers used to get knotwood from trees in this area for making mauls. The knots, being hard, made excellent hammers for use on pioneer farms. Nightly visits by whip-poor-wills. Ten feet beyond the spring is a better one, according to "Vagabond Vinny" of '91.

> Wildlife: *Wild turkeys are excellent flyers, but you will probably see them on the ground, since they prefer to walk or run when threatened. Years ago, they wandered around in flocks of hundreds but were hunted to near-extinction. They have reestablished themselves and are thriving in many areas. Turkeys roost in trees and ground feed on insects, berries, seeds, and nuts. Males put on a spectacular strutting display in mating season, and females are good mothers to as many as three dozen chicks, sometimes boldly charging hikers that get too close.*

Chestnut Knob Shelter: The best water source for northbounders is the pond 1.7 miles before the shelter. A small piped spring is located at the northern edge of the pond. Southbounders should get water at Walker Gap before heading up. This shelter is said to have a severe mouse problem.

Walker Gap: spring 300 feet to the right, off the road to the left. Follow the blue-blazes, which were easy to see last year.

Clubnote: The next 28 miles are maintained by Virginia Tech Outing Club volunteers.

Davis Farm Campsite: highly recommended by several thru-hikers, with a grand view of Burke's Garden. What about it? Look for a double-blue-blazed tree marking the side trail (thanks, Cindy and Maggie).

Little Wolf Creek: can be a joy on a sunny day but is very dangerous after a few days of heavy rain. In 1990, it was waist-deep during one especially rainy period. If the upper crossings of the creek are tricky, turn around, and take the high-water route. This is no place to take chances. The high-water trail is a blue-blazed old forest road designated for use by hikers when the creek route is precarious (in other words, the blue-blazed route *becomes* the A.T. during high water). It comes out on gravel Va. 615. Turn right, and follow the road to the A.T., which goes off to the left. Southbounders should turn right on Va. 615 and go past the Trail Boss Trail to the blue-blazed high-water trail to the left.

U.S. 21/52: On A.T.—several houses just before Trail reaches the road. At the house with a satellite dish, Mr. Morehead will call Ron Pauley, a friend of hikers known locally as "Dr. Frog" (703-688-4231 or 688-3733) for shuttle to Bland, or Levi Long for shuttle to Bastian. *Right 2.5m*—to the town of Bland. *Left 1.8m*—to the town of Bastian.

♦ **BLAND, VA.** (pop. 684): *Services*—Big Walker Motel: $24S $27D (1 bed) $31D (2 beds) $4EAP, 5 max, $3 for roll-a-way bed; a/c, cable, phone in room, small pets only (MC, Visa, Dis); located on Interstate 77, possible shuttle to A.T. at manager's convenience • Lion's Park: area for tenting behind school-board office • Bland Square Restaurant: B/L/D, home-cooked meals, ham and eggs, biscuits, burgers, chicken dinners, salads, daily luncheon specials; open Mon-Fri 6am-8:30pm, Sat 7am-8:30pm, Sun 8am-7pm • Burger Boy: fast-food walk-up, open 7 days 7am-10pm • Scott's IGA Supermarket: good for long-term resupply; open Mon-Sat 7am-10pm, Sun 8am-10pm • Bland Laundri-Mat: no soap or change on premises, dryers very hot; open 7 days, 7am-8pm • bank • pharmacy •

W&W Napa, a hardware store • doctor • dentist • UPS pickup. *PO-ZIP 24315:* Mon-Fri 7:30am-4pm, closed Sat; 703-688-3751; LY-50.

♦ **BASTIAN, VA.** (pop. 300): *Services*—Levi Long's Corner Diner & Hostel (P.O. Box 42, Bastian, Va. 24314; 703-688-4982): home-cooked meals, cornbread and beans, burgers, milkshakes, snacks, drinks, and hiker registers from years past. Free hostel downstairs in "Mama Kate's" house across the road from the diner, has mattresses on the floor for sleeping, common area with sofas and tables, kitchen with sink and refrigerator, electric lighting, and privy. Levi will shuttle to and from the Trail and hold maildrop packages if sent c/o Levi and Jan Long. • Jay Fred's Market: good for short-term resupply; open Mon-Sat 7:30am-9pm, Sun noon-6pm • doctor • health clinic. *PO-ZIP 24314:* Mon-Fri 8am-noon and 12:30-4:30pm, Sat 8-10:30am; 703-688-4631; LY-100+.

Mountain music: Levi Long grew up surrounded by mountain music and learned to play the fiddle from his father at an early age. In 1949, Levi began playing on the radio in Bristol, Va., but found over the years that he was having trouble finding younger fiddlers to join him. He realized that mountain music was dying and began encouraging parents to teach their sons and daughters the music of the mountains. In 1967, he started training and bringing people together to play and sing at his diner. "Sunday Gatherings" have been happening ever since, helping to pass on the traditions of mountain music in this region. Levi says modestly, "We're just old boys that like to pick." Truth is, they are some of the best.

Helveys Mill Shelter: a good place to crash after pigging out at Levi's. Water from creek quite a distance down from shelter.

Jenny Knob Shelter: water from creek down blue-blazed path in same direction as privy. Small creek in opposite direction is closer but may not be running in dry years.

> Wildlife: *Phoebes are the birds you find as your shelter mates, especially between Bastian and Troutville. They build their nests under the eaves of shelters, sometimes even inside, and seem to tolerate the activities of hikers without too much anxiety. Phoebes eat large quantities of insects.*

Kimberling Creek: Warren Doyle's bathtub in the creek just before the register mailbox. The tub, considered to be the ultimate in litter by some and praised by others as harmless Trail humor, was once kept stocked with sodas and beer for hikers, but local kids made one too many visits, and the tradition died. Now, it's usually just full of silt.

Lickskillet Hollow (Va. 608): *Right 0.8m*—to Barnard's Grocery & Hardware.

♦ Barnard's Grocery & Hardware: limited hiker supplies, outside drink machine, and unleaded gas.

Clubnote: The next 29 miles are maintained by Roanoke A.T. Club volunteers.

Va. 606: a roadwalk along a busy highway, so watch for speeding logging trucks and other traffic on curves. New relo and suspension bridge shorten the roadwalk shown on older

Trail maps. Just before turning into the woods at log steps, go straight ahead 0.2 mile to Trent's Grocery, good for short-term resupply, with snack foods, drinks, deli section (sandwiches, *etc.*), Coleman fuel, water from faucet on front of store, picnic table for hikers, and outside public telephone; open 7 days, 9am-9pm.

Dismal Creek Falls: "Hunter" of '90 says, "Definitely take the time to visit the falls. You'll walk farther just to get to a privy in Maine." **Caution:** Bottom of pool has broken glass.

Pond: off to the left about a mile south of the Wapiti Shelter, exactly what your mind conjures up when you hear the term "swimming hole."

Wapiti Shelter: Water source is the creek just before the side trail to the shelter.

> Wildlife: *Wapiti formerly roamed the woods of the East but now can be found only in isolated areas of the western states. The word is Indian for "white," which refers to the rump of this large deer. Several attempts have been made in this century to reestablish the wapiti (or elk) in the East, with no success.*

Sugar Run Gap: Right 0.6m—to Woodshole. Directions: At gap, turn right on dirt/gravel road, bear left at the fork, and go 0.5 mile down the road to Woodshole on right.

♦ Woodshole Hostel: an old homestead discovered by Roy and Tillie Wood while Roy was doing a study of elk in the early 1940s. The hostel, first opened to hikers in 1986, welcomes long-distance hikers during May and June, possibly longer this year. It features an 1880s log farmhouse and barn converted to a hikers' bunkhouse. The bunkhouse, with mattresses in the loft for sleeping, and nearby solar shower are free. Sodas, candy, and Coleman fuel are for sale. An authentic Southern breakfast, "around the table in the big house with Tillie," is available to the first eight hikers who make reservations; $3.50 donation. No other meals are available. A telephone is available for making credit-card or collect calls only. It might be noted that Tillie appreciates help with mowing the lawn, cutting wood, and other light-maintenance jobs. Last year, 200+ thru-hikers stayed overnight. A typical thru-hiker comment, "Woodshole is terrific, and Tillie is, too. I highly recommend it." Address: Tillie Wood, Rt. 2, Box 332A, Pearisburg, Va. 24134 (do not use as maildrop).

Shumate Bridge: On A.T.—Wade's Food Supermarket: good for long-term resupply, deli and bakery; open 7 days, 6:30am-10pm. *Right 2m*—to the city of Pearisburg. (If you walk into town, keep to the right through the interchange.)

♦PEARISBURG, VA. (pop. 2,500): The A.T. skirts the edge of town and hiking is not one of the important things taking place in the lives of most residents. Nevertheless, the people are friendly, and the town, proud of its association with the A.T., offers most major hiker services. The only problem is that everything is spread out, requiring you to put on more town miles than you'd prefer. *Hostel*—Holy Family Hospice (703-921-3547 church, 703-921-9816 hostel), operated by the Church of the Holy Family for thru-hikers only. The barn-shaped hostel, located behind the church, offers foam pads on the floor for sleeping, a kitchen with stove and refrigerator, bathroom with hot shower, dining booth, library with writing table, penny scales (pennies supplied), barbells (nothing like pumping iron during a hike, is there?), and public telephone. A nearby gazebo on the expansive lawn is often used for sleeping. No alcoholic beverages are permitted on the property, but pets are welcome. Normal stay is limited to two days (if you need to stay longer, see Pastor Thomas Welch). A donation of $5 per night is suggested. Grass-cutting or wood-chopping may be substituted and is appreciated. Friends and relatives are welcome to visit but may not stay overnight. UPS packages can be found inside the church entrance. Directions to the church: From the PO, go left two blocks to the traffic light, turn left on Wenonah Ave., go 0.8 mile to the 7-Day Market, turn left on Gale Rd., turn left on Mason Ct., and go uphill to the church on the right. *Other lodging*—Rendezvous Motel: $19S $24D, 2 max; a/c, cable, no pets inside (may tie outside), one-time free shuttle to and from town, shuttles to other points by arrangement, may make telephone calls from manager's office (3-minute limit) • Plaza Motel: $28S $34D $5.33EAP, 4 max; a/c, cable, phone in room, no pets, picnic tables outside for cooking • Holiday Motor Lodge: $36S $46D (economy rooms $22S $32D) $4EAP (but not in economy), 4 max; a/c, cable, phone in room, pool (MC, Visa, AE). *Places to eat*—The Holiday Restaurant: B/L/D, home cooking, open 7 days, 6am-9pm • Eric's Restaurant: L/D, fine dining but casual (hiker attire welcomed), American (prime rib, steaks, Texas fried chicken, country ham, seafood, *etc.*) and continental (scampi, fettucine alfredo, chicken Kiev, *etc.*), daily salad bar; open Sun and Mon 11am-3pm, Tues-Sat 11am-9pm (MC, Visa). • Big Tee Family Restaurant: B/L/D, eat-in and take-out, burgers, hot dogs, fries, open 7 days, 5am-10pm • Dairy Queen: open Mon-Thur 5:30am-9pm, Fri-Sun 'til 10pm • PJ's Deli: hot lunches and subs • Papa's Pizzeria: L/D, take-out, pizza, subs, salads; open 7 days, Sun-Thur until 9pm, Fri and Sat until 10pm • Pizza Hut: AYCE salad bar, open Fri and Sat until 1am • Hardee's • Burger Queen. *Groceries*—Food Lion Supermarket: good for long-term resupply; open Mon-Sat 8am-10pm, Sun 9am-9pm • Rex Food Center: good for long-term resupply; open Mon-Sat 8am-10pm, Sun 9am-9pm • 7-Day Market: convenience store near hostel, open 7 days, 6am-midnight. *Laundromats*—Carroll's Quickclean: FLW, detergent and change at store next door; open 7 days, 7:30am-9:30pm, last load 8:45pm • E-Z Way Laundry: FLW, open 7 days, 6am-10pm, last load 9:30pm. *Stove fuel*—Little Giant Grocery: Coleman by the pint. *Cobbler*—Mutter's Shoe Repair: overnight service on boots; open Mon-Sat 8am-5pm, closed Wed. *Other services*—banks • Western Union at Stafford's Express Studio, closed Sun • Most • discount pharmacy • hardware store • department store • doctor • dentist • hospital • veterinarian • municipal pool with dressing rooms and snack bar, across from 7-Day Market, $1.25 adults, open Memorial Day-Labor Day (Mon-Sat noon-6pm, Sun 1-6pm) • UPS/FedEx pick-up • Pearisburg Cab Service (703-921-2736) and Curtis Robbins Cabs (703-921-3201) • light sewing available at dry cleaners. *PO-ZIP 24134:* Mon-Fri 8:30am-5pm, Sat 8:30am-noon; 703-921-1100; LY-150. The nearest outfitter is Blue Ridge Outdoors (703-552-9012) in Blacksburg (Kelty, Camp Trails, Gregory, Lowe, Sierra Designs, Eureka!, Hi-Tec Sports, Merrell, Vasque, MSR, Optimus/Svea, Peak 1, Marmot, Thermarest, ThorLo, Wigwam); open Mon-Sat 10am-9pm, Sun 1-6pm (MC, Visa, AE, Dis).

New River: supposedly the second-oldest river in the world (after the Nile), flows into the Ohio River system to empty into the Gulf of Mexico. All major rivers crossed on the A.T. north of here flow into the Atlantic.

Clubnote: The next 19 miles are maintained by Kanawha Trail Club volunteers.

Campsite: four miles north of town, with good spring and level tentsites. A good place to aim for if you're having trouble getting out of town. (In a register several years ago, someone drew Pearisburg with a giant magnet hovering overhead, pulling a heavy-laden northbound hiker back into town. I'm sure you can relate.)

Symms Gap: views into West Virginia, tentsites, no dependable water.

Pine Swamp Branch Shelter: creek is water source. Use small spring on A.T. 0.5 mile before shelter as an alternative.

Clubnote: The next 85 miles are maintained by Roanoke A.T. Club volunteers.

War Spur Shelter: surrounded by *mountain laurel*, which can be spectacular in full bloom. Flat areas for tenting are numerous near the shelter. Creek is water source.

Laurel Creek Shelter: Water source is creek beyond on A.T. Go downstream for a cold dip in small pools.

In memory: Andy Layne, dedicated Trail volunteer and "the heart and soul" of the Roanoke A.T. Club, died of natural causes last year. Several years ago, Andy was pictured in the National Geographic Society book, *Mountain Adventure*, doing what he liked best—maintaining. He devoted thousands of hours to A.T. maintenance, and even did Trail work with the Konnarock crew at the tender age of 77. Andy was also a member of the Natural Bridge A.T. Club and a former member of the Tidewater A.T. Club. Known for his sense of humor and zest for life, Andy Layne was an inspiration to all who knew him.

Sinking Creek Valley (Va. 42): *Right 0.2m*—to Level Green Christian Church, where Pastor Jack Ford sometimes allows hikers to stay overnight in the pavilion, but ask permission first. *Left 1.6m*—to small Twin Oaks Grocery. *Right 8m*—to the town of Newport.

♦ Twin Oaks Grocery: good for short-term resupply; open Sun-Thur 6am-9pm, Fri and Sat 6am-10pm.
♦ Newport, Va. (pop. 500): grocery store and ATC Regional Rep Mike Dawson (offices in The Newport Hotel, 703-544-7388), who sometimes can put up hikers for the night. Shuttle to outfitter can be arranged for emergency gear replacement.

Keffer Oak: large white oak (more than 18 feet around, fattest tree on the Trail?) in Sinking Creek Valley, about 0.25 mile north of Va. 630, with stile attached; estimated to be more than 300 years old. When you cross the field beyond, turn around and look at this magnificent tree before you go into the woods. Ponder the fact that trees this size were common in the forest the settlers found.

Trail Fact: *Each mile of the A.T. has an average elevation gain of 217 feet, which means that a thru-hiker will climb and descend a total of 88.3 miles between Springer and Katahdin. That's the equivalent of going from sea level to the summit of Mt. Everest and back more than sixteen times.*

Sarver Cabin: a poor man's Woodshole with several old homestead buildings. The main building, which can be used as a shelter, is kind of snaky looking, definitely leaky, and rumored to have a ghost, but the spring is cold and dependable. The 0.3-mile side trail is steep and is marked by signs. A visit to this place will show you what life in the mountains must have been like a hundred years ago. Could you have endured it?

Niday Shelter: water source is small creek across the A.T. down blue-blazed trail. If the upper creek is dry, go down a few hundred feet to the larger stream.

Brush Mountain: Trail relocated by the Roanoke A.T. Club and Konnarock crew to eliminate the infamous "ins and outs," a tedious section where the Trail crossed 33 hollows. The new route adds great views of Sinking Creek Mountain. At the top of Brush Mountain, the route follows a road now closed to vehicles. The relo also gives access to the Audie Murphy Memorial, honoring this country's most decorated WWII hero.

> Wildlife: *Copperheads are one of two poisonous snakes you will encounter on your hike. They are pit vipers, with heat sensors located between the eye and nostril (if you can see the pits, you are too close!), allowing the snake to detect warm-blooded prey. The copperhead can be 24-48" in length, with a copper, orange, or pinkish-colored head, and vertical pupils. They like rocky areas and are often found near water. Copperheads range as far north as Massachusetts on the A.T.*

Pickle Branch Shelter: on a seemingly endless blue-blazed side trail that crosses a dirt road. The shelter sits on the edge of a beautiful forest area. Water is down a blue-blazed trail behind the shelter. A spring flows from under a large tree adjacent to the stream.

Dragons Tooth: a spectacular rock outcropping on a blue-blazed side trail just before you start the sometimes hand-and-foot descent off the ridge. This is a great place to view a sunrise.

Va. 624: Left 0.3m—to Va. 311, then left 0.1 mile to the Catawba Grocery, good for short-term resupply, with microwave foods, ice cream, T-shirts, and hiker's register; open 7 days, 6am-9pm. A public telephone is outside. Water is available from a faucet on the right side of the building. Friendly owner Carol Caldwell may permit you to camp at the nearby pond, or, on a rainy night, in the "Catawba Hilton" next door. The latter is a shelter of last resort.

Va. 311: Left 1m—to the community of Catawba.

♦ **CATAWBA, VA.** (pop. 245): *Services*—The Home Place Restaurant: L/D, family-style dinners (fried chicken, country ham, roast beef, pork barbeque on Thur, vegetables, biscuits, cobblers) in the $8-$10 range (MC, Visa); open Thur-Fri 4:30-8pm, Sat 4-8pm, Sun 11am-6pm; closed week of July 4th. Looks country-fancy, but grubby hikers are welcomed by both management and guests as adding to the ambiance of this special place. Considered by many thru-hikers to serve the best food on the Trail. Typical comment: "Just like dinner at grandma's; the best chicken I've ever had." • grocery store with limited hiker supplies, closed Wed afternoon. *PO-ZIP 24070:* Mon-Fri 8am-noon and 1-5pm, Sat 8-10:30am; 703-384-6011; LY-100.

Boy Scout Shelter: the first shelter after the road. The newer Catawba Mountain Shelter is one mile north.

Catawba Mountain Shelter: Water source is small spring to the left, just before the shelter.

McAfee Knob: probably the best photo opportunity on the Trail, with a large anvil-shaped slab of rock jutting out into space, overlooking a magnificent valley. Tinker Cliffs can be seen to the right in the distance. Across the valley is North Mountain, where the A.T. was located prior to a 1987 settlement of a land dispute and subsequent return to the present historic route. Camping is not permitted at the overlook, but the new Campbell Shelter with water is just 0.7 mile north, close enough to come back for a sunset.

Campbell Shelter: one of the nicer shelters in this section. Water is available from a piped spring down blue-blazed trail, to the left as you look into shelter, across a dirt road.

Lamberts Meadow Shelter: copperheads reported in the rocks of the firepit for several seasons, a reminder that extra caution should be exercised around all rocky areas, especially during summer months. From now on, use a flashlight to check where you are stepping during the night. Water source is the creek.

> Wildlife: *Moles are responsible for the broken mounds of earth crossing the Trail. The shallow tunnels are evidence of their foraging for earthworms and larvae close to the surface. You may occasionally see a dead but uneaten mole in the treadway, probably killed by another mole, since these animals cannot tolerate each other except during the (brief) mating season. The eastern mole is mouse-like, with a pointed nose.*

Cloverdale/Troutville: The small residential towns of Cloverdale and Troutville are four miles apart on U.S. 11. Midway between them on U.S. 11 (which parallels Interstate 81) is the U.S. 220/I-81/U.S. 11 interchange. The Trail first crosses U.S. 220, avoids the interchange area, goes under I-81 on a back road, then crosses U.S. 11 near Troutville before heading north. You can reach the interchange area (which has most of the services you will need) by going right on either U.S. 220 or U.S. 11. From the interchange, the Cloverdale PO is 1.2 miles farther on U.S. 11, then left on Read Mountain Road. To reach the Troutville PO, cross U.S. 220 (it's a busy road, so be careful), follow the A.T. through the woods to U.S. 11, then go left 0.8 mile to the PO. On the way to the Troutville PO, you'll pass Doc's Chili Dogs Diner (B/L, fresh cinnamon biscuits for breakfast, luncheon specials for $4, burgers, fries, *etc.*), managed by friendly Millie Horton, open Mon-Sat 6am-6pm, closed Sun.

U.S. 220 (where A.T. crosses)—Best Western Coachman Inn (235 Roanoke Rd., Daleville, Va. 24083): special rates only for hikers of $34S/D $5EAP, 5 max; a/c, cable, phone in room, pool, washer/dryer, pets allowed, will hold mail or UPS packages, Coleman by the pint available, Italian-American restaurant in motel (MC, Visa, AE, Dis, DC) • Howard Johnson's Motel: $34S $43D (rates include hiker discount) $5EAP, 4 max; a/c, cable, phone in room, use of refrigerator, pool, washer/dryer, pets allowed (MC, Visa, AE, Dis, DC) • Western Sizzler: B/L/D/, AYCE salad bar $4; open 7 days, 7am-10pm • Pizza Hut.

♦ Interchange area: *Lodgings*—Travelodge: $27S $34 (2-4 persons) (rates include hiker discount), 4 max; a/c, cable, phone in room, pool, pets allowed, movie rentals and free popcorn each evening, donuts and coffee each morning (MC, Visa, AE, Dis, DC) • Comfort Inn: $45S $51D $5EAP, 5 max; a/c, cable, phone in room, pool, pets allowed (MC, Visa, AE, Dis, DC) • Daystop Motel (Truckstops of America): $38S $43D $5EAP, 5 max; a/c, cable, phone in room, laundromat (open to public), no pets (MC, Visa, AE, Dis, DC) • shower only: available at Truckstops of America for $5 ($10 deposit) and at Pilot Truckstop for $5 with towel furnished. *Places to eat*— Shoney's: AYCE breakfast buffet • Country Cookin' Restaurant: L/D, home-style meals with AYCE salad-vegetables-bread-desert buffet for $3.50 (MC, Visa); open 7 days, 11am-10pm • Burger King • Hardee's • McDonald's • Waffle House. *Groceries*—Winn-Dixie Supermarket: good for long-term resupply; open Mon-Sat 8am-11pm, Sun 8am-10pm • Pilot Food Mart: snacks. *Other services*— laundromat: inside at Truckstops of America, open 24 hours • pharmacy • bank • Western Union at Truckstops of America • Plus, Cirrus.

♦ **CLOVERDALE, VA.** (pop. 100): *Services*—Traveltown Motel: $23S $30D $5EAP, 5 max; a/c, cable, phone in room, use of refrigerator, pets allowed (MC, Visa, AE, DC); located on U.S. 11 about one mile beyond the interchange • Greenway Market: convenience store located just past Traveltown on U.S. 11; open 7 days, 7am-11pm • Coleman by the pint at Peck's Hardware on U.S. 11, 0.3 mile beyond the Traveltown Motel. *PO-ZIP 24077:* Mon-Fri 8am-noon and 1-5pm, Sat 9am-noon; 703-992-2334; LY-35; located on Read Mountain Road, to the left just beyond the Traveltown Motel.

♦ **TROUTVILLE, VA.** (pop. 575): *Services*—Thriftway Supermarket: good for short-term resupply. *PO-ZIP 24175:* Mon-Fri 8:30am-noon and 1-5pm, Sat 8:30-11:30am; 703-992-1472; LY-100; located on U.S. 11.

♦ Blue Ridge Outdoors (703-774-4311): outfitter located in nearby Roanoke, Va. (Tanglewood Mall), with large selection of gear (Kelty, Camp Trails, Gregory, Lowe, Sierra Designs, Eureka!, Hi-Tec Sports, Merrell, Vasque, MSR, Optimus/Svea, Peak 1, Marmot, Thermarest, ThorLo, Wigwam), possible shuttle to and from store; open Mon-Sat 10am-9pm, Sun 1-6pm.

Fullhardt Knob Shelter: reached after a long climb, especially difficult if you've just pigged out at Country Cookin' or Shoney's. Water is available behind the shelter from the last cistern remaining on the Trail. A seasonal spring is located 0.4 mile north on the A.T.

Clubnote: The next 88 miles are maintained by Natural Bridge A.T. Club volunteers. These folks can often be seen out on weekends clearing weeds, especially nettles, which are in full growth by early summer when most thru-hikers come through.

Bobblets Gap Shelter: maintained by Runnin' Richard, who sometimes shows up with sodas and other treats for thru-hikers. OK, the chairs are not "wilderness," but they sure feel good to a tired back.

Bearwallow Gap (Va. 43): *Right (north) 5m*—on the Blue Ridge Parkway (BRP) to Peaks of Otter Recreation Area. *Left 5m*—to the town of Buchanan.

♦ Peaks of Otter Recreation Area: campground equipped for tents $8 per night, lodge with snack bar and restaurant (B/L/D, casual, fine dining, $6 AYCE breakfast 'til 10:30am, MC, Visa, open 7:30am-11pm), and camp store with very limited supplies; open May-Oct.

♦ **Buchanan, Va.** (pop. 1,205): pronounced "Buck-cannon." Not recommended as maildrop location because of difficulty hitching in and out of town (best time to hitch in, 3-4pm; out, 6-8am). *Services*—motel • La Pizza • diner • grocery store • convenience store • laundromat • bank • pharmacy • Buchanan Hardware Store with UPS pickup • department store • doctor • dentist • Greyhound bus service.

Cove Mountain Shelter: no water at shelter, so you must pack it in from the small spring at Bearwallow Gap, or follow a steep, unmarked trail from the shelter 0.5 mile to a good stream. "The Happy Feet" jokingly suggest you use this shelter as practice for Pennsylvania, where, they say, "water is even harder to get!"

Jennings Creek (Va. 614): *Right 0.3m*—to Middle Creek Picnic Area with water from well. *Left 1.5m*—to small grocery store (possibly closed, no recent reports). In 1989, a thru-hiker, sleeping under the Jennings Creek bridge, was bitten by a copperhead while he slept. He recovered without permanent injury but lost several weeks from his hike.

> Wildlife: *Mink are quite common in the mountains but, being nocturnal, are rarely seen by thru-hikers. The best place to see them is along the bank of a lake or stream, where they feed on small animals and a variety of aquatic life, especially crawfish. Mink are rich dark brown in color, with a white chin patch and the long, slender body characteristic of the weasel family.*

Va. 714: Right 0.7m—to intersection with Va. 618, then right 0.7 mile to Jellystone Park Campground.

♦ Jellystone Park Campground: cabins $40 per night (2 people, $5EAP), campsites $14.50 per night (2 people, $3EAP), pool, showers ($3 if not camping), laundromat, and camp store with limited supplies, ice cream, Coleman by the gallon. Shuttle back to the Trail is sometimes available. Warning: Do not sit in Yogi's basket, because his owner will not be pleased.

Apple Orchard Mountain: proposed reroute will take the Trail over the open summit, which was the original A.T. route until the 1950s.

Thunder Hill Shelter: maintained by Laurel and Bill Foot, "The Happy Feet," who entertain a number of thru-hikers in their home each year with food and slides of their 1987 thru-hike. Bill is a new member of the ATC Board of Managers.

Matts Creek Shelter: new footbridge across the creek, dedicated by NBATC to Hank Lanum; natural bathtubs in the creek in front of the shelter; watch for snakes.

> *In memory:* Hank Lanum, long-time supervisor of trails for NBATC, died in the summer of 1991, at the age of 74, while working on trails in Idaho. Hank was often seen with his weed-eater, shin guards, face guard, and day pack, heading up and down the A.T. to clear the way for other hikers. He was himself a 2,000-Miler, completing his hike in 1987. Hank leaves boots that will be hard to fill.

James River (U.S. 501/Va. 130): *Right 4m*—on U.S. 501 to the little community of Big Island. *Left 7m*—to the town of Glasgow.

♦ **BIG ISLAND, VA.** (pop. 325): *Services*—H&H Food Market (a combination gas station-store-restaurant): limited hiker supplies, country-style short-order food served 7 days, 5:45am-9:45pm. *PO-ZIP 24526:* Mon-Fri 8am-12:30pm and 1:30-5pm, Sat 8-11am; 804-299-5072; LY-48

♦ **Glasgow, Va.** (pop. 1,259): *Services*—motel (closed in 1991, may be reopened this year) • Balcony Downs B&B: $40-$50S $50-$60D (20% discount for thru-hikers) $10EAP, 3 max; TV, kitchen privileges, pool, washer/dryer, pets allowed conditionally, will shuttle back to A.T. • The Crossing Restaurant • Food Mart Supermarket: good for long-term resupply • 24-hour convenience store • laundromat: detergent at Food Mart • bank • hardware store • doctor • dentist. *PO-ZIP 24555:* Mon-Fri 8am-4:30pm, Sat 8-11pm; 703-258-2852; LY-25.

Johns Hollow Shelter: Water source is the creek. Notice that small "spring" to the left flows from below the privy area.

Bluff Mountain: site of memorial to "Little Ottie," no kin to Audie. Black spruce and view at site of old firetower.

Punchbowl Shelter: small pond adjacent, so count on hearing frogs and peepers singing to you all night long. Don't drink any more pond water if you start singing back.

Va. 607: Do not use this road as an approach to Buena Vista.

Pedlar Dam: holding back the drinking water for the city of Lynchburg. No fishing or swimming is permitted here. The footbridge at the base of the dam replaces a rickety old structure that used to shake and twist as hikers passed over, causing many a pilgrim to fear that his adventure would end in the creek. "Ringo" of '91 spotted a bobcat near the dam.

> Wildlife: *Frogs were once extremely abundant in lakes and ponds but, like other amphibians, are in serious decline worldwide due to destruction of wetland habitat and pollution. They are usually greenish or brownish in color and have irregular dark spots on their bodies. The bullfrog is the most prominent member of this group.*

Brown Mountain Creek Shelter: small spring to the left as you look into shelter. Level tentsites across creek. Lower Brown Mountain Creek valley full of old fields, fences, and chimneys; settled by freed slaves after the Civil War.

U.S. 60: Left 1.2m—to Hamm's Country Store. *Left 8m*—to the large town of Buena Vista. Note: The Parkway Motel has closed, so there are no groceries, lodging, or meals 2.5 miles left; as indicated in some older guidebooks.

♦ Hamm's Country Store: snack foods, sodas, and telephone, no ice cream last year; open 7 days, 9am-7pm.
♦ **Buena Vista, Va.** (pop. 9,000): pronounced "Bee-you'-nuh." Not recommended as a maildrop location by past thru-hikers because of difficulty hitching in and out of

town. *Services*—Buena Vista Motel: $40S $42D $3EAP, 4 max; a/c, cable, phone in room, pets allowed (MC, Visa, AE, DC) • Glen Maury Park family campground with shower and pool, $10 • Green Forest Restaurant (in Buena Vista Motel): B/L/D, country-casual, home-cooked meals, lunch and dinner buffet; open 7 days, 7am-8pm • Hardee's • Pizza Hut • Kenny's Diner • Food Lion Supermarket: good for long-term resupply • bakery • laundromat • cobbler • pharmacy • hardware store • department store • doctor • dentist • veterinarian • UPS pickup • taxi service.

Cow Camp Gap Shelter: replaces the Wiggins Spring Shelter, which has been demolished. Good piped spring near shelter.

Hog Camp Gap: After passing through stile, watch for right turn to newly developed Tarjacket spring with decent campsites, located 0.3 mile from Trail. *Left 0.5m*—to Wiggins Spring.

♦ Wiggins Spring: one of biggest springs near the A.T. Site of former shelter, which was removed because of overuse and abuse by groups coming in by road. The left-over materials were used to build the Campbell Shelter near McAfee Knob.

Tar Jacket Ridge: New relo gives great views, taste of balds past and future. The stone wall breached by the A.T. was built by slaves in the 18th century. There were reports of a mountain lion in the area in 1990, but no confirmation.

Seeley-Woodsworth Shelter: gushing piped spring, usually.

Fish Hatchery Road (Va. 690): *Left 1.6m*—to an intersection, passing the fish hatchery on the way, then left 0.3 mile to the community of Montebello. Note: There is virtually no traffic on this road.

♦ MONTEBELLO, VA. (pop. 300): *Services*—store and part-time restaurant (if they can get a cook!). A pay-for-what-you-catch fishing lake is located across from the store. Two blocks from the PO is a campground with $9 tentsites, showers, laundromat, and apartments to rent. Townspeople are often available for shuttle back to Trail. *PO-ZIP 24464:* Mon-Fri 8am-noon and 12:30-4:30pm, Sat 9-11:30am; 703-377-9218; LY-65.

Spy Rock: unusual dome-shaped rock formation with superlative overlook, off A.T. 200 yards to the right. Confederate soldiers used this location to spot activities of Union troops during the Civil War, hence the name.

Sentinel Pine: on new relo after descending Maintop Mountain; rock outcropping with majestic pine tree.

Va. 826: Left 0.5m—to a campsite, then another 0.5 mile or more to Crabtree Falls, with five cascades. One thru-hiker raved about this place. Another said it was a disappointment. Perhaps recent rain and the eye of the beholder make the difference. Be careful on the slippery rocks. A 1986 thru-hiker fell to his death here.

The Priest Shelter: excellent cold spring to the left looking into the shelter. Area heavily used by large groups, especially on weekends, but they rarely use the shelter.

Tye River (Va. 56): *Right 1.4m*—to the hamlet of Tyro.

♦ **TYRO, VA.** (pop. 50): *PO-ZIP 22976* (Mon-Sat 9am-2pm; 804-277-5731; LY-59) in Bradley's Store (store open Mon-Sat 8am-6pm, closed on Sun). Store has ice cream, snacks, sodas, limited groceries, Coleman by the pint, and UPS/FedEx service. If you don't see what you're looking for at first glance, check again, since the shelves in this store are somewhat like a treasure hunt. No public telephone is available, but the Bradleys have let many a hiker place collect or credit-card calls from the store telephone. An apple-packing warehouse is across the road and will sell apples in any quantity in season.

Clubnote: The next 11 miles are maintained by Tidewater A.T. Club volunteers.

Mau-Har Trail: a shortcut around Three Ridges. The blue-blazed trail descends to a scenic waterfall and several swimming holes, then ascends steeply over rocks to Maupin Field Shelter.

> Wildlife: *Veeries are the birds making that strangely resonant, downward-spiraling sound you've been hearing. Many have likened its call to someone whistling into a metal tube. The veery is a member of the thrush family and feeds on the ground. It is 7" in length, cinnamon-brown above, and whitish below. You may not see one, but you will never forget its ethereal song. They are rarely heard north of Maryland on the A.T.*

Harpers Creek Shelter: the last water until you reach the Maupin Field Shelter area. Spring up creek to the left; privy next to shelter.

Three Ridges: spectacular views back to The Priest and down into the Tye River valley. The summit is dry, so take plenty of water with you from Harpers Creek. Note: The Three Ridges area is being considered for wilderness designation.

Maupin Field Shelter: with caretaker service during the busy summer months. Northbounders can get to Rusty's "Hard Time Hollow" from here. To do so, go back to the A.T., turn left, and follow the dirt access road 1.3 miles to the Blue Ridge Parkway, turn left (south) on the BRP and go 1.2 miles to Rusty's gate on the left at mile 16.7 (gate has his name on one end). The posted warnings along the driveway are there to discourage people other than hikers.

♦ Rusty's "Hard Time Hollow": open year-round for thru-hikers; a place for old-time Appalachian Mountains hospitality, with lots of sharing and fellowship (often there's a good-natured party going on until early morning), enjoyed by more than 2,000 thru-hikers since Rusty opened his doors in 1982. The "Hollow" offers a porch and bunkhouse that will accommodate 20+ hikers on mattresses and has a good springhouse (serves as the refrigerator), cold shower, no electricity, no running water, no telephone, ping-pong table, one-of-a-kind privy, and a precision urinal. No dogs are permitted on the property (they chase the chickens), and smoking is not allowed in or near the buildings because of the fire hazard. Rusty, an inventor by trade (ask him about his latest patent), is a very generous individual who will literally give you the shirt off his back, but don't abuse his kindheartedness. Keep in mind that this is Rusty's home. Make yourself feel comfortable, but don't take over. When you arrive, don't expect a ride to town right away (Rusty likes to consolidate trips, since the round trip to Waynesboro is more than 36 miles). If you can afford it, chip in for some gas. Also, no matter how much you enjoy your stay, don't put directions to Rusty's in any registers near the hollow. In the past, neighbors have caused him problems. Note: Rusty has dreams of thru-hiking the Trail in 1993, if he can find someone responsible to run the "Hollow."

Va. 664 (Reeds Gap): Southbounders can go right (south) on the BRP from here to reach the entrance gate to Rusty's, on the left at milepost 16.7 (see above).

Clubnote: The next 17 miles are maintained by Old Dominion A.T. Club volunteers.

Cedar Cliff: view to the west overlooking the Sherando Lake valley, an excellent place to view a sunset.

Paul Wolfe Memorial Shelter: new shelter on Mill Creek, located 13.2 miles north of Maupin Field Shelter. Creek is water source; waterfall and excellent swimming hole 200 yards downstream, along old road (look for large sycamore tree).

Rockfish Gap (BRP/Interstate 64/U.S. 250): The A.T. comes out of the woods and turns left on the Blue Ridge Parkway, crossing over I-64 and U.S. 250, as it heads north toward Shenandoah National Park. To go into town, follow the BRP (A.T.) for a short distance, take the first left, going past Howard Johnson's Restaurant (as of late 1991, open 7 days, 7am-9pm), a gift shop/gas station, and a tourist information center, to reach U.S. 250, which goes three miles to the city of Waynesboro. Also in the gap, above HoJo's on a side road—Skyline Parkway Motel: $21S/D $5EAP, 4 max; a/c, TV, no pets (MC, Visa) • Holiday Inn: $50S $55D $6EAP, 4 max; a/c, cable, phone in room, pool, Dulaney's Steak & Seafood Restaurant in motel, major credit cards honored; will hold packages for hikers.

♦ **WAYNESBORO, VA.** (pop. 18,000): one of the largest towns you will visit during your hike, with all services needed by thru-hikers. As with most of the larger towns, it isn't hiker-oriented, and the people are generally unaware of the A.T. Nevertheless, this is a friendly town, and you will be treated with courtesy, and perhaps curiosity, during your stay. *"Hostel"*—The Waynesboro Fire Department, in the center of town, allows hikers to use the firefighters' restroom and showers and pitch tents overnight on a grassy area behind the building (or sleep inside, if it's raining); stay limited to 48 hours, unless you are sick or injured. If no one is around when you arrive, you may go inside. Instructions for checking in and house rules are posted on a wall near the restroom. When you sign in, be sure you pick up a "Hospitality Packet," which includes a map of the city, discount coupons for local restaurants, and information about free shuttles back to the Trail. This packet, the only one of its kind on the A.T., is the project of Waynesboro residents Brian Shirley and Tom Diamond (Many thanks, guys!). *Other lodging*—Exxon Cabin Court: $24 for a cottage, 2 max; a/c, cable, house-broken pets allowed (MC, Visa, AE, Dis) • Budget West Lawn Motel: $27S $31D $5EAP, 6 max; a/c, cable, phone in room, small pets allowed (MC, Visa) • Deluxe Budget Motel: $30-$42S $32-$45D $4EAP, 4 max; a/c, cable, phone in room, pool, no pets (MC, Visa, AE, Dis, DC) • Comfort Inn: $38S $48D $5EAP, 5 max; a/c, cable, phone in room, pool, small pets allowed (MC, Visa, AE, Dis, DC CB); continental breakfast in lobby. *Places to eat* (near the fire station)—Weasie's: B/L/D, home-cooked meals (meat and vegetables), formerly Dairy Queen and still essentially the same; $2 AYCE pancake special available anytime, a hiker favorite (some hikers have eaten as many as 18 pancakes at one sitting!); open Mon-Thur and Sun 5:30am-9pm, all night Fri-Sat • Kroger: deli with hot meat and veggie lunches to go • Sub City: L/D, Jersey-style subs, Philly-style cheese steaks, chili, home-made soup, deli salads, AYCE spaghetti (Mon-Wed); open Mon-Sat 10am-9pm, Sun noon-6pm • Apple Blossom Restaurant: B/L/ D, home-cooked meals, daily luncheon buffet 11am-2pm, dinner buffet Fri and Sat 4-9pm, breakfast buffet Sat 7-11am, $5-6 dinner specials Mon-Thur 4-9pm; open Mon-Sat 7am-9pm • Purple Foot Deli: patio lunches (sandwiches, soups, quiches, crepes, salads, desserts, wines), open Mon-Sat 11am-2pm • Little Caesar • Fox & Hounds: L/D, English pub and fine-dining restaurant, regional food (MC, Visa, AE); open for lunch Mon-Fri 11:30am-2pm, for dinner Mon-Sat 5-9:30pm • General Wayne Inn: L/D, country-casual, country-style buffet Sat 5:30-8pm, Sunday brunch 10:30am-2pm (MC, Visa, AE). *Places to eat* (in fast-food district, about one mile from fire station)—Arby's • Burger King • McDonald's • Hardee's • Shoney's with AYCE breakfast and salad bar • LJ Silver's • Subway • Bonanza with super $5 salad-fruit-hot bar • Pizza Hut • Scotto's Italian Restaurant • Golden China: full Chinese menu • Golden Corral: steaks • Peck's Bar-B-Que. *Groceries*—Kroger Supermarket: good for long-term resupply, open 24 hours • Valley Fresh Supermarket: good for long-term resupply; open Mon-Sat 7am-10pm, Sun 8am-8pm • Nick's Supermarket: good for long-term resupply; open 7 days, 7am-9pm. *Laundromats*—Two locations, one near the fire station, the other near the high school, both with FLW, last load 8pm. *Stove fuel*—Coleman by the pint at True Value Hardware, across from the fire station. *Cobbler*—Graham's Shoe Service: overnight boot and pack repair; open Mon-Sat 9:30am-5:30pm, located near fire station. *Outfitter*—Rockfish Gap Outfitters (703-943-1461) with full selection of backpacking gear (JanSport, Kelty, Camp Trails, Gregory, Mountainsmith, Lowe, North Face, Sierra Designs, Eureka!, Moss, Hi-Tec Sports, Danner, Merrell, Vasque, MSR, Optimus/Svea, Peak 1, Thermarest, ThorLo, Wigwam), repair service, MC, Visa; owners Matt and Dorothy McCall, have been helpful to many thru-hikers; located on U.S. 250 about one mile from the firehouse; open Mon-Thur 10am-6pm, Fri until 7pm, Sat 9am-5pm, Sun noon-4pm. Even if you don't need to buy anything, stop by, and check out the photo board to see who's ahead and to have your own photo added to the collection. *Other services*—banks • Western Union • Most • pharmacies • drug stores (Haney's has a soda fountain with good milkshakes) • department stores • doctors • dentists • hospital • veterinarian • barber with $3 basic cut • library with huge selection of magazines • movie theatre • UPS/FedEx pick-up • taxi service. *PO-ZIP 22980:* Mon-Fri 8:30am-5pm, closed Sat; 703-949-8129; LY-200+.

Wildlife: *River otters are usually seen swimming and are often mistaken for beavers. The otter has a 24-36" weasel-like body and a long, furry tail tapering toward the tip. These animals are very playful and like to vocalize with each other. You will be enthralled if you are lucky enough to see a mother training her young to swim, dive, and hunt along a river bank, as one thru-hiker did from the bridge near Weasie's several years ago.*

Shenandoah National Park

This chapter takes you from Rockfish Gap, Virginia, to Front Royal, Virginia, and corresponds to *Data Book* chapter seven.

Shenandoah National Park (SNP): playground of the nation's capital, containing 290 square miles of reclaimed backcountry connected by more than 500 miles of hiking trails. The A.T. runs the length of the park, with a smooth, wide treadway and moderate grades most of the distance. Along the way, animals, conditioned by years of protection, are plentiful and seem tame. Skyline Drive is crossed frequently, usually at scenic overlooks, and, to the delight of many thru-hikers, restaurants, camp stores, and shelters are never far away. Shelters in the park are called "huts." They are maintained by PATC (Potomac A.T. Club), which would like to make these facilities available free of charge but is required by park regulations to request a donation of $1 per night, payable on the honor system last year. Camping is difficult because of park regulations and terrain. Campsites must be located 250 feet from the A.T. or any other trail, 0.5 mile from any road, building, shelter, or other developed area, and out of sight. As you will find, there aren't many places that meet all requirements. Violation, however, can result in a $25 fine. As in the Smokies, thru-hikers must obtain a backcountry hiking permit before entering the park (see below). For information about the park, call the backcountry ranger (703-999-2243).

Notice: Listed dates and hours of operation for facilities in SNP are those for 1991. Information for 1992 was not available at time of publication. Check ahead, if you plan to use these facilities early or late in the year, by calling ARA Virginia Sky-Line Co. (703-743-5108).

Rockfish Gap: The Trail actually enters SNP eight miles north of here, but a backcountry permit should be obtained at the Skyline Drive entrance booth, located just north of Rockfish Gap, before you enter the park. Directions: After crossing the bridge over I-64, continue on the paved entrance to Skyline Drive for a short distance, follow the A.T. to the right into the woods for 0.8 mile to a blue-blazed side trail on the left (at sign), then go 0.2 mile on this side trail to the entrance booth, or, continue on the paved road from the bridge directly to the entrance booth, then take the side trail back to the Trail. A self-registration board is located near the booth, where you can sign in and attach a permit to your pack.

Clubnote: The next 238 miles are maintained by PATC volunteers.

Spring: located three miles past the gap, just off the A.T. 15 feet to the right, but it may be hidden by bushes. Be careful when you go off the Trail: You're in rattlesnake country.

Bear Den Mountain: Dire warnings about snakes and an excellent view greet you from the summit. Old tractor seats make an interesting grandstand. The next 0.3 mile has strawberry fields, with berries usually ripe and juicy by June.

Calf Mountain Shelter: your introduction to the infamous SNP bear poles for protecting food. There is a trick to hanging your bag without looking foolish, but it would spoil the fun if revealed here. The privy was once the most literate on the Trail. Sojourners could ponder *Atlantic Monthly* and *The London Literary Gazette*, but the reading rack was empty last year. Perhaps this is a good place to leave a register.

Wildlife: *Long-tailed weasels are sometimes seen scurrying from shelters as you approach. They are small, brown, squirrel-sized animals, with a long slender body, long neck, and a distinctive tail with a black tip. Weasels eat many small mammals, especially rats and mice, sometimes daring to enter occupied shelters at night to grab a gorp-fattened rodent. In northern states, they turn white during the winter, except for the tip of their tails.*

Jarman Gap: You are now in the park, officially.

Black Rock Hut: typical of the shelters in the park, and, for northbounders, the first on the A.T. to request a donation for overnight stay. A small pipe collection box is attached to the shelter. Numerous bears and a few bobcats were sighted north of this shelter in the early-morning hours last year. Piped spring usually gushes.

Browns Gap: site of ancient Indian ceremonial grounds. In autumns past, tribal hunters would gather for ceremonies, led by their medicine men and chiefs, to invoke a bountiful hunt. Excavations here in 1985 revealed pottery shards more than 8,000 years old.

Gypsy Moths: Hordes devastated the southern section of the park in 1990, leaving much of the Trail exposed to the sun. The forest looked like autumn; the heat felt like summer. The effect was eerie and depressing. Many people are hoping this nonnative insect, which escaped into the natural environment earlier in the century, can be controlled in some manner that does no additional harm to the balance of nature.

Loft Mountain Campground: bordered by the Trail for more than a mile. You can follow a side trail (straight ahead at the first concrete marker you encounter) through the amphitheater to the camp store, or stay on the A.T. for 0.7 mile to the marker indicating the camp store 250 feet to the left. The store has a limited hiker-food selection, coin-operated laundromat and pay showers (both open 7:30am-8pm), outside public telephone, and picnic tables; store open May 24-June 16 (9am-6pm), June 17-Sept 1 (9am-7pm), Sept 2-Oct 27 (9am-6pm). Campsites are $8. From the camp store, the paved road leads about 0.8 mile to the right to Loft Mountain Wayside with breakfast and grill (burgers, milkshakes), open 9am-5:30pm.

Deadening Nature Trail: left to Loft Mountain Wayside.

Pinefield Hut: one of the most landscaped shelter areas on the Trail. A few folks don't like the ambiance ("It isn't natural"), but most agree the paths and gravel help minimize damage to the surrounding grassy areas. Larry, the volunteer maintainer, makes frequent visits and often brings his family for cookouts with any hikers in for the night. Deer almost come into the shelter.

Hightop Hut: off the Trail to the left, with good piped spring.

South River Picnic Grounds: 500 feet to the left on a side trail, with water fountain, picnic tables, restrooms, and (usually) treats offered by generous picnickers. This is a good place to practice your yogi-ing skills on weekends, but remember: It isn't yogi-ing if you ask for a handout; let them offer.

Lewis Mountain Campground: similar to Loft Mountain, but smaller. The camp store can be reached via a side trail to the left through the campground. The store has a limited hiker-food selection, coin-operated laundromat and pay showers inside, and a drink machine and public telephone on the front porch; open May 9-May 31 (9am-5:30pm), June 1-Sept 2 (9am-8pm), Sept 3-Oct 28 (9am-5:30pm). Campsites are $8. A group cabin, with four bunks (cabin can sleep eight comfortably), electric lights, no running water, antique woodstove, and restrooms nearby, is available for $12 per group per night.

Bearfence Mountain Hut: with small spring that has very poor flow. Get water at Lewis Mountain Campground.

Lewis Springs: a gushing spring 50 feet off the Trail to the left, with Lewis Falls farther down the side trail that goes beyond the spring. The service road to the right leads 0.2 mile to Skyline Drive, where you can go left another 0.2 mile to Big Meadows Wayside (see below for alternate route).

> Wildlife: *White-tailed deer are now the most abundant hoofed wild mammals in North America, and you will see them often. Unlike most animals, they have benefitted from the cutting of forest and clearing of land. Males have antlers, which they shed each winter. Females are frequently seen with fawns. The tail, which shows white when raised, is used to signal alarm and serves as a moving "white blaze," so deer can follow each other through the brush when fleeing.*

Big Meadows: a large complex spread out over a one-mile area. The A.T. borders the camping-picnic-amphitheater section. Big Meadows Lodge has rooms and cabins available Mar 28-Dec 1. A dining room in the lodge is open from 7:30am-9pm (with "killer apple pie," according to "Connecticut Yankee" of '90); taproom with entertainment open until 11pm; public telephone in the lobby. The campground near the lodge and picnic area has campsites with pay showers and coin laundromat for $10 per night. An easy mile away via the paved lodge entrance road, at the intersection with Skyline Drive, is the Big Meadows Wayside with store, restaurant, and visitors center. The store (good hiker-food selection but expensive) is open Mar 1-Mar 28 (9am-5:30pm, Sat and Sun until 7pm), Mar 29-June 6 (9am-5:30pm), June 7-Sept 2 (8am-8pm), Sept 3-Dec 1 (9am-5:30pm). The restaurant with dining room and grill is open 9am-5:30pm. An outside public telephone is nearby. The visitors center features exhibits, movies about the history and wildlife of SNP, a great front-porch view of the meadows, and daily wagon rides through them (ask at desk).

Rock Spring Hut: adjacent to the Rock Spring Cabin (locked), with good spring and privy.

Joe's best day: "Joe Knothead" of '88 had an early breakfast at Big Meadows, hiked eight miles to Skyland for a big lunch, rested briefly, then hiked nine miles to Panorama for dinner before sundown. That evening at Pass Mountain Shelter, he was heard to comment that this had been his "best day on the A.T. so far," and he wasn't referring to mileage.

Skyland Lodge & Restaurant: now bypassed and not visible from the A.T. An unblazed side trail cuts over to the Skyland area but was hard to see last year. The surest way to reach the lodge and restaurant area is to go to the road just before the Stony Man parking area. Turn left on that road, at the sign indicating the way to the "Dining Room." The lodge has motel rooms, $63-$70, and cabins, $34-$66 (you may be able to bargain for better rates if they have vacancies). The restaurant, which is open Mar 28-Dec 8 (7:30am-9pm), doesn't quite know what to do with grubby thru-hikers, but most report good service and fairly good food, and breakfast comes highly recommended by several thru-hikers. A taproom is open until 11pm during the summer.

Stony Man Nature Trail: added to the A.T. in 1990 and a scenic improvement over the old route. Pick up a self-guiding brochure at the entrance for full enjoyment of the nature trail.

Byrd's Nest #3 Picnic Shelter: for picnickers only, and, yes, rangers do check at night. Water from springfed fountain.

Mary's Rock: on short side trail to the left, with view worth the detour.

Thornton Gap (U.S. 211): *Right 0.1m*—to Panorama with restaurant and AYCE salad bar, gift shop, and public telephone in the parking lot; open Mar 15-June 6 (9am-5:30pm), June 7-Sept 3 (9am-7pm), Sept 4-26 (9am-5:30pm), Sept 27-Oct 27 (9am-7pm), Oct 28-Nov 17 (9am-5:30pm).

Pass Mountain Hut: down long blue-blazed side trail to the right, with good spring, famous for the "kissing trees."

Wildlife: *Cottontails deserve their reputation for being prolific. Females can produce three litters a season, and rabbits born in early spring can breed by summer. Owls, foxes, hawks, bobcats, and man help to keep them in check, with more than 80% of the rabbit population being killed by predators each year. Few individuals live longer than nine months. Some of the eastern cottontails you encounter will seem remarkably tame, but remember that they are wild, and resist the urge to feed or pet them.*

Elkwallow Gap: Right 0.1m—to Elkwallow Wayside Store & Grill with limited groceries, burgers, milkshakes (the Mountain Blackberry is their specialty), patio tables, picnic tables, gas station, restrooms, and outside public telephone; open Apr 12-June 28 (9am-5:30pm), June 29-Sept 1 (9am-7pm, grill closes 5:30pm), Sept 2-Nov 3 (9am-5:30pm). No shower or laundromat.

Gravel Springs Hut: last shelter in SNP, dependable spring.

Trash cans: recently removed from parking areas in the northern half of SNP to encourage park users to dispose of trash outside the park, something easily accomplished by motorists but a hassle for thru-hikers.

Northern park boundary: self-registration station with backcountry hiking permits for southbounders (see comments at beginning of this chapter).

Tom Floyd Wayside: a PATC shelter, not a SNP restaurant. Tom, a longtime volunteer maintainer and Trail supervisor, built this shelter for thru-hikers when the park closed its shelters to hikers in the early 1980s (another silly episode, like the current experiment with the trash cans mentioned above). This was the first shelter to have a deck, a feature liked by thru-hikers. Water for this shelter is 0.2 mile down the mountain on a blue-blazed trail, from a piped spring to the left at the bottom. Two primitive tentsites are nearby.

Va. 602: Left 0.3m—to 4-H Center with large pool visible from the Trail, open to hikers afternoons only last year; admission fee. A blue-blazed trail to the left, about 0.7 mile beyond Va. 601, leads to the pool.

U.S. 522: Left 4m—to the city of Front Royal.

◆ **FRONT ROYAL, VA.** (pop. 11,000): *Lodging*—Front Royal Motel: $22S $28D (1 bed), or $32D (2 beds) (rates slightly higher on Fri-Sat) $4EAP, 4 max, $4 for roll-a-way bed; a/c, cable, phone in room, pool, pets allowed with $25 deposit (MC, Visa, AE, Dis, DC); located about one mile from downtown • Center City Motel: $25S; a/c, cable, phone in room (MC, Visa, AE, Dis, DC) • Mid-town Motel: $35S (but they claim they've never lost a hiker yet and will deal on rates); a/c, cable (MC, Visa, AE, Dis, DC); possible shuttle back to A.T. by maintenance man. *Places to eat*—many restaurants • L-Dee's Pancake House: B/L, home-cooked meals and short-orders; open Mon-Sat 5:30am-2pm, Sun 7am-1pm • McDonald's • Hardee's • KFC • Burger King • Pizza Hut • Wendy's • Arby's • Golden Corral • Tastee Freeze. *Other services*— several supermarkets, all good for long-term resupply (closest one located on U.S. 522 within three miles of the A.T.) • Better Thymes Natural Foods (Royal Plaza) • bakery • laundromats • Stokes General Store: some Hi-Tec boots, military surplus • bank • pharmacy • hardware store • doctor • dentist • hospital • veterinarian • UPS pickup • taxi service. *PO-ZIP 22630:* Mon-Fri 8:30am-5pm, Sat 8:30am-2pm; 703-635-4540; LY-45.

In memory: John Miller, PATC ridgerunner until 1989, died last year of cancer. For many years, John was seen patrolling Hwy. 602 on weekends, looking for folks in need of a ride to Front Royal. Many a thru-hiker benefitted from his generosity and from his efforts to make hiking the A.T. a safe and enjoyable experience.

Northern Virginia-West Virginia-Maryland

This chapter takes you from Front Royal, Virginia, to the Maryland-Pennsylvania line and corresponds to *Data Book* chapter six.

National Zoo compound: home for many rare and endangered animals from all over the world. Formerly a military reservation, the buildings and lands cover thousands of acres. Exotic birds comprise a major part of the collection, and herd animals adapt particularly well to the rolling landscape. You are most likely to see African donkeys near the fence that parallells the Trail. A nearby facility, part of a former U.S. Cavalry Remount Station, is used to train dogs for DEA duties.

PATC sign: adjacent to the zoo, saying "No Trespassing. Violators Will Be Eaten." This sign is famous in A.T. circles (thanks for the updated version, Carl!) but can be slightly hidden by brush in midsummer.

Mosby Campsite: on a side trail to the right, a primitive area with reliable spring and flat spots to pitch tents.

Jim and Molly Denton Shelter: showplace of PATC with furnished patio, cooking pavilion, and shower that is a magnificent engineering feat. Caretakers keep the place immaculate and often join hikers for cookouts on weekends.

> *Trail Fact: A hiker who burns 4,000 calories a day (and many thru-hikers burn considerably more) is expending an amount of energy equivalent to running two 26-mile marathons. For a five-month hike, that's the same as 300 marathons. You will possibly consume more than half a million calories of food between Springer and Katahdin. (How many M&Ms is that?)*

Va. 638: Left 0.5m—on busy, narrow road to Linden. Be careful of traffic here! Better yet: Use Va. 55, usually an easy hitch.

Va. 55: Left 1m—to the crossroads community of Linden.

♦ **LINDEN, VA.** (pop. 165): No services (the grocery store closed in 1991), outside public telephone; good alternative to Front Royal as a maildrop location if you don't need services. *PO-ZIP 22642:* Mon-Fri 8am-noon and 1-5pm, Sat 8am-noon; 703-636-9936; LY-67.

Manassas Gap Shelter: good, reliable spring; small tentsites nearby.

Trico Tower Trail: leads left 0.4 mile to firetower with good views.

Dick's Dome Shelter: built in 1989 by PATC member Dick George and sons, Sky and Everett, as a family project; a 12-foot geodesic-dome structure, one of the most unusual shelters on the A.T. The area around is rocky, with limited tentsites. Water source is the creek in front of the shelter.

Sky Meadows State Park: marked by wooden bench and sign on A.T., right 1.5 miles to a visitors center with soda machine. The park has shelters, tentsites, and picnic area. You will often meet park naturalists leading nature hikes on the Trail.

Northern Virginia Trail Center: located 0.6 mile to the right on blue-blazed side trail (0.2 mile north of where A.T. crosses Va. 602). Hikers may camp on lawn, get water from hose. PATC caretaker lives at the center.

Rock wall (just before U.S. 50): laid out by surveyor George Washington.

Ashby Gap (U.S. 50): *Right 0.1m*—to Papa Nick's Restaurant: B/L/D, home-cooked country-style meals, burgers, fries, salads, Nick's Special (3 eggs, bacon or sausage, home fries, toast, juice), Bubba Special (Can you guess what this is?), daily luncheon special $4, "mouthwatering" milkshakes (so Nick claims); open Mon-Fri 4:30am-9pm, Sat 6am-9pm, Sun 7am-9pm. *Right 1m*—to the community of **Paris, Va.** (pop. 100), with closed PO and no services.

Rod Hollow Shelter: built in 1985, initiating a new phase of shelter-building by PATC. This shelter was a prototype for other shelters, most notably the Denton Shelter. In recent years, it has suffered from heavy use by groups from nearby Washington, D.C., and Baltimore. One evening last year, 48 people camped in the area.

Rod Hollow Shelter to Blackburn A.T. Center: looks benign on the profile maps, but is actually a roller-coaster section with 17 ascents totaling about 5,000 feet.

Bears Den Mountain: site of world's first aerial wireless telegraphy transmission, by Dr. Mylan Loomis in 1888, using kites flown with copper wires. If Ben hadn't "discovered" lightning, Mylan might have!

Bears Den AYH Hostel (Rt. 1, Box 288, Bluemont, Va. 22012, 703-554-8708): located off the Trail 150 yards to the right at Bears Den Rocks. Originally built as a summer home during the 1930s, the quartzite "castle," now owned by ATC, was transformed into a 20-bed hostel by the ATC and AYH a few years ago. The hostel offers a hot shower, bunk, sheet sleepsack, and cooking privileges in a well-equipped kitchen, $9 for AYH, ATC, and A.T. club members, $12 nonmembers. Camping on lawn with full use of inside facilities, $4 for members, $7 nonmembers. Laundry is $2 per load, including detergent. Trail foods (Lipton dinners *etc.*), candy, ice cream, cold drinks, lemonade, and Coleman by the pint for sale. A shower without stay is $2 with towel, soap, and shampoo. The telephone is available for guests only. Check-in time: 5pm-9pm (hostel building usually closed during the day). Houseparents John Vassar and Jennifer Wampler welcome all hikers, and they will hold packages. Taxi, shuttle, and slackpacking services available for a fee by arrangement. Water is always available outside, from a faucet to the left at the front entrance.

Snickers Gap (Va. 7/679): *Left 0.2m* (on Va. 679)—to Horseshoe Curve Restaurant: L/D, third-generation family pub with sandwiches, burgers, and fries; open Tues-Sat noon-11pm, Sun noon-7pm, closed holidays. Owner Tracee Wink says, "Hikers are always welcome, and I enjoy talking to them." *Right 1.8m*—to the town of Bluemont.

♦ **Bluemont, Va.** (pop.100): *Services*—Snickersville General Store (est. 1846): general merchandise (including Coleman fuel), full range of deli sandwiches and salads, home-made cookies/breads, hand-dipped ice cream, milkshakes, and the trademark "Snickersville Donuts" made fresh each morning (still warm at 6:30am!). Owners Mark and Kate Zurschmeide welcome hikers.

> Wildlife: *Box turtles always seem to be going up a mountainside, never down, for some reason. These reptiles can live to be more than 100 years old and grow to about 9" in length at maturity. They are brown to black, with yellow, orange, or olive lines or spots, and have a hinged lower shell. Whatever you do, don't let one pass you on the Trail.*

Blackburn A.T. Center: reached via 0.3-mile side trail to the right that descends steeply. The center is owned by PATC. During the summer, it is staffed by caretakers (for the past four years by thru-hiker couples of the previous year) and open to hikers free of charge. The main building has a large, screened porch with sofas, picnic table, hiker register, and public telephone (703-338-9028). Water is available from plastic jugs on the porch. Inside are books, games, and other entertainments. A small cabin near the main building has been converted to a hiker hostel with bunk beds and a woodstove. Sleeping space is also available in the carriage house if the hostel is full. The shower is a fill-the-bucket-yourself type located in the woods below the center. If you are lucky, you'll arrive to find a barbeque or seafood festival in full swing. Washington, D.C. is visible on clear days.

David Lesser Memorial Shelter: new in late 1991, located two miles south of Keys Gap, off the A.T. to the right. Replaces the old, abused Keys Gap Shelter north of Rt. 9.

Keys Gap (W.Va. 9): *Left 0.1m*—to Mountaineer Mini-Mart: limited groceries, snack foods, and ice cream; open 7 days, 5am-9pm.

Loudoun Heights: the name of the ridge that overlooks Harpers Ferry on the south. The heights, bare of trees in the 1860s, were an important strategic location during the Civil War. A blue-blazed side trail, continuing past the point where the A.T. leaves the ridge, will take you to a fine view of Harpers Ferry. As you descend to the Shenandoah River, the Trail weaves in and out of old trenches that were used to protect riflemen more than 125 years ago.

Shenandoah River Bridge: narrow sidewalks and fast two-lane traffic, so be especially careful crossing it. At the end of the bridge, continue past the park entrance sign, and cross the paved side road to a guardrail. The Trail going north ascends into the woods behind the guardrail.

HARPERS FERRY, W. VA. (pop. 1,500): hometown of ATC and the psychological halfway point for most thru-hikers. The town itself, founded in 1747, is a sleepy little residential community dominated by the Harpers Ferry National Historical Park. It has few hiker services, but the nearby towns, accessible by local bus, have most of the major services needed by thru-hikers. *ATC headquarters (304-535-6331)*—The ATC offices are located at the corner of Washington and Jackson streets. (Directions from the A.T., using the 0.2-mile blue-blazed side trail: Go up rock steps to the left, follow blazes through the former Storer College campus, turn left on Fillmore Street, then right one block on Jackson Street to the white building on your right); open year-round, Mon-Fri 9am-5pm; also mid-May through October, Sat-Sun 9am-4pm. When you walk through the door weekdays, information specialist Jean Cashin, who serves double-duty as everybody's "Trail mother," will probably be the first to greet you. Jean will take your picture for the Class of '92 photo album. After that formality, you should sign the hikers' register and check the letter box for mail from home and messages left by other thru-hikers. A doctor's scale for checking your weight, located in the restroom, is accurate (dieting staffers disagree) but eccentric. In the lobby, guidebooks, maps, and other Trail paraphernalia are on sale. Coleman fuel is available by the pint for a donation. If you are not an ATC member, this is a very good place to become one. Also, if you have a few hours, you may want to help stuff envelopes or do another volunteer chore with Jean or in the sunny new shipping area upstairs. By so doing, you'll get a chance to meet some of the staff (most work upstairs) and make a contribution to the Trail effort. *Lodging*—Hilltop House Hotel: $20S $35D $5EAP, 8 max; a/c, phone in room, no pets (MC, Visa, AE, DC); rates subject to space available, and you must state that you are a thru-hiker; located three blocks from ATC • Comfort Inn: $50S $58D $6EAP, 5 max; a/c, phone in room, cable , no pets (MC, Visa, AE, Dis, DC); free complimentary breakfast; located near the PO • several b&bs (ask Jean about availability) • Harpers Ferry Camp Resort: a full-service campground with cabins for $30D, tentsites (listed at $18, but hikers get huge discount, usually $4 per person), showers free for guests ($4 for nonguests), small campstore (milk, eggs, snacks, sodas), indoor and outdoor pools, game room, and coin-operated laundromat open to public 8am-10pm. The campground is located 1.4 miles west of ATC, accessible by the bus service described below; open Apr 15-Dec 15. *Places to eat*—King's Pizzeria: open Tues-Sun 11am-11pm, closed Monday (closed August 1992 for remodeling) • Hilltop House Restaurant: B/L/D, fine dining with AYCE breakfast and AYCE dinner buffet (Fri- Sat only), open 7 days. *Groceries*—three convenience stores with limited groceries (about one mile from ATC) • *Other services*—laundromat (at campground) • bank • Most • doctor • dentist • UPS/FedEx pick-up at ATC. *Transportation*—Bus service is available from the ATC building to Charles Town. A one-way trip costs $1; buses run four times a day. Bus schedule and a Charles Town shopping guide with map are posted on the front bulletin board at ATC. • Amtrak (1-800-USA-RAIL; $13 one-way, $20 round trip) and commuter trains (1-800-325-RAIL; $6.50 one way, $12 round-trip) go to and from Washington, D.C. *Harpers Ferry National Historical Park*—Many exhibits and free guided tours will acquaint you with the varied history of the Harpers Ferry area. It's a good place to spend a leisurely morning or afternoon browsing around. Adjacent to the park are shops and a few restaurants mostly geared to tourists. Little Ponderosa BBQ: in old train car, welcomes hikers, serves healthy portions, 8am-5pm, closed Wed. *PO-ZIP 25425:* Mon-Fri 8am-12:30pm and 1:30-4pm, closed Sat; 304-535-2479; LY-465. *Nearby town*—Charles Town (6 miles west).

♦ **Charles Town, W.Va.** (pop. 2,857): *Services*—Turf Motel: $32S $46D $2EAP, 4 max; a/c, cable, phone in room, pool (MC, Visa, AE, Dis, DC); in motel, Turf Restaurant with seafood and prime rib • Donna's Washington St. Deli & Cafe: mainly sandwiches • Charles Washington Restaurant: fine dining, lunch and dinner specials, Sunday brunch, reservations suggested • Shu Chen's Family Restaurant: full chinese menu • McDonald's • Hardee's • KFC • Pizza Hut • Dairy Queen • Subway • LJ Silver's • Wendy's • Denny's • Golden Corral • Ponderosa with weekend breakfast bar • Food Lion Supermarket: good for long-term resupply, located in Somerset Village Shopping Center on U.S. 340, about five miles from ATC • Barnhardt's Supermarket: good for long-term resupply, located across from Food Lion in Charles Town Shopping Center; laundromat next door • bakery • whitewater outfitter with no backpacking supplies • sporting goods store • bank • Western Union • Cirrus • pharmacy • Valley Hardware Store • JC Penny Department Store • doctor • dentist • health clinic • hospital • veterinarian.

Potomac River: crossed on the 600-foot-long Goodloe Byron Memorial Pedestrian Walkway, built by the NPS and dedicated in 1987, restoring the original route of the A.T. across the Potomac. At the north end of the bridge, the Trail turns right onto the C&O Canal towpath, which it follows for about three miles. You can reach spectacular Maryland Heights by turning left and going 0.5 mile upriver on the towpath, then taking the orange-blazed Grant Conway Trail; side trail from it to the right leads to the familiar postcard view overlooking Harpers Ferry from the north.

C&O Canal: an enterprise dating back to colonial times. George Washington was one of the investors and reportedly rode his horse down the towpath (now the A.T.) to check on his investment. Mules used the towpath to pull barges filled with goods headed for the frontier, which was not too far beyond Harpers Ferry in the 1700s.

Sandy Hook: with hostel, reached by following a blue-blazed side trail to the left immediately after going under the Sandy Hook (U.S. 340) bridge. Cross the C&O Canal on a small footbridge, then head across railroad tracks to Sandy Hook Road. A small grocery store is located to the left. Go right on the road 0.4 mile to the Sandy Hook AYH.

♦ Sandy Hook AYH: bunkrooms, laundromat, kitchen, and hot showers; open 6pm-10pm for registration. Bunkroom is $10 for members, $13 nonmembers. Camping on lawn is $5 for members, $8 nonmembers. Campers may use inside facilities. ATC members are given AYH member rates, but you must have your membership card with you. Doing a chore is part of your payment, standard practice at AYH facilities. Pets must remain outside. For the past few years, quite a few thru-hikers reported that they felt unwelcome at this hostel, but it is under new management in 1992, and the new managers, PATC members Nancy McDonnell and Tom Kenny, welcome thru-hikers and want to change the image of the hostel.

Weverton Cliffs: the place pictured on the cover of the *National Geographic* book, "the one with the yuppies on the cover," as one wag put it. Those very neat people were not thru-hikers, but let's try not to feel too smug about our dirt and miles. More than three million other hikers use the A.T. every year, most for short hikes. In a way, thru-hikers are the ones out of step, if anyone is.

Wildlife: *Opossums are America's only marsupial. They are nocturnal and usually go unnoticed by hikers, although you may see a female foraging during the day, sometimes with wide-eyed babies clinging to her back. Under stress from predators, these mammals curl up in a trancelike state that may last for several hours, hence the term "playing possum." Opossums look like very large rats, with a pointed face and hairless tail.*

Gathland State Park: notable for its large stone monument to war correspondents, but also of importance to thru-hikers because of its drink machine (have 50¢ in coins ready). Restrooms, water, and a picnic pavilion make this a good place to cook dinner if you are heading for Crampton Gap Shelter. Camping is sometimes available, check at park office above the restrooms. Jim Preston, longtime superintendent and friend of hikers, retired in 1991 and will be missed.

Md. 572: Right 1.2m—to the community of **Burkittsville, Md.** (pop. 220) with The Dreaming Deer (hand-crafted jewelry made from deer antlers found in the area), no other services.

Crampton Gap Shelter: on blue-blazed side trail to the right, easily missed; has variable spring, so you may want to carry water from the park.

Rocky Run Shelter: lovingly cared for by the overseer, Karl. Swing in front.

Dahlgren Backpack Camping Area: the only place on the A.T. with state-provided hot showers for hikers. This 24-hour facility has restrooms, showers, picnic tables, and a camping area; all free. Watch your gear while showering, since U.S. 40A is nearby.

Turners Gap (U.S. 40A): *Left 0.1m*—to Old South Mountain Inn: L/D, upscale fine dining, prime rib, seafood, and good wine list (MC, Visa, AE, DC); open Tues-Sat 11:30am-2:30pm, Sat 4-10pm, Sun 10am-8pm, closed Mon. If you don't feel dressed suitably for dining inside, request seating on the dining patio. *Left 2m*—to the town of Boonsboro, Md.

♦ **Boonsboro, Md.** (pop. 2,600): *Services*—restaurant • grocery store • laundromat • bank • Cirrus, Most, MAC • pharmacy • doctor • dentist • veterinarian. Watch your gear in town. A pack was stolen here in 1990.

Washington Monument State Park: with soda machines, picnic tables, and a public telephone on the road just before the park entrance. The park is built around the first Washington Monument, an unusual structure built in 1827 by the citizens of nearby Boonsboro, that affords excellent views of the surrounding countryside from an observation area on top. A 1988 thru-hiker, upon first sighting the monument, was heard to mutter admiringly, "What a bunch of crock." George would have probably agreed.

I-70 footbridge: a puzzle to some thru-hikers. The drivers in cars and trucks going from your right to the left often honk their horns and wave. Those going in the opposite direction rarely do the same. Can you see why? While you are pondering the mystery, the A.T. turns left and passes under the U.S. 40 bridge. If you go up to U.S. 40 and go left for 0.4 mile, you will come to Greenbrier State Park with campground (tentsites $10 per site with shower, shower $2 if not camping), camp store, and swimming ($2 per person). Across the road from the park are the Greenbrier Inn with pizza and seafood, open 7 days, noon-midnight; and a small grocery store with limited groceries, ice cream, and a public telephone, open Mon-Fri 5am-9pm, Sat and Sun 7am-7pm.

Pine Knob Shelter: not marked by a sign on the A.T. Instead, a sign saying "spring" points left down an overgrown woods road. The spring sign may have a small notation about the shelter. For the past few years, a mother gray fox has led her kits past the shelter to the spring at dusk. Partying neighbors sometimes visit on weekends.

Pogo Memorial Campsite: good spring and privy, site of former Blackwater Hotel.

Hemlock Hill Campground and Shelter: within sight of Wolfsville Road, built as a Scout project in the late 1960s. Water may be obtained by going north 0.1 mile on the A.T., across the road, to an abandoned gray/green house just off the Trail to the right. A concrete block springhouse is behind the house, but the spring is not dependable in dry times. If it's running, you will need a cup for dipping. The house is off-limits to hikers.

Wolfsville Road (Md. 17): *Left 2.4m*—to the town of Smithsburg.

♦ **Smithsburg, Md.** (pop. 1,000): *Services*—Dixie Eatery: B/L, home-cooked meals, steak and cheese subs, luncheon specials daily; open Mon-Thur and Sat 7am-2pm, Fri 7am-8pm, closed Sun • Vince's Pizza: L/D, casual and take-out, pizza, subs, lasagna, salads; open Mon-Fri 11am-11pm, until midnight on weekends • Dairy Queen • Smithburg Market: neighborhood grocery store, good for short-term resupply; open Mon-Sat 8am-9pm, Sun 9am-5pm • Smithsburg Home-style Laundry: FLW, open 6:30am-10:30pm • bank • Cirrus, Most, MAC • Smithsburg Plaza (on Md. 64) with Tastee Freeze, High's convenience store, Family Medical Center (doctor, dentist), pharmacy, and hardware store.

> Wildlife: *Foxes are members of the canine family and seem to be holding their own in the modern world. You may see two varieties. The red fox is usually reddish with black feet and legs or can be dark gray, but has a white-tipped tail. The gray fox has a bushy, black-tipped tail. It can also climb trees. Both are about 24" in length and den in hollow logs, tree trunks, or rock caves.*

Md. 77: water sometimes available from the South Mountain Rod & Gun Club.

Camp David: presidential retreat in the Catoctin Mountains, located a few miles from the Trail somewhere in this vicinity. Camping by invitation only!

Devils Racecourse Shelter: a bit dilapidated and a long way back down the mountain you have just climbed to reach the shelter turn-off. Water is from the spring just before the shelter.

Pen Mar County Park: featuring sunset and picnic pavilions and restrooms. The sunset pavilion overlooks Maryland and Pennsylvania farmland to the west and is visited by many neighbors on a clear night. Nearby, an A.T. mileage sign and American flag make a good place to have your picture made for the folks back home. The park ranger usually allows hikers to sleep in one of the picnic pavilions, but ask permission before you move in. A public telephone is located in the ranger office, which, along with the restrooms, is locked when the ranger leaves at 8pm.

♦ Decker's Supermarket & Deli (good for long-term resupply; open Mon-Fri 7am-9pm, Sat 8am-8pm, Sun 9am-3pm) and Rocky's Pizza are located about 1.5 miles from the park. At park entrance, go left on High Rock Road, continue past traffic light, on past the Fort Richie entrance, under RR bridge to intersection, then right to the market. The park ranger usually goes to Decker's for coffee around 6pm and sometimes offers a ride, especially if you offer to buy the coffee.

Pennsylvania

This chapter takes you from the Maryland-Pennsylvania line to Delaware Water Gap, Pennsylvania, and corresponds to *Data Book* chapter five.

Pa. 16: Right 2.2m—to the town of Blue Ridge Summit. *Left 5m*—to the city of Waynesboro.

♦ **Blue Ridge Summit, Pa.** (pop. 2,500): *Services*—diner: with good breakfast; open 7 days, 7am-11pm • Summit Plaza Restaurant: B/L/D, home-cooked meals, burgers, fries, soups, hearty daily specials under $4; open 7 days, 6am-8pm; located across from the library (old train station). • High's convenience store.
♦ **Waynesboro, Pa.** (pop. 9,800): *Services*—Best Western Motel (on far side of town) • restaurants • Keystone Kountry Kitchen • McDonald's • Hardee's • KFC • Pizza Hut • Dairy Queen • Bonanza with AYCE salad and food bar • Golden Corral • several supermarkets good for long-term resupply • bakery • laundromat • cobbler • bank • Western Union • pharmacy • hardware store • department store • doctor • dentist • hospital • veterinarian • movie theatre • UPS/FedEx pick-up.

Game lands: The A.T. goes through state game lands in Pennsylvania, where hunting in season is allowed. Game-land boundaries are marked with white splotches of paint. These splotches are often on trees near the Trail and resemble blazes but are generally larger and irregular. Pay attention. Follow only the standard 2" x 6" blazes.

Deer Lick Shelters: the double-shelter style used in much of southern Pennsylvania. A lumber company donated the logs for these two shelters and for quite a few others that you will see in the next few days. Pennsylvania Conservation Corp crews built them, under the supervision of Michaux State Forest personnel. Thanks to all concerned. Water from large spring on a blue-blazed trail, reportedly worth the long walk.

Antietam Shelter: located on Antietam Creek, which is great for wading (the minnows nibble your toes) but not potable. Get water from springhouse faucet at Old Forge Park, a few hundred feet north on the A.T. Water in this area contained *giardia* in 1989 but was deemed safe to drink late last year. Look for signs posted on park fountains and at the springhouse.

Tumbling Run Shelters: double shelters new in 1990, watched over by caretaker Rex "Loonie Boonie" Looney, who often brings treats for thru-hikers. The old shelter has been demolished. Cold spring nearby.

Rocky Mountain (Jim Thorpe) Shelter: water can be found by going 0.2 mile on the dirt road in front of the shelter to a paved road, then left 100 yards to spring in the woods, on the right.

Pa. 233: Right 1.6m—to the town of South Mountain.

♦ **South Mountain, Pa.** (pop. 2,000): *Services*—convenience store good for short-term resupply • tavern with grill. "Geek" of '90 said, "Town is very friendly. I camped in a clearing behind the PO, but ask first." *PO-ZIP 17261:* Mon-Fri 8am-noon and 1-5pm, Sat 8am-noon; 717-749-5833; LY-25.

U.S. 30: Left 0.5m—to Poorman's Pizza, closed Monday; 0.4 mile farther to Hinicle's Grocery. *Left 3.5m*—to the town of Fayetteville. *Right 15m*—to the historic town of Gettysburg.

♦ Hinicle's Grocery: good for short-term resupply, excellent deli (hot foods prepared daily); open 7 days, 8am-9pm.
♦ **Fayetteville, Pa.** (pop. 4,000): *Services*—motel • restaurant • convenience store • laundromat • doctor.
♦ **Gettysburg, Pa.** (pop. 7,194): *Services*—many motels and restaurants • Chambersburg Street AYH, $8 for members, $11 non-members, plus $1 for sleepsack, located within one mile of the Gettysburg National Battlefield (Civil War exhibits, guided tours, site of Lincoln's famous address) • Beanie's Shoe Repair: boots and packs repaired while you wait, if possible; open Tues-Fri 7am-6pm, Sat 7am-noon, closed Mon.

Caledonia State Park: with picnic area, restrooms, pool, public telephone, and campsites ($6 per person with shower, maximum of 4 people per site, no pets). Pool, with place to store packs inside fenced area, and concession stand with fast food, snacks, ice cream, and Slurpies; open 7 days, 11am-7pm; $2 pool fee. The historic Thaddeus Stevens blacksmith shop is located near the park entrance.

Quarry Gap Shelters: double shelters, spring at head of creek, campsites in woods across creek in front of shelter area, smallest picnic table on the A.T. You may want to cook at the park, where water is available from spigots, before heading to this shelter for the night.

Milesburn Cabin: locked PATC cabin with privy. A small spring is located down the road, to the left about 100 yards, then off to the right about 100 feet on a blue-blazed side trail. Unofficial campsites are available on the A.T. south and north of the cabin.

Toms Run Shelters: two new ones in place last year, old ones now demolished; fireplaces built as a Scout's Eagle project, occasional problems with weekend parties. Water from spring behind the old chimney.

> *Wildlife: Bats often dart in and out of shelters on a hot night, and you may feel the breeze from their wings (which are actually hands) as they change direction. If this gives you the creeps, remember that bats eat the hungry mosquitos hovering just above you. You may also encounter a bat hanging upside-down in the corner or under the eave of a shelter. Don't try to handle or remove it. Come nightfall, it will leave of its own accord.*

Pine Grove Furnace State Park: campsites $5 per site (maximum of 5 people per site), Fuller Lake beach and swimming area (free, open 7 days, 11am-7pm, with concession stand), camp store, hostel, and historic furnace used to smelt iron during the Revolutionary War. A public telephone is outside at the park office but can be cantankerous. No pets (thru-hiker dogs may pass through) or alcohol are permitted in the park, which is open from dawn to dusk year-round (camping and other facilities Memorial Day-Labor Day). *Hostel*—Ironmaster's Mansion AYH (717-486-7575): in building dating back to colonial times, one of the places George and Martha Washington are known to have stayed overnight, during the wedding of the ironmaster's daughter. Today, the hostel caters primarily to cyclist and large groups; operated by hostlers Bob and Joan Beard. (Tom Martin will be your host from May 15 to late August, while Bob and Joan tandem-cycle across the U.S.) Bunk with shower and kitchen privileges, $8 for members, $11 nonmembers, plus $1 for sleepsack. ATC membership is honored as AYH membership for one night only. Laundry is extra: $1 for wash with detergent, $1 for dryer. A shower without stay is $2.50 with towel, soap, and shampoo. Video movies and a Jacuzzi ($3.50 for 30 min., non-guests must take $2.50 shower first) are available. Check in after 4:30pm. Check out before 9:30am. *Camp Store*—Pine Grove Furnace Store: located next to the hostel, home of the "Half-Gallon Club." Anyone who has hiked here from Georgia or Maine may join this wacky thru-hiker tradition. All you have to do is buy a half-gallon of your favorite ice cream as soon as you arrive, and eat (not drink) it as fast as you can. You are permitted to wash it down with hot coffee or soda if you have the stomach for it. Those who finish their half-gallon are given a commemorative wooden spoon as a membership token and are invited to draw a cartoon depicting the event. The drawings are displayed at the store all summer. Limited hiker foods and snacks are also available; open 7 days, 8am-9pm, closed after Labor Day.

Clubnote: The next 17 miles are maintained by Mountain Club of Maryland volunteers.

Midpoint marker: located just north of Pine Grove Furnace State Park. The actual halfway point moves from year to year, due to relocations, but stays in this vicinity, so this spot is as good a place to have a midpoint marker as any. "Woodchuck" of '85 built and erected the marker and register box.

Tagg Run Shelters: 0.2 mile off the Trail, with good piped spring on blue-blazed trail beyond the shelters.

Earl Shaffer: the first person to hike the A.T. in one continuous journey. Earl lives nearby and is seen on the Trail in this area from time to time. His written account of that first hike, *Walking With Spring*, is a classic. Count yourself lucky if you have a chance to spend an evening with him. Earl is a gentleman and a poet.

Pa. 34: Right 5m—to the community of Gardners, Pa.

♦ **Gardners, Pa.** (pop. 1,213): *Services*—restaurant • small grocery store • pharmacy • doctor • dentist • health clinic.

Pa. 94: Left 2.5m—to the town of Mt. Holly Springs.

♦ **Mt. Holly Springs, Pa.** (pop. 4,068): *Services*—hotel • several restaurants • sandwich and sub shop • supermarket • convenience store • laundromat • hardware/sporting goods store • bank • MAC • pharmacy • doctor • dentist • movie theatre.

Sheet Iron Road: Left 0.3m—to a private campground with camp store.

Wildlife: *Timber rattlers are pit vipers that will not always rattle as you approach, so you should watch where you place your feet and hands, especially in rocky areas or when you step off the Trail into the brush. Rattlers vary in color from reddish-tan in the South to yellow-black or black in the North. They are not aggressive toward man, but hearing one "sing" will bring out the fear in you. Resist the urge to kill them. Enjoy these beautiful animals from a distance. Rattlesnakes can be seen as far north as Massachusetts on the A.T.*

Alec Kennedy Shelter: completed in 1991. Look for new sign indicating location of the shelter, which is just before Center Point Knob on a side trail to the right. Water source is the creek 300 yards before the shelter.

Center Point Knob: site of a monument to mark the original midpoint of the Trail. Midpoint and plaque marking it have long since gone wandering.

Clubnote: The next 18 miles are maintained by Cumberland Valley A.T. Management Association volunteers, who comprise the newest A.T. club, approved in 1990.

White Rocks Ridge: the end of the Blue Ridge Mountains, which you have been following since Georgia.

Notice: No camping is allowed along the A.T. in the Cumberland Valley between Alec Kennedy Shelter and Darlington Shelter.

Cumberland Valley Relocation: now open almost all the way across the valley. The new route forsakes the increasingly congested valley roads for scenic farmland, making melting asphalt a thing of the past for this year's thru-hiker. It also adds Boiling Springs to the list of Trail towns, and this charming little community will undoubtedly become a hiker favorite in years to come. Unfortunately, the "Ice-Cream Lady" is no longer able to greet overheated thru-hikers with a smile and an icy scoop of double-dip chocolate, as she did for so many seasons. Look for notices giving information about the relo, since some maps for this area may not reflect the new path.

BOILING SPRINGS, PA. (pop. 1,521): an 18th-century iron-industry settlement that became a 19th-century tourist village and recreational area. Today, it is primarily a residential community, listed in the National Register of Historic Places. The springs are some of the largest in Pennsylvania, with a flow of 24 million gallons bubbling up per day (the local high school teams are known as "The Bubblers"). The town was new to the A.T. in 1990, but its residents are already adapting to the flow of hiker traffic that comes through each summer. *Services*—The Garmenhaus B&B: $50S/D $25EAP, 4 max; tenting in backyard for $1 per night (does not include bathroom or shower privileges; house and refreshments are for b&b guests only), shower only $5, laundry $2, breakfast $5; owned by John Garmen • Highland House: $50S/D (special rate for hikers, weekdays only); a/c, pool, no pets; hosted by a retired production executive with ABC's "Wide World of Sports" (Tell him about the agony of *de feet!*) • Boiling Springs Tavern: L/D, casual fine dining, steaks and seafood, reservations required for dinner, five-drink limit at bar; open Tues-Sat 11:30am-10pm • 3rd Street Deli & Oriental Food: L/D, cafeteria-style and take-out, sandwiches, subs, fried chicken, fish, ice cream, and milkshakes; open Mon-Thur 10am-9pm, Fri-Sat 10am-10pm, Sun 10am-9pm • Anile's Italian Restaurant: pizza, Italian dishes, open 11am-11pm • Karns Grocery Store: good for short-term resupply; open 7 days, 8am-10pm • laundromat • bank • MAC • Boiling Springs Pool: $3.50 admission, open daily 11am-7pm • park and lake (with black swans) • ATC Regional Office (717-258-5771) with swing and grassy yard on A.T., but city ordinances prevent camping, so don't ask. *PO-ZIP 17007:* Mon-Fri 8am-1pm and 2-4:30pm, Sat 8am-noon; 717-258-6668; LY-50+.

U.S. 11: crossed on the new pedestrian footbridge opened in autumn of 1990. *Left 0.2m—* to Pleasant Inn: $34S $37D $3EAP, 5 max; a/c, cable, phone in room, washer/dryer, continental breakfast 7am-10pm, pets allowed (MC, Visa, AE, Dis) • Appalachian Trail Inn: $45D $3EAP, 5 max; a/c, cable, phone in room, some rooms with Jacuzzi, pets allowed, Trailside Restaurant in motel (MC, Visa, AE, Dis, CB); no relation to ATC • Horizon Restaurant: B/L/D, country-casual, family-style meals, salads, short-order favorites (MC, Visa); open 7 days, 6am-10pm • Hardee's. *Right 0.2m—*to Gina's Italian Luncheonette with tasty subs and friendly conversation, open daily 7am-3pm, but hours may vary; closed month of August (and possibly all of 1992). *Right 0.4m—*to Carlisle 24-Hour Truck Plaza: restaurant (B/L/D, trucker-style meals, burgers, fries, ice cream, pies), laundromat, Western Union, public telephones, and small store for snacks; open 7 days, 24 hours.

Conodoguinet Creek: water from spigot on right side of house; owned by NPS and used by ATC and local volunteers; located just beyond the north end of the bridge across the creek, signs show the way. A few hundred feet farther, entrance to a trailer park with campstore (looks like a red barn, good for short-term resupply; open 7 days, 7am-9pm) and laundromat.

Clubnote: The next 13 miles are maintained by Mountain Club of Maryland volunteers.

Darlington Shelter: water from spring a long way down the blue-blazed trail in front of the shelter (take a cup). Consider carrying water from the piped spring halfway up Blue Mountain, 30 feet to the left at the point where the Trail crosses the jeep road.

Rocky I: The next 10 sometimes rocky, sometimes smooth miles into Duncannon will give you a good idea of what the A.T. is like in the remainder of Pennsylvania.

Thelma Marks Shelter: water down steep, blue-blazed trail in front of the shelter. Take a cup or small water bottle for dipping, since the spring source is nestled in rocks.

Memorial trees: planted beside the Trail in memory of 1990 thru-hikers Geoff Hood and Molly LaRue.

Hawk Rock: overlook with view of Duncannon and the Susquehanna River valley for many miles north. An unofficial campsite 0.1 mile south of the overlook has no water. Susquehanna A.T. Club officials are sworn in at this overlook, a long-standing club tradition.

DUNCANNON, PA. (pop. 2,445): once called "the jewel of the Susquehanna," but considered by many of its residents to be a small, blue-collar town that has probably seen its better days. From a thru-hiker standpoint, it still provides basic services and is also fairly convenient, since everything is located within a few minutes of the central business area. Hiking is not of major interest to the town's people, though they are quite friendly to A.T. hikers that pass through their community. *Lodging*—Doyle Hotel (717-834-3020), legendary in thru-hiking circles. Built around the turn of the century by Anheuser-Busch, the hotel was purchased by the Doyle family four decades ago. Most of the early thru-hiking pioneers stayed here (check the old registers), and many a hiking tale has been told around the bar on the ground floor. Today, it's a bring-your-own-toilet-paper kind of place that caters to short-term renters and to hikers during the summer months. Rooms are inexpensive, $10.60 per person, and come supplied with bed linens, a dresser, an electric light, and dust bunnies, some of which may have been on the loose since the early 1980s. Most rooms have keys, but none have air conditioning or fans. Shared bathrooms, two per floor, have only tubs, and the toilets are vintage (notice the name on the front of the toilet bowls, perhaps the inspiration for the phrase, "going to the John"). A public telephone is available in the lobby. The bar features television, air conditioning, and draft beer for 60¢ a glass. Patrons begin arriving around eight in the morning, and you will never see the bar without at least one regular holding down the fort. The bar and hotel are closed Sunday (you can stay in the hotel Sunday if you check in Saturday). One final comment: The Doyle obviously isn't 5-star, but the folks who run it are friendly and make thru-hikers feel at home. *Other lodging*—Riverfront Campground (near Clarks Ferry Bridge): tentsites with few amenities for $3 per tentsite, pay showers. Railroad tracks are quite close, and trains pass often, so don't expect to get much sleep • Clarks Ferry Truckstop (at U.S. 22/ 322): no longer a motel but has showers available. *Places to eat*—Sorrento's Italian Restaurant: pizza, subs, stromboli (Can anyone eat a whole one?), all considered excellent by thru-hikers of past years. • 3B's Ice Cream Shop: located about 0.6 mile north of the Doyle, open daily 11am-10pm. *Groceries*—Mutzabaugh's Market: large grocery store, good for long-term resupply • 24-hour convenience store, located behind the Doyle. *Laundromat*—FLW, centrifugal water extractor, good place to wash a synthetic sleeping bag; open 7 days, 8am-9pm. *Stove fuel*—Coleman by the pint at True Value Hardware. *Other services*—bank • pharmacy • newsstand • doctor • dentist • health clinic. *PO-ZIP 17020:* Mon-Fri 8am-4:30pm, Sat 8am-noon; 717-834-3332; LY-300. *Nearby town*—Harrisburg (about 15 miles southeast).

♦ **Harrisburg, Pa.** (pop. 53,264): a large city with all major services, including a great backpacking store, Wildware Outfitters (717-564-8008) with Lowe, Gregory, Mountainsmith, Camp Trails, Kelty, JanSport, Peak 1, Sierra Designs, Moss, Eureka!, The North Face, Vasque, Merrell, Hi-Tec Sports, Danner, Timberland, MSR, Optimus/Svea, GAZ Bluet, and repair services; open Mon-Fri 10am-9pm, Sat 10am-5pm.

Susquehanna River: the longest river crossed by the Trail, 444 miles in length. The Connecticut River is second at 411; the Potomac, third at 383; the James, fourth at 340; and the Hudson, fifth at 315.

Clubnote: The next 8 miles are maintained by York Hiking Club volunteers.

Peters Mountain flag: first flew in the 1940s, a permanent landmark since then; 10 x17-foot flag cleaned and maintained by local Boy Scouts once a year.

Rocky II: Just when you thought all those stories about rocks were exaggerated, the fun begins. From here to Delaware Water Gap, you will have rocks of one kind or another. Some sections will have large rocks, allowing you to hop from rock to rock and make good time. Other sections will have pointed little rocks that slow you down. You'll also have to be extra alert for rattlesnakes and copperheads, now that the weather is getting really hot. Fortunately, the ridges are fairly level, so you won't have many long climbs.

Clarks Ferry Shelter: bunks, picnic table, and dependable cold spring; recently built to replace the old Susquehanna Shelter. Take enough water from here to get to the Peters Mountain Shelter, since water is scarce on this ridge.

Clubnote: The next 9 miles are maintained by Susquehanna A.T. Club volunteers.

Zeager Shelter: great view in front, but no water for miles.

Peters Mountain Shelter: formerly called the Earl Shaffer Shelter, but he asked that his name not be used when the floor was added. Earl believes that earthen floors are more in keeping with the Trail experience. Water is far down a rocky blue-blazed trail in front of the shelter. A 1987 thru-hiker commented in the register, "The reason the spring is so cold, it's in Canada."

> Wildlife: *Coyotes will probably be the closest you come to seeing a wolf on your hike. They look like a small wolf with a bushy tail but have reddish-gray flanks and rust-colored legs, feet, and ears. Very noticeable is their habit of running with their tails between their legs. Coyotes have extended their range into the northeastern states, from Pennsylvania to Maine, by coming up the back side of the Appalachians via the Ohio River valley, and they seem to adapt well to the presence of man. You may hear their series of high-pitched yaps in the evening, or you may catch a glimpse of greenish-gold eyeshine.*

Clubnote: The next 12 miles are maintained by Brandywine Valley Hiking Club volunteers.

Rausch Gap Shelter: off the A.T. 0.3 mile to the right (sign easy to miss going north). Shelter has unique table for cooking, "running water," and privy to the left a hundred yards from the shelter. The area is overused by weekenders, who have easy access from a nearby forest road. Good campsites can be found near the shelter.

Rausch Creek experiment: to the left where the Trail crosses the creek on a dirt road. A large, eight-foot diameter pipe is filled with limestone. Water from the creek is diverted through it to remove acidity caused by seepage from old mines. If the wire cover is removed, some hikers swear the pipe looks like a hot tub, but quickly add that it doesn't feel like one.

Clubnote: The next 62 miles are maintained by Blue Mountain Eagle Climbing Club volunteers.

Bleu Blaze Hostel: at bottom of Second Mountain, where A.T. makes sharp right turn onto dirt road. To reach hostel, don't turn right, but continue straight ahead and follow blue blazes 600 feet to the home of ATC members Dick and Ann Tobias (717-397-0851). Hostel is in their carpet-covered garage addition, with some beds, toilet, sink, solar shower, over-stuffed chairs, electric lights, and a radio; free to thru-hikers for the past three years.

Pa. 443: Trail passes by Larry's Greenpoint Grocery. Larry sells insurance and is never around but usually has a resident manager who lives in the adjacent house. The store carries bread, canned goods, pasta, toiletries, ice cream by the pint, chips, sodas, juices, and candy; open Mon-Fri 7am-6:30pm, Sat 7am-7pm, Sun 9am-6pm. A public telephone and drink machine are located outside. Note: Don't count on this store for resupplying. It has opened and closed several times in recent years.

Waterville Bridge: built by the Berlin Iron Bridge Co. using wrought iron instead of steel. It is a fine example of the lenticular-truss bridge and is listed in the National Register of Historic Places. The bridge was scheduled to be demolished but was restored and moved to this location over Swatara Creek in 1987. A piece of history has been saved and put to good use.

Blue Mountain Campsite: on A.T. with good piped spring 100 yards down a blue-blazed trail. This place was the scene of a theft in 1985. "Indiana John" had everything stolen as he slept. People in a nearby town helped him reequip, and he was able to finish his thru-hike, another instance of the good folks outnumbering the bad. A new shelter is planned for this location and may be open for 1992 thru-hikers.

Pa. 501: Immediately after crossing paved Pa. 501, go left on the blue-blazed side trail 0.1 mile to the Blue Mountain Eagle Climbing Club Shelter, always open, free to thru-hikers. The shelter is an enclosed building with bunks (no mattresses), table and chairs, skylight (a potter once had her wheel underneath), privy, and solar shower. Water is available from a faucet at the caretakers' house. Caretakers George and Joan Shollenberger (717-933-4858) are usually around and offer ice cream and sodas in exchange for a small donation. Emergency transportation is available at their discretion. Check the register here for news of hiker-helper "$2 Bill," who sometimes greets hikers in the Port Clinton area. *Left 3.3m*—to the town of Pine Grove.

♦ **Pine Grove, Pa.** (pop. 3,200): *Services*—motel • Scotty Lynn Family Restaurant (located 0.5 mile east of town on Rt. 443): B/L/D, varied open menu, smorgasbord, usually five different meats, AYCE for $7.25; described by "$2 Bill" as a "hiker's paradise; nobody leaves here hungry" • pizzeria • McDonald's • Hardee's • supermarket • grocery store

• convenience store • laundromat • hardware store • 5&10¢ store • doctor • dentist •
veterinarian • movie theatre • UPS pick-up • Capitol Trailways bus service.

Pilger Ruh: on side trail to right, with marker explaining its name and history.

Shower Steps: on side trail to right; an oldtime commercial tourist attraction.

Fort Dietrich Snyder Marker: the site of a fort built during the French and Indian War.
Construction of the fort was supervised by Benjamin Franklin, who probably camped in
the area and drank from the (now piped) spring reached by following the blue-blazes down
the road, then into the woods to the left.

Sand Spring: if unusable in dry weather, reportedly has a spring a few hundred feet farther
down the mountain. Any update?

Eagle's Nest Shelter: replacement for the old Ney Shelter, which has been torn down.
Water source is the creek you cross on the way to the shelter.

Shartlesville-Cross Mountain Road: Right 3.6m—to the town of Shartlesville.

♦ **Shartlesville, Pa.** (pop. 196): *Services*—Haag's Hotel: $20S $25D, no a/c or TV,
pets allowed if house-broken. In the hotel, Haag's Restaurant offers breakfast and
AYCE "Pennsylvania Dutch" meals served family-style, prices ranging from $8.50
(one meat) to $10 (four meats); open 7 days, 7:30am-7:30pm • Dutch Motel: $30S $32-
$37D $7EAP, 4 max; a/c, cable, dogs allowed (MC, Visa, AE); shuttle back to A.T. •
small grocery store.

PORT CLINTON, PA. (pop. 400): founded in the late 1700s on the Schuylkill River.
Twelve-year-old Daniel Boone, who was born south of here, once got lost and camped
overnight on the riverbank near where the Trail crosses a bridge into town. The A.T. was
routed through town in 1928, and the friendly townspeople have looked forward to the
yearly parade of hikers ever since. The town, which now bills itself as the "buzzard capital
of the Northeast," has few hiker services, but the nearby town of Hamburg has just about
everything hikers need. *Town pavilion*—a covered wooden structure, has been used as a
shelter by thru-hikers for many years. Water is available from a nearby hand pump, and
a privy is located across the road near the river. As you enter town, turn left on Penn Street
and follow the blue-blazes to the large pavilion on the right beyond Ravine Street.
Lodging—Port Clinton Hotel, another legendary hiker haven from the early days of thru-
hiking (ask to see the old registers). The hotel is owned and operated by Helen Carbaugh,
who seems a bit gruff at times but is really a sweetheart. Check-in time is after 2pm (Sunday,
knock on back door). Room with shower, $20S $26D. The bar on the ground floor has good
food (menu varies according to what Helen has on hand), 45¢ draft beer, a healthy bowl
of ice cream for 75¢, and television (Helen picks the programs). A public telephone and
soda machine are outside. Unfortunately, Helen had the hotel listed for sale last year, and
it may not be open in 1992. • Union House B&B: no rates available, a/c, cable, pets outside,
restaurant on premises (MC, Visa, AE). *Other services*—3C's Restaurant (located 0.5 mile
beyond pavilion where Penn Street joins Pa. 61): B/L/D, varied menu, breakfast anytime,
daily luncheon specials; open Mon-Fri 4am-4pm, Sat 6am-2pm, Sun 7am-2pm • peanut
shop with nuts and candies • museum • library with 24-hour "hiker library" on outside

of building (unique on the A.T.) *PO-ZIP 19549:* Mon-Fri 7:30am-12:30pm and 2-5pm, closed Sat; 215-562-3787; LY-100+.

Pa. 61/Pa. 16 (where A.T. goes under bridge): *Right 3m*—on Pa. 16 to the town of Hamburg. *Right 5.7m*—on Pa. 61 to Tom Schaeffer's Camping Center.

♦ **Hamburg, Pa.** (pop. 4,011): *Services*—Regal Restaurant & Motel: $30D, may give shuttle back to the Trail • Wisser's Bar & Restaurant: B/L/D, country-style meals, seafood, "Shrimp Nite" on Wed; open Tues-Sat 6am-9pm, Sun 8am-7pm • Pizza Como Restaurant: L/D, casual fine dining, Italian meals served family-style, sandwiches, hoagies; open 7 days, 9:30am-10:30pm • Chinese restaurant: L/D, open 7 days, 10:30am-10pm • Di Maio's Italian Restaurant: knockout chicken tetrazzini • Acme Supermarket: good for long-term resupply; open Mon-Sat 7am-9pm, Sun 7am-6pm • King's Supermar-ket: good for short-term resupply; open 24 hours Mon-Fri, Sat until 11pm, Sun 7am-11pm • bakery • laundromat • cobbler Mike Wengert closed in 1991 • bank • pharmacy • hardware store • department store • doctor • dentist • health clinic • veterinarian • movie theatre • Greyhound bus service • Jim Weaknecht Sporting Goods (215-562-3370): Coleman by the pint, some food items, hiker register. Jim will shuttle to and from A.T. for small fee. He will also accept UPS packages (you must show ID for pickup).
♦ Tom Schaeffer's Camping Center (215-562-3071): large selection of outdoor gear (JanSport, Camp Trails, Mountainsmith, Lowe, Eureka!, Moss, Walrus, Slumberjack, Hi-Tec Sports, Danner, MSR, Optimus/Svea, Peak 1, Thermarest, Wigwam); open Mon-Fri 9am-9pm, Sat 9am-5pm, closed Sun.

Windsor Furnace Shelter: Water source is creek of questionable quality, so you may want to carry water from Pocahontas Spring.

> Wildlife: *Hawks are daytime hunters and the bird of prey most often seen on the A.T. The red-tailed hawk is the large bird you will likely see riding the wind, as if glued to the same spot in the sky, and it also hunts from exposed perches, such as dead treetops. The red-shouldered hawk soars less frequently and perches below treetop level. Both types eat primarily small mammals, especially rodents.*

The Pinnacle: great view overlooking Pennsylvania farmland.

Hawk Mountain Road: Right 0.2m—to Eckville Hiker's Center (RD 2, Box 194, Kempton, Pa. 19529), located on the right side of the road. The shelter is the white building behind the house of BMECC caretakers Dave and Connie Crosby (in residence mid-June through Sept). The shelter has bunks, portatoilet, water from tap on the back porch, solar shower across the road, and a picnic table. No smoking is permitted inside the shelter, and no alcohol may be consumed on the premises. Pets are welcome, as long as they get along with the caretaker's dogs (Dave trains two Siberian husky sled dogs for racing) and you take care of their sanitary needs. The center may be used as a maildrop location, but it might be wise to verify that caretakers are in residence before you send a package; call 215-376-5967, which is Dave and Connie's home number in Reading. *Left 1.4m*—to the entrance of the Hawk Mountain Sanctuary.

♦ Hawk Mountain Sanctuary: an internationally recognized mecca for hawk watching as well as a center for raptor research. A visitors center has exhibits and viewing windows; open 7 days, 8am-5pm, small admission fee charged. The fall hawk migrations are an awesome sight. One September day in 1978, 21,488 raptors were recorded as passing over Hawk Mountain, one every two seconds!

Clubnote: The next 11 miles are maintained by Allentown Hiking Club volunteers.

Allentown Hiking Club Shelter: spring often slow or dry in drought years.

Pa. 309: Trail virtually goes in the back door of Gambrinus German Restaurant & Bar, which his good food and many labels of imported beer, public telephone, television in bar; open Tues-Sun noon-10pm, closed Mon. You possibly can camp out back on the big grassy area, but ask permission. Get water here. The next 16 miles are very dry, even during wet seasons, and springs are not dependable. Note: Gambrinus' was for sale in late 1991; status and hours are uncertain for 1992.

Clubnote: The next 4 miles are maintained by Blue Mountain Eagle Climbing Club volunteers.

New Tripoli campsite: left 0.3 mile; dependable water on new side trail north of powerline that avoids steep gravel road at powerline.

Bake Oven Knob Shelter: check the lower spring if the upper one is dry; a distant third spring, also on blue-blazed trail, is usually dependable. Tentsites nearby.

Clubnote: The next 10 miles are maintained by Philadelphia Trail Club volunteers.

George Outerbridge Shelter: the piped spring on the A.T. 200 feet north of the shelter is the exception on this water-scarce ridge. It usually gushes and never stops. Read EPA warning before drinking. Shelter visited by neighbors on weekends.

Lehigh Gap (Pa. 873/Pa. 248): *On A.T.*—soda machine where Trail reaches Pa. 873. *Left 2m*—on Pa. 248, after crossing the Lehigh River, to the town of Palmerton.

♦ **PALMERTON, PA.** (pop. 5,855): *"Hostel"*—The city allows hikers to stay in a basement room in the borough hall police station at no charge; one-night limit. Check in at the clerk's desk to the right after you enter the building (after hours, call 215-826-2311 for admittance). A hot shower is available (no towel). Cooking must be done outside the building. No pets are allowed inside, and you must obey the leash law outside. Anita Harry works in the borough office, and is a friend of hikers. *Other lodging*—Palmerton Hotel: $60S per week, $65D per week, rooms by the week only. *Places to eat*—Bert's Steak House: B/L/D, home-cooked meals, cheese steaks, fries, soups; open Mon-Sat 6am-11pm, Sun 9am-11pm • Big S Restaurant: B/L/D, home-cooked meals, steak sandwich, home-made soups, salads; open Mon-Wed and Sat 6am-2pm, Thur and Fri 6am-8pm, Sun 6am-noon (breakfast only), closed first two weeks in July • Tony's Pizza: pizza, pasta, and subs; open 7 days, 11am-10pm • J's Subs: pizza, subs, hoagies; open 7 days, 11am-10pm • Lucky House: Chinese takeout, open 7 days, 11am-10pm. *Groceries*—Golden Key IGA: good for long-term resupply; open Mon-Fri 8am-9pm, Sat-Sun 8am-7pm • Acme Super market: good for long-term resupply; open Mon-Fri 8am-9pm, Sat-Sun 8am-7pm • Food Mart: 24-hour convenience store • discount bakery. *Laundromat*—Towne Laundry: FLW, open 7 days, 5:30am-8pm, closed holidays. *Other services*—Shea's Sporting Goods • banks • MAC • pharmacy • Steimer's hardware with Coleman by the gallon • doctor • dentist • hospital • library • UPS pickup • taxi service. *PO-ZIP18071:* Mon-Fri 8:30am-5pm, Sat 8:30am-noon; 215-826-2286; LY-50+.

Rocky III: The fun continues as you scramble up out of Lehigh Gap. If it's a sunny day, the heat radiating off the rocks will make you think you're in a scene from Dante's *Inferno.* The view at the top is fantastic, though, even if the countryside does resemble the Badlands. The former zinc-smelting plant by the river was the culprit. It no longer belches fumes, and the ridge is slowly being reclaimed by greenery. One of our own, Mark D'Andrea ("Sojourner" of '91), was involved with the EPA project that monitors this area. Note: The Trail here may be temporarily rerouted in 1992 as NPS and Pennsylvania DOT try to alleviate a hazardous rockfall problem.

Spring: four miles north of the gap, to the left. Look for small sign on a tree, about eight feet above the ground, barely readable because of bullet holes from "hunter's" weapons. Also, look for a grassy clearing to the left about 25 feet off the footpath. From the clearing, a blue-blazed trail goes 200 feet down to the spring, which flows even in dry years (but read the EPA warning before drinking).

Clubnote: The next 16 miles are maintained by AMC-Delaware Valley Chapter volunteers.

Smith Gap Road: Left 1m—to Linda and John's Blue Mountain Dome, where you can get water from an outside spigot at the rear of the house. Owners John Stempa and Linda Gellock are maintainers with the Keystone Trails Association, have hiked all of Pennsylvania, and enjoy meeting thru-hikers.

Leroy A. Smith Shelter: water from spring down old road in front of shelter. If first or second spring is dry, the third spring is usually flowing, but it's a long way down. Two bears were spotted near the shelter in 1991.

Wind Gap (Pa. 33): *Left 0.2m*—to the Gateway Motel: $32S $37D $5EAP, 4 max; a/c, cable, phone in room, use of refrigerator, pets allowed (MC, Visa, AE, Dis); will often give rides to restaurant and laundry; public telephone outside. *Right 1m*—to the town of Wind Gap.

♦ **Wind Gap, Pa.** (pop. 2,800): *Services*—Wind Gap Motel: good verbal reports from several hikers last year, but no details sent in • Caesars Restaurant with pizza • McDonald's • Burger King • supermarket • laundromat • bank • pharmacy • doctor • dentist • veterinarian.

Clubnote: The next 8 miles are maintained by Batona Hiking Club volunteers.

Rocky IV: The section from Wind Gap to Delaware Water Gap is perhaps the most tedious underfoot of any section on the A.T. This is where the local clubs are rumored to sharpen the rocks each spring. If your feet and ankles have just about had it, hang in there. You're almost through Pennsylvania.

Clubnote: The next 7 miles are maintained by Springfield Trail Club volunteers.

In memory: Wilma Flaig, long-time maintainer with the Springfield Trail Club and ATC Board member from 1977-1983, died of bone cancer last spring at the age of 79. Thru-hikers over the years often met Wilma—always with a hammer and a grin—building shelters and outhouses, painting blazes, clearing blowdowns, and serving the Trail project wherever there was a need. She was a joy to all who knew her, and, as a friend observed, "the world is a lovelier place for her efforts."

Kirkridge Shelter: Water source is a faucet. It can be found about 200 feet up the blue-blazed trail (to the left as you face the shelter). The folks at the nearby retreat center are kind enough to let us use this spigot. Be sure the water is turned off when you're done.

DELAWARE WATER GAP, PA. (pop. 800): primarily a tourist community. You'll see more automobile tags from New York and New Jersey than from Pennsylvania. The village itself has very few basic services for hikers. For those, you will need to go to East Stroudsburg, a large college town several miles away. No bus service is available, but the outfitter runs a shuttle service for thru-hikers (check hostel bulletin board for details). *Hostel*—Located in the basement of the Presbyterian Church of the Mountain (Pastor Karen Nickels, 717-476-0345) and operated year-round for thru-hikers only. The hostel has a bunkroom with mattress bunks, hot shower with towels provided, and a sitting room. If crowded, hikers may pitch tents on the church lawn. A $3 donation is requested after the first night. At 6pm on Thursday nights (June 1-Sept 1), the members of the church put on a covered-dish cookout for hikers in residence. This event has been a highlight for past thru-hikers. Sunday worship service is at 10am, and you are welcome in hiker attire. Free Sunday-afternoon concerts (often jazz) are held in July and August. Friendly "Pastor Karen" is available to help with any problems you may be having (with one exception: She won't pick up mail for you, so don't call ahead to ask). The church piano and organ are available for musical hikers missing the ivories. A public telephone is located across the street. Hiker vehicles may not be parked in the church parking lot, but a parking area at the Trailhead is available. UPS does not deliver to the church. Also, don't send mail to the church. To reach the hostel, turn right on paved Mountain Road, follow the white blazes downhill to Pa. 611, turn left and go past the Deerhead Inn to the church driveway on the left. *Other lodging*—Water Gap Motor Court: $25 for cottage with double bed, private bath, no a/c, cable; basic, but clean. "Grandma" Gatewood stayed here on her 1957 hike • Ramada Inn: $58S $64D $8EAP, 5 max; a/c, cable, phone in room, pool, restaurant on premises (MC, Visa, AE, Dis, DC). *Places to eat*—Water Gap Diner: B/L/D, home-cooked meals, varied menu (American, Italian, seafood, burgers, pies, *etc.*) and generally good food; open 7 days, 5:30am-11pm • Rumours: bar food, pizza, sandwiches, and snacks. *Outfitter*—The Pack Shack: backpacking items (Camp Trails, Sierra Designs, Eureka!, Merrell, Vasque, MSR, Optimus/Svea, Peak 1, Thermarest, Wigwam), Coleman by the pint, repair capabilities, rental tubes for fun on the river; 10% discounts to thru-hikers, even on candy bars; owned by John Green, who will arrange shuttles for slackpacking.

Other services—Bakery/fruitstand: bread, pastries, fresh fruits and vegetables in season • fudge shop. *Points of interest*—The Deer Head Inn, next to the hostel, is a regional jazz center. Jazz groups often perform Saturday night, and a week-long jazz festival is held in September • The Water Gap Trolley is an hour-long ride that touches the scenic and historic points of interest in the gap area. Tour buses depart every half hour from the center of town; fare is $4. *PO-ZIP 18327:* Mon-Fri 8:30am-12:15pm and 1:30-5pm, Sat 8:30-11am; 717-476-0304; LY-200+. *Nearby town*—East Stroudsburg.

♦ **East Stroudsburg, Pa.** (pop. 8,039): a big college town, spread out over a very large area, with just about every service you need as a hiker, including cobbler, banks, department stores, doctors, dentists, and so on (check the *Yellow Pages* for specific services). It also has dozens of restaurants and motels. Basic services are available in a small shopping mall (near the McDonald's), which has a Shop-Rite Supermarket (good for long-term resupply, deli, open 7 days), coin-operated laundromat, pharmacy, department store, and pizzeria. You may also wish to go to Stroud Mall, which has many stores, a movie theatre, and a laundromat nearby (across the highway).

New Jersey-New York

This chapter takes you from Delaware Water Gap, Pennsylvania, to the New York-Connecticut line and corresponds to *Data Book* chapter four.

Delaware River: famous in American history for " Washington crossing the Delaware" on Christmas Day 1776, on his way to defeating the British (actually the Hessians), a key event in the Revolutionary War.

Clubnote: The next 164 miles are maintained by New York-New Jersey Trail Conference volunteers.

Delaware Water Gap National Recreation Area: host to the Trail for the next twenty miles or so. A visitors center at the east end of the Delaware River Bridge has restrooms, water fountains, and information about weather and trail conditions ahead. You can't camp just anywhere in New Jersey, so ask about Campsites #1 and #2 (both supposedly dry) if you're getting a late start out of DWG.

Rocky V: The next few miles will remind you of Pennsylvania, and your feet and ankles will probably begin to rebel once again. Don't despair. Even though you'll have rocks under foot all the way to Katahdin, the Pennsylvania-type rocks will soon be behind you for good.

Sunfish Pond: the first glacial pond encountered going north on the A.T. It was almost lost years ago when a power company wanted to use it as a cooling pond. Public outcry prevented that from happening. Today, it is a popular spot with dayhikers and often crowded on sunny weekends. Swimming is not allowed, but hardly anyone can resist the temptation. Camping is prohibited, and thru-hikers should observe this prohibition. The "Ed Garvey, spring" is located about 0.5 mile north of the pond on the A.T., to the left on a blue-blazed side trail, but is usually dry.

Herbert Hiller memorial: off the Trail to the left, attached to a rock on Kittatinny Mountain about two miles north of Sunfish Pond, a tribute to Herbert Hiller, long active in the A.T. project and the 23rd person to hike the A.T. from end to end.

Mohican Road: Left 0.5m—to Mohican Outdoor Recreation Center with campground, covered shelter area, restrooms, and hot shower (solar-heated, no towels); $5 per person. Check in at the house to the left at the second gate. Water is available from a spigot near the gate if you aren't staying. Note: This facility was marginal last year, may not be available to hikers in 1992.

Rattlesnake Spring: about 0.6 mile past Catfish Fire Tower, 50 feet to the left on a dirt road.

Flatbrookville Road: water pump to the left just before the paved road.

Brink Road Shelter: remodeled in early 1990. Dependable spring and several rocky tentsites in the vicinity.

Culvers Gap (U.S. 206): *On A.T.*—Worthington's Bakery, a tradition on the Trail and a favorite stop for thru-hikers for more than 40 years. The bakery has pastries, pies, cinnamon rolls, hot coffee, limited groceries, fresh fruit, and a deli section; open July 1-Labor Day, daily 8am-6pm, closed Tues; remainder of year, Fri-Sun only, 8am-6pm. "Grandma" Gatewood stayed with the Worthingtons on one of her treks. Also in the gap, Texaco station with telephone, Gyp's Tavern overlooking Kittatinny Lake, and a small outdoors shop with no Coleman fuel and few backpacking items. *Right 3.4m*—to the town of Branchville.

♦ **Branchville, N.J.** (pop. 1,000): *Services*—motel • restaurant • small grocery store • bank • MAC • pharmacy • veterinarian.

Gren Anderson Shelter: Water source is spring to the left looking into shelter; flat areas for tenting nearby.

Sunrise Mountain: with covered pavilion. No water, and no camping allowed.

> Trail Fact: *Assuming he or she is always the first person on the Trail each day, a thru-hiker must eat two extra Snickers bars to have the additional energy needed to break all the spider webs encountered across the Trail from Georgia to Maine.*

Mashipacong Shelter: Water source is a pump 0.2 mile north on the A.T. across nearby paved Deckertown Turnpike. The water, tested and approved by state agencies, has high mineral content and looks icky, but there have been no reports of illness from past thru-hikers who have braved using it.

Rutherford Shelter: down to the right on blue-blazed trail. Water source is small spring you pass on way to shelter. Flat, grassy tentsites are available behind the shelter.

N.J. 23: On A.T.—High Point State Park headquarters (201-875-4800): information desk, restrooms, water fountain, and outside public telephone; open 7 days, 9am-11pm during the summer. Park Superintendent John Keator and "Ranger Ed" Pomeroy and the rest of the staff are friends of hikers, often driving them to nearby grocery stores and McDonald's if they aren't too busy. You may use the HQ as a maildrop. Address: H.P.S.P., RR 4, Box 287, Sussex, N.J. 07461. The park also has swimming in Lake Marcia, cold showers, a picnic area, and the High Point monument, all off the Trail.

Observation platform: with great views of the surrounding countryside from the highest area in New Jersey. Some claim that New York City can be seen from here on a clear night.

High Point Shelter: water source is small spring about 250 feet up old road behind the shelter. Several flat areas for tenting are nearby. Maintained by Vincent "Vagabond Vinny" Pernice, who plans to make frequent visits bearing gifts.

Pastures and swamps: Agriculture and wetlands in this section make the Trail a bit challenging at times, especially to the local maintaining club responsible for keeping the A.T. passable. Countless hours are spent erecting posts for blazes in pastures, only to have cattle eventually knock them over, and days are spent building bog bridges. As you walk through this section, focus on the many habitats you see. On no other section of Trail will you see so much diversity in so short a distance.

Vernie Swamp: One of the finest examples of freshwater wetland habitat on the Trail, with lush growth and plenty of wildlife. The 111 bog bridges that allow you to go through this area without wading were installed by 14 club volunteers and a Trail crew of four during a busy weekend in 1987. Thanks for the elevated footpath, folks.

Lott Road (paved road with pond on north side): *Left 0.4m*—to the town of Unionville, passing a rubber company and cemetery on the right as you head into town.

UNIONVILLE, N.Y. (pop. 560): *Restaurant/hostel*—Unionville Inn & Hostel (P.O. Box 358, Unionville, N.Y. 10988; 914-726-3956), owned and managed by Rick Bohnsack and Patti "Mr. B's Millipede" Muchmore. Rick has six years of culinary training; Patti is certified in restaurant management (she's also a veteran canoeist and hiker). They want to have the best food on the A.T. ("Mr. Greenjeans" of '91 thinks they already do) and welcome your feedback. Some of the items on the menu include sandwiches, burgers, steaks, stuffed chicken breast, "Veal Bohnsack," seafood, and pasta and vegetarian delights. Thursday nights feature a 20 oz. rib-eye with baked potato, veggies, and salad for $9.99. A bar adjacent to the dining room opens at noon. Rick and Patti will fill your water bottles and let you use their telephone. The restaurant is open Memorial Day-Labor Day (Tues-Sun 11:30am until there are no more customers). The hostel, open even when the restaurant is closed, was new in 1991, as a temporary room with bunks until Rick can erect a separate building for hikers. Hostel is $2 for bunk, $5 for bunk and hot shower with towel, $3 for shower only; camping in yard available. "Buzzy and Tag A Long" of '90 said in the register, "A definite A.T. experience, so very glad we didn't pass by." Note: Unfortunately, Rick and Patti were considering selling the inn in December, so it may not be available for hikers in 1992. If so, the slow economy is the culprit (as probably it has been for many other places you've found closed or changed). *Other places to eat*—Side Road Kitchen: B/L/D, home-cooked meals; open Mon-Fri 7am-2pm and 4-7pm, Sun 7am-7pm. *Other services*—Horler's General Store: good for short-term resupply, deli, medicines; open Mon-Sat 7am-7pm, Sun 8am-1pm • public telephone next to PO • water fountain in town playground for filling water bottles • Camping is no longer permitted behind the Fire Department building. *PO-ZIP 10988:* Mon-Fri 8am-1pm and 2-5pm, Sat 8am-noon; 914-726-3535; LY-60+.

Wallkill River Valley: one of the richest agricultural regions in the nation. Black loamy soil goes down hundreds of feet. The A.T. crosses the Wallkill River on a paved road, then turns right on a dirt road bordering a sod farm. Sod from this farm is shipped all over the Northeast.

Pochuck Mountain Shelter: new in 1990. It has no water, but a well near where the Trail crosses Liberty Corners Road serves as the shelter's water source.

County Road 565: Left 1.1m—to the small hamlet of Glenwood.

♦ **Glenwood, N.J.** (pop. 217): *Services*—Apple Valley Inn (201-764-3735): owned by Alabamians John and Mitzi Durham, offering a combination of New Jersey sophistication and southern hospitality in a beautifully restored three-story rural house dating back to 1831. A private room with shared bath, breakfast, and dinner is available at very reasonable rates for thru-hikers. Mitzi can host only five thru-hikers at a time, so call ahead for confirmation. Be sure to mention that you're hiking the entire A.T. No pets. Possible shuttle back to Trail. "High Pocket" of '90 said, "This is one of those special Trail places that gets my highest rating. Wonderful food and fellowship." • Farmer's Market: limited hiker supplies, deli; open 7 days, 6am-6pm. *PO-ZIP 07418:* Mon-Fri 8am-noon and 1-5pm, closed Sat; 201-764-7280; LY-30.

County Road 517: Left 1.1m—to Glenwood (see above).

Relocation: 1991 relo follows Maple Grange Road halfway through "the Flats," turns left and follows Canal Road for 0.5 mile, then turns right and cuts across five open fields with sweeping views of the surrounding ridges. The new route crosses N.J. 94 about 0.5 mile north of old A.T. crossing, near Price's Switch.

N.J. 94: Right 1.4m—to Appalachian Motel (manager usually referred hikers to the Apple Valley Inn in 1991). *Right 2.3m*—to the town of Vernon.

♦ **VERNON, N.J.** (pop. 1,468): *Fire-department pavilion* (near PO and stores)— available free for overnight stay by thru-hikers. Check in at the police department, and ask them to notify someone about unlocking the restroom. The fire horn, used to summon distant volunteer firefighters, will take years off your life. *Services*—Dairy Queen • pizzeria • A&P 24-Hour Supermarket: good for long-term resupply; open 7 days, closes 9pm on Sun (you figure it out) • laundromat: on outskirts of town, not convenient to A.T. or pavilion • MAC • pharmacy • hardware store • doctor • dentist • health clinic • veterinarian. *PO-ZIP 07462:* Mon-Fri 8:30am-5pm, closed Sat; 201-764-2920; LY-40+.

Wawayanda Shelter (Wawayanda State Park): located 0.4 mile north of Wawayanda Road, to the right on 0.1-mile blue-blazed side trail. A new shelter in 1991, it is already being called the "Wawayanda Hilton." Water can be obtained by going north 0.1 mile on A.T., then right 0.2 mile on blue-blazed side trail leading to the park headquarters, which has an information desk, restrooms, and very cold water from fountain inside. After hours, get water from a hose at nearby maintenance yard. Bears were reported in this area last year.

Wildlife: *Raccoons are chiefly nocturnal and occasionally visit shelters along the Trail. If you leave dirty dishes on a picnic table until morning, these crafty animals may carry them off to who knows where and clean them for you. They are undisturbed by the presence of man and are among the few creatures still expanding their range. Raccoons prefer to feed along stream banks and will eat almost anything. Big ones can weigh up to fifteen pounds in the wild.*

Warwick Turnpike: Right 0.1m—to L&L Farm (named for owner Lila Lee, who's been keeping a hiker register since 1983) with fresh fruit in season, homebaked goods, ice cream, hot dogs, and sodas; open Thur-Sun 10am-7pm. Water is available from an outside hose on the far end of the barn; Lila says, "Help yourself!" *Left 0.7m*—to Willow Brook Inn: no recent hiker reports.

Roger's Appalachia Cottage: an old A.T. tradition. For many seasons, author, weather expert, and grand host Roger Brickner entertained thru-hikers at his cottage just off the Trail overlooking Greenwood Lake. In 1990, Roger moved to New Hampshire but still opens the cottage for hikers on occasion; available this year June 12-28. Look for a metal information box that marks the side trail down to the cottage. Also, check for notices on the bulletin board at the Presbyterian hostel in Delaware Water Gap.

N.Y. 17A: Left 1.6m—to the village of Bellvale. *Left 2.6m*—to the town of Warwick. *Right 2m*—to the town of Greenwood Lake.

♦ **Bellvale, N.Y.** (pop. 1,643): *Services*—Iron Forge Inn: a restaurant located in 1790 colonial house; open Wed-Sat 5-9pm, Sun 2-8pm • Bellvale General Store: very limited hiker supplies, snacks; open Mon-Fri 5:30am-6pm, Sat 7am-6pm, Sun 8am-1pm • outside public telephone (still only 10 cents!) • bus service to NYC • taxi service.

♦ **Warwick, N.Y.** (pop. 5,320): *Services*—Warwick Motel: $45S $55D $5EAP, 5 max; a/c, cable, phone in room, pool, no pets (MC, Visa, AE, Dis, CB) • First Motel: $45S $50D $10EAP, 4 max; a/c, cable, use of refrigerator, washer/dryer, pets allowed (MC, Visa, AE) • Warwick Gardens Restaurant: L/D, Sunday brunch • Grand Union Supermarket: good for long-term resupply • laundromat • Western Union • pharmacy • doctor • dentist • UPS pickup.

♦ **GREENWOOD LAKE, N.Y.** (pop. 4,807): *Services*—Breezy Point Inn: $45S $55D $5EAP, 5 max; a/c, cable, no pets, restaurant (burgers to fine dining), lounge, dock, boat rentals • Lakeside Diner: open 7 days, 6am-4pm • supermarket: good for short-term resupply • bank • pharmacy • doctor • dentist. *PO-ZIP 10925:* Mon-Fri 7am-5pm, Sat 9:30am-noon; 914-477-8005; LY-50+.

Mombasha High Point: occasional view of New York City (compass heading to the Empire State Building: 160-170°).

Orange Turnpike: Right 0.5m—to piped spring, dependable even in dry weather periods and used by many folks who drive from places as distant as NYC to get this water. Before you laugh at them for driving so far, remember how far you've *walked* to drink it. Top off your water bottles, and drink up. The next section is water-scarce.

N.Y. 17: Left 0.7m—to the village of Arden. *Right 1.5m*—to small grocery store; 0.3 mile farther to Red Apple Restaurant and Tuxedo Motel. Short Line bus can be flagged down in front of restaurant; goes to **Monroe, N.Y.**, with supermarket, laundry, and bank; fare is $1.20 each way.

♦ **ARDEN, N.Y.** (pop. 400): *Services*—small grocery store with very limited supplies in same building as post office. *PO-ZIP 10910:* Mon-Fri 7:30am-noon and 2-5:15pm, Sat 7:30am-noon; 914-351-5341; LY-40.

♦ Red Apple Restaurant: B/L/D, cafeteria-style meals, burgers, soup, sandwiches, milkshakes, ice cream, outside public telephone; open 7 days, 6am-9pm.
♦ Tuxedo Motel: $30S $34D $2EAP, 4 max; a/c, TV, pool, no pets (MC, Visa).

In appreciation: Elizabeth Levers, after decades of involvement with the Trail project and many years of tireless service with the NY-NJ Trail Conference, retired in 1991. Her list of accomplishments is too long to be included here, but, suffice it to say, you will not hike a mile in this section without benefitting from her labors in some way. She'll probably still be out checking on "her" trails from time to time, so some of you may be lucky enough to meet her. Thanks so much for everything, Elizabeth.

Harriman State Park: New York's second-largest park, encompassing 46,000 beautiful wooded acres. The terrain in the park is different from any other section on the A.T., with many small ascents and descents. You'll get quite a workout before you reach the Hudson River. Shelters in the park are reserved for thru-hikers; stay limited to one night. Fires are permitted only in fireplaces.

Lemon Squeezer: This narrow crevice will have you between the proverbial rock and a hard place. You'll be in good company, though. Some of the folks who have squirmed their way through this opening are Benton MacKaye, Myron Avery, Earl Shaffer, Emma Gatewood, and, according to an eyewitness met here in 1989, Marilyn Monroe. Near here, a female osprey defending her nest and chicks "buzzed" several hikers in 1990.

Fingerboard Shelter: No water source nearby, so you must go 0.5 mile to Lake Tiorati on the blue-blazed Hurst Trail, which begins in front of the shelter. Treat the water, since the lake is used as a swimming hole by much of New York City.

Arden Valley Road (the crossing north of the Lemon Squeezer): *Right 0.3m*—to Lake Tiorati Circle with bathhouse (free shower), restrooms, beach, concession stand (expensive burgers, sodas, snacks), and picnic area with tables and water fountains. A public telephone is next to the information station. Tiorati is an Indian word meaning "sky-like."

William Brien Memorial Shelter: rebuilt after being lost in a 1988 forest fire. Water of questionable quality is sometimes available from a well in front of the shelter on blue-blazed trail. It's best to carry water from Tiorati Circle.

Palisades Interstate Parkway: a comment on modern American life. Notice that the cars heading toward NYC are traveling 55 mph, while those heading out are doing at least 70. Maintainers are trying to get a better sign to alert drivers, but, meanwhile, use care!

West Mountain Shelter: no water at the shelter (undependable spring 0.5 mile left on blue-blazed TT Trail), so you may want to bring some from the creek you cross about 0.3 mile north of the parkway. New York City is visible from here. On a clear night, you can see the tops of skyscrapers, the George Washington Bridge (headlights will twinkle as they go behind the girders), and the Meadowlands in New Jersey, if it's lit up for an event. On a clear morning, the sunlight glints off the windows of Manhattan.

Bear Mountain: formerly called Bare Mountain by travelers on the Hudson, because iron miners had chopped down all the trees on the summit. Later, a map-maker misspelled it "Bear Mountain," and the name caught on. The summit is now topped by a stone observation tower, restrooms, a water fountain, and, once again, by trees.

Bear Mountain State Park: part of the Palisades Interstate Park system. The first section of footpath built for the Appalachian Trail project was constructed in this park in 1922-23. You are literally walking on Trail history as you go along. At the base of Bear Mountain, you will come to the developed part of the park, which includes a post office, inn, and nature museum/zoo. **BEAR MOUNTAIN, N.Y.**—*PO ZIP 10911* (Mon-Fri 7:30am-1pm and 2:30-5pm, Sat 7:30-11:30pm; 914-786-3747; LY-80+), located across the road from the administration building, behind the maintenance garage, about 0.2 mile off the A.T. Ask directions at the inn or administrative offices. *Lodging/Restaurant*—Bear Mountain Inn has a cafeteria on the first floor, the Wildflower Restaurant on the second floor (L/D, American fare, chicken, seafood, MC, Visa, AE; open Mon-Sat 11am-3pm, Sat and Sun 5-9pm); also Coke and snack-food machines, restrooms, and public telephones. Overnight accommodations: $49S/D (weekdays) $84S/D (weekends) $10EAP, 4 max; a/c, TV, phone in room, pool, no pets (MC, Visa, AE). In the lodge area, adjacent to the restaurant, is a link of the chain stretched across the Hudson to prevent the British from sailing upriver during the Revolutionary War. Hessian Lake is behind the inn. *Museum/Zoo*—Trailside Museum & Zoo, built in 1927 at the urging of Benton MacKaye, among others, features some of the nation's oldest nature trails. The A.T. goes through Trailside, passing geology, nature study, small animal, and history museums, as well as a memorial to Walt Whitman. The nature exhibits and zoo feature plants and animals native to the Bear Mountain area, in an attempt to inspire in the urban visitor an appreciation for the wonders of nature. Trailside is visited by more than half a million people annually. Note: Seeing animals in cages will make you appreciate the unfettered natural wonders you have been seeing and experiencing day after day on the A.T. Just remember, most Americans aren't as fortunate as you.

Bear Mountain Bridge: keeps you from having to swim the Hudson River, which is almost half a mile wide here. The A.T. emerges from Trailside at the west (south) end of the bridge. To go into the town of Fort Montgomery from where the Trail exits the zoo, turn left and go to a traffic circle, bear right around the circle, exit right on U.S. 9W, cross a bridge across a large creek (great photo of Bear Mountain Bridge possible from here), turn left on Old 9W just past the bridge, and go 0.8 mile to the town center. Be careful in this area; traffic can be unreal.

Notice: The pedestrian walkway giving access to Fort Montgomery on U.S. 9W was being rebuilt in 1991 and is not scheduled for reopening until late 1992. Use the Bear Mountain post office for your maildrop (see above) and do not count on access to other services listed in Fort Montgomery unless you can get a ride across the U.S. 9W bridge.

♦ **FORT MONTGOMERY, N.Y.** (pop. 1,950): *Services*—Bear Mountain Bridge Motel: $36S $40D $5EAP; a/c, TV, no pets (MC, Visa) • Old Oak Inn: $20S $40D, some rooms have a/c, no pets • Reborn Acorn Restaurant (in Old Oak Inn): B/L/D, American fare (MC, Visa, AE) • KC's Pizzeria: good pasta meals, open Mon-Sat 11am-10pm • M&R Grocery & Deli: sandwiches to go, very limited hiker supplies. *PO-ZIP 10922:* Mon-Fri 8:30am-

5pm, Sat 8:30am-noon; 914-446-2173; LY-50+. *Nearby towns*—West Point and Highland Falls have motels, restaurants, McDonald's, supermarket, convenience store, bakery, laundromat, bank, drugstore, hardware store, doctor, dentist, veterinarian, and the U.S. Military Academy.

Anthony's Nose: whimsical designation for the prominent mountain in front as you head north across the Bear Mountain Bridge. It was named after the navigator on Henry Hudson's *Half Moon*, which was sailed up this river more than 350 years ago. Journals record the crew's astonishment at the beauty of the Hudson highlands, the area now called the Palisades. Wonder what they would think now?

U.S. 9/N.Y. 403: Right 4.5m—to the city of Peekskill.

♦ **Peekskill, N.Y.** (pop. 18,236): *Services*—motel • restaurant • McDonald's • KFC • Burger King • supermarket • grocery store • convenience store • bakery • laundromat • cobbler • bank • Western Union • Cirrus • pharmacy • hardware store • doctor • dentist • health clinic • veterinarian • barber • beautician • library • swimming pool • movie theatre • local bus service • taxi service.

Graymoor Monastery: home of the Franciscan Friars of the Atonement and the birthplace of the Christian Unity movement in America. Many ecumenical conferences are held each year at the Graymoor facilities, and the outreach of the friars is worldwide. A.T. thru-hikers have been welcomed to stay overnight for more than 17 years. Recommended check-in period is 3:30-5pm. A friar will greet you and show you to your private room with bed, sink, and writing table. A hot shower with towel and soap is available down the hall. Public telephones are available just off the lobby. An AYCE dinner is served promptly at 5:30pm (late check-ins should not expect dinner). An AYCE breakfast is served at 7am. If you have a pet, you can use all inside services but will be asked to sleep outside with your pet. No smoking is permitted in the buildings, and no alcohol is permitted on the premises. Do not use Graymoor as a maildrop location. Stay is limited to one night (for thru-hikers only; no friends or relatives). Check-out time is 10am. Donations are accepted and needed to keep this hiker service available. Directions to Graymoor: Cross U.S. 9, and go 0.5 mile through the woods on the A.T. When the Trail comes out on a paved road with red wooden shed on the left, turn right, then bear right at fork, and continue to the brick monastery building. Enter via steps to the ground-floor lobby, take the elevator to the floor indicated on the directory. Quite a few hikers echoed the sentiments of one who said, "The most pleasant surprise on the whole Trail for me." Another added, "Even as a devout atheist, I felt comfortable here. The friars were perfect hosts."

Dennytown Road: water pump on side of stone building next to road, and campsites available about 0.2 mile north on the A.T. Avoid camping in sight of the road. The area is heavily used by college and Scout groups, especially on weekends.

> Wildlife: *Striped skunks, larger than their spotted cousins, are the animal you probably picture when someone yells, "Skunk!" They are nocturnal and unafraid of man. If one is provoked, it will stomp its front feet and shuffle backward as a warning. Should one do this to you, you should hastily do (the latter) likewise, before it sprays. The stripped skunk is very fond of grasshoppers, ground beetles, and bees, excavating nests to get at larvae.*

N.Y. 301: Right 1m—to Clarence Fahnestock State Park.

♦ Clarence Fahnestock State Park: at entrance, go right 0.2 mile to campground with shelters, hot showers, and restrooms (first night free for thru-hikers); or, at entrance, turn left 0.3 mile to free Canopus Lake swimming area with beach, concession stand (open late June-Labor Day), restrooms, cold shower, and picnic tables. No pets are allowed on the beach or in the picnic area. Said several thru-hikers, "The park superintendent is friendly to hikers; he made us feel at home."

Viewpoint: located 2.2 miles north of N.Y. 301, overlooking Canopus Lake swimming area (see above). Supposedly a trail leads from this viewpoint to the beach below. Can anyone find it?

Notice: Do not take the Taconic State Parkway as a shortcut to RPH Cabin. The parkway has no shoulders where it has been cut into cliffs, so you could be injured by speeding traffic that has no room to dodge you. State troopers will pick you up and issue a stiff fine for endangering your life and theirs.

Hortontown Road, RPH Cabin: a house that borders the Trail, once known as Ralph's Peak Hikers Cabin, after the club that originally maintained it. Now the property is assigned to the NY-NJ Trail Conference. Joe Hrouda (914-221-9014) is the caretaker, and you will no doubt meet him when he comes by in the evening (after 5pm) to chat and sometimes shuttle hikers to a nearby shopping area. The cabin has bunk beds and is free. Water with high iron content is available from a pump out back. Several years ago, a 12-foot pile of dirt occupied the front lawn and was dubbed "Ralph's Peak" by thru-hikers, but the little peak served a more useful purpose as fill dirt around the water pump. The privy usually has flags flying and helps hikers get better acquainted with their knees. Bicycles ("The Shenandoah Shuttles") in the garage can be used to go to the grocery store down the road. RPH Cabin is open June 1 to mid-September (door facing the road is padlocked during the day, but side door facing the Trail is usually left unlocked); garage is open year-round. You can use this shelter as a maildrop location. Address packages to yourself, c/o RPH Cabin, 275A Hortontown Road, Hopewell, N.Y. 12533, and put your expected arrival date on the package. A thru-hiker commented, "This is a great place to kick back and relax. Thanks, Joe." *Left 1.1m*—on Hortontown Road to the Shenandoah General Store.

♦ Shenandoah General Store: good for short-term resupply, subs; open Mon-Sat 6:30am-6pm, Sun 8:30am-4pm, but hours may vary. The store has been in business for more than 100 years, owned by the Pavelock family and operated by friendly Andrew P. today.

Taconic State Parkway: can be very dangerous, especially at rush hour. Cars turning left at Miller Hill Road (which the A.T. follows for a short distance) have been running up guardrails and overturning at openings. New York DOT is installing a flashing traffic light to help alleviate the problem. Use care when crossing here.

Bailey Spring Campsite: stagnant water, bad mosquitos, and a long, steep descent reported last year.

N.Y. 52: Right 0.4m—then 0.1 mile on side road to Mountain Top Store with groceries, very good subs, ice cream, public telephone, and a hiker register; open 7 days, 6am-8pm. *Left 1.9m*—to the town of Stormville, N.Y.

♦ **Stormville, N.Y.** (pop. 2,100): *Services*—Harold's Five Restaurant • pizzeria • small grocery store with deli.

Morgan Stewart Shelter: very old well is the water source. Last year, it was found to have a high bacteria count, so be sure you treat the water.

Nuclear Lake: a pond 0.3 mile from the A.T. that may have been contaminated in 1972 by the processing of low-level radioactive materials. The lake area, still off-limits to the public, is monitored by NPS. A blue-blazed alternate route that takes you farther from the site is used by few thru-hikers, since the danger is very low, almost nonexistent. No glowing hikers have been spotted in recent years.

N.Y. 55: Left 1.5m—to the town of Poughquag.

♦ **Poughquag, N.Y.** (pop. 439): *Services*—Pine Grove Motel: $38S $40D $5EAP, 3 max; a/c, cable, kitchen privileges, washer/dryer, pets outside (MC, Visa, AE) • 7 Stars Restaurant • ice-cream parlor • Cumberland Farms Market: good for short-term resupply • bank • dentist • UPS pickup • Beekman Taxi Service (914-226-5773).

Telephone Pioneers Shelter: Water source is small trickle you pass on side trail to shelter. Caretaker often brings water for thru-hikers.

County Road 20 (West Dover Road): *Right 2.9m*—to the town of Pawling and to Murrow Park.

♦ **PAWLING, N.Y.** (pop. 1,996): *Services*—supermarket • laundromat • cobbler • restaurant • bakery. *PO-ZIP 12564:* Mon-Fri 8:30am-5pm, Sat 9am-noon; 914-855-1010; LY-40+.
♦ **Murrow Park:** named for broadcaster Edward R. Murrow, a native son of Pawling; operated by the Lions Club, which allows thru-hikers to sleep in the pavilion at the park with cold shower, beach and lake for swimming, soda machine, and telephone, $2 admittance; closed after Labor Day. You can bypass the town of Pawling and go directly to the park by turning right on Lakeside Road and continuing one mile to the park entrance.

Appalachian Trail Station: just before N.Y. 22, a stop on the Metro-North Commuter Railroad (Harlem Line). You can go into NYC from here. Trains go to Grand Central Station at 3:42pm and 6:32pm, return at 8am and 10:41am, weekends and holidays only. Fare is about $10 one way. For information, call 1-800-METRO-INFO.

N.Y. 22: Right 0.5m—to Tony's Deli with limited groceries, good sandwiches and subs, ice cream, sodas, hot coffee, and picnic tables out front; open 7 days, 6am-midnight. A public telephone and soda machine are available outside.

Old Route 22: The old water tower to the right is being preserved by local groups, ATC, and the NY-NJ Trail Conference as a historic structure.

Webatuck (Wiley) Shelter: water from cistern-spring 100 feet down the path in front of the shelter. Be glad that manhole covers are round, since they can't be dropped in the hole.

Hoyt Road: Left 3.3m—to the town of Wingdale.

♦ **Wingdale, N.Y.** (pop. 400): *Services*—motel • restaurant • pizzeria • grocery store: good for short-term resupply • bank.

Connecticut-Massachusetts

This chapter takes you from the New York-Connecticut line to the Massachusetts-Vermont line and corresponds to *Data Book* chapter three.

Hoyt Road: Pick up a free map from the box on the tree just north of the road. This schematic map shows the Trail route, shelters, and campsites in Connecticut. Pay attention to the location of designated campsites, because you can't camp anywhere else. You can't build fires, either. Ridgerunners patrol during the summer months and on spring and fall weekends.

Clubnote: The next 51 miles are maintained by AMC-Connecticut Chapter volunteers.

Ten Mile River: spanned by the Ned Anderson Memorial Bridge, named for the man who laid out the original Trail route in Connecticut and maintained it for 20 years. Campsites and a privy are near the bridge. Don't mistake the overgrown area at the sign for the campsites. Look for the grassy areas bordering the Housatonic River, 100 feet off the Trail, to the right at the bridge's south end.

Bulls Bridge Road: A.T. goes left on the road, then back into New York for a brief visit. *Right 0.2m*—(across two bridges, one modern, the other an early 1800s covered wooden bridge not visible from the A.T., at site where George Washington thrice crossed) to the Country Mart: good for short-term resupply, sandwiches, Ben & Jerry's, hiker register, outside telephone; open 7 days, Mon-Thur 6am-9pm, Fri until 10pm, Sat 7:30am-10pm, Sun 8am-10pm; friendly owner Patty will fill water bottles • Bull's Bridge Inn: L/D, country casual, roast turkey, steaks, seafood, vegetarian meals (MC, Visa, AE); open Tues-Fri 4pm-10pm, Sat-Sun noon-10pm, closed Mon.

Schaghticoke Mountain: easier done than said. The Trail crosses back into Connecticut as you go over the summit.

Indian Rocks: fine views of the Housatonic Valley. The Trail in this section passes through the Schaghticoke Indian Reservation.

Mt. Algo Lean-to: water from creek, plenty of flat spots for tenting nearby. This structure could just as easily have been called a shelter. From here to Katahdin, the terms "shelter" and "lean-to" are used interchangeably. By the way, Katahdin is beginning to seem real again, isn't it?

Conn. 341: Right 0.5m—on paved road through the campus of The Kent School, then across the Housatonic River to the village of Kent.

♦ **KENT, CONN.** (pop. 2,800): an upscale New England village with lots of activity on weekends. *Lodging*—Fife 'n Drum Inn: (special rates for hikers) $75D $12.50EAP, 4 max; a/c, TV, no pets (MC, Visa, AE, DC); restaurant in inn (B/L/D). *Places to eat*— Filippo's Italian Restaurant: L/D, varied pasta meals, steaks, inside public telephone; open 7 days, 11am-11pm • Kent Pizza Garden: L/D, casual eat-in or take-out, pizza, steak, chicken, seafood (MC, Visa, AE, DC); open 7 days, 11am-11pm • The Villager: B/L/D, country-casual, varied inexpensive menu, burgers, fries, luncheon specials; open Mon-Fri 6am-4pm, Sat 7am-3pm, Sun 8am-2pm, dinner Wed-Fri 5:30-8pm • Shanghai Chinese Restaurant: eat-in and take-out; open Mon-Thur 11am-10pm, Fri-Sat 11am-11pm, Sun 11:30am-9:30pm. *Groceries*—Davis-IGA Supermarket: good for long-term resupply; open Mon-Thur and Sat 8:30am-6pm, Fri 8:30am-8pm, Sun 9am-2pm • Kent Market & Deli: good for short-term resupply, sandwiches to go; open 7 days, 6am-9pm • bakery. *Laundromat*—Kent Laundromat: FLW, place for gear on back porch (don't block customers inside); open Mon-Sat 8am-8pm, last load 7pm, closed Sun. *Other services*— The Sports Scene (203-927-3852): good selection of backpacking gear (JanSport, Kelty, Lowe, The North Face, Sierra Designs, Eureka!, Merrell, Vasque, MSR, Optimus/Svea, Peak 1, Thermarest, ThorLo, Wigwam), Coleman by the pint, other fuels (MC, Visa, AE, Dis); open Mon-Sat 9am-6pm, Sun noon-4pm; owned by Chris and Helen Larvick, who go out of their way to help thru-hikers with equipment problems. Water can be obtained from a spigot on the outside of the building (make sure it's turned off!). • bank • pharmacy • hardware store • doctor • dentist • UPS/FedEx pick-up • Last year, the only outside public telephone was in front of the Sunoco gas station, on the right as you intersect U.S. 7 coming into town. *PO-ZIP 06757:* Mon-Fri 8am-1pm and 2-5pm, Sat 8am-12:30pm; 203-927-3435; LY-100+.

St. Johns Ledges: a steep descent that will put the hurt on your knees. The area is used by rock climbers to practice their art. A camping area at the base is heavily used by groups.

The River Walk: a flat section of Trail along the river that contains archaeologically interesting sites estimated to be more than 9,000 years old. The river valley is prime habitat for a wide variety of flora and fauna, including coyotes, bear, beaver, bobcat, wild turkey, and numerous types of waterfowl. The river itself is a favorite whitewater spot, with a slalom racing course for canoes and kayaks visible from the A.T. at the northern end.

Red-pine plantation: an eerily beautiful experiment that failed; the trees are dying. Red pines are not native to Connecticut and have a hard time growing in this climate. Trees from this stand have been used to build some of the nearby shelters.

Stewart Hollow Brook Shelter: Water from nearby brook flows from an old pasture. Level tentsites abound in the area.

Piped spring: located 25 feet to the right where the A.T. crosses dirt River Road, 2.4 miles north of Stewart Hollow Brook Shelter.

Silver Hill "Shelter": burned to the ground in early 1991. Cause of the fire was a faulty fireplace. This was a fine shelter, an enclosed cabin with sofa, magazines, loft for sleeping, porch, swing, and covered outdoor cooking area. The spring, which flows through a wall to a hand-pump faucet, is still usable. Said a 1990 thru-hiker, "This place is outstanding.

Wonder if all shelters will be like this in 25 years?" Good question. The AMC-Connecticut folks are considering what to do with the site. Usable in 1992 for camping.

Conn. 4: Right 0.9m—to the village of Cornwall Bridge.

♦ **CORNWALL BRIDGE, CONN.** (pop. 200): *Services*—Baird's General Store: good for short-term resupply, deli, sandwiches and grinders to go, outside public telephone; open Mon-Fri 7am-6pm, Sat 7:30am-6pm, Sun 8am-4pm • New England Catering: pastries, baked items, ice-cream parlor; open Sun-Thur 9am-6:30pm, Fri until 8pm, Sat until 7pm • veterinarian: Vet-Pet Care • Cornwall Package Store: owned by Richard and Patty Bramley, who invite you to stop and sign their hiker register; open Mon-Thur 9am-7pm, Fri 9am-8pm, Sat 9am-7pm, closed Sun. Water spigot and other cold drinks available. Note: The bridge has a history connected with the underground railroad. *PO-ZIP 06754:* Mon-Fri 7:15am-5pm, Sat 7:15am-noon; 203-672-6710; LY-80+.

West Cornwall Road: Right 2.2m—to the village of West Cornwall.

♦ **West Cornwall, Conn.** (pop. 600): *Services*—several restaurants and a grocery store.

Pine Swamp Brook Lean-to: water source is creek flowing from the swamp. As always, be sure to treat it, and watch out for "swamp things."

Sharon Mountain: offering good views of the valley. If you hear a lot of screeching tires below, it's not a rash of accidents happening before your ears. The test facility of a company that evaluates brakes for automobile manufacturers is located at Lime Rock Race Track, at the base of the mountain.

Belter Campsite: good place to tent; spring dependable except in driest years.

Conn. 112/U.S. 7: On A.T.—Lime Stone Auto: best to pass this place without stopping. Beyond, where the A.T. turns left on Warren Turnpike, cross the bridge over the railroad tracks, then continue 0.2 mile on U.S. 7 to the Village Coffee Shop & Restaurant (B/L/D, home-cooked meals, burgers, fries, ice cream, pies, and outside public telephone; open Mon-Fri 7am-7:45pm, Sat 7am-2:45pm, Sun 8am-1:45pm). Behind the restaurant, cottages with showers are available for $50D, no pets inside (MC, Visa); available May-Oct. Bonanza Bus stops daily in front of the coffee shop. The blue-blazed Mohawk Trail, marked by a sign across the highway, leads 0.2 mile back to the A.T.

Warren Turnpike: Water no longer available from spigot at side of school offices. Blue-blazed trail to the right 150 feet beyond the school offices leads across railroad tracks 0.2 mile to U.S. 7 (see above).

Iron Bridge over the Housatonic: On A.T.—picnic area with picnic tables, privy, no water, located to the left immediately after crossing river. (How many times does the Trail cross the Housatonic, anyway?). *Right 0.5m*—to the town of Falls Village.

♦ **Falls Village, Conn.** (pop. 552): *Services*—motel • The Inn Restaurant: L/D, home-cooked meals, prime rib, shrimp, grilled pork chops, roast duck, homemade soup, Mon-

Thur dinner special $12.95 (MC, Visa, AE); open Mon-Fri 5pm-9pm, Sat 11:30am-3pm and 5pm-10pm, Sun noon-8pm • Bonanza bus service • bank • outside public telephone. *PO-ZIP 06031:* Mon-Fri 8am-noon and 1-5pm, Sat 8am-noon; 203-824-7781; LY-21.

Great Falls: visible from A.T. to the right. Spectacular after a lot of rain. In 1989, when a storm had destroyed the power company's spillway and all the excess went over the dam, a thru-hiker reported that "the ground shook for hundreds of feet in every direction. It sounded like Niagara." Last year, the falls were back to normal, just a trickle.

Spring: off the Trail about 30 feet to the right as you ascend Prospect Mountain.

Limestone Springs Lean-to: reached by 0.5-mile side trail to the left. Blue-blazed loop leads back to A.T. Dependable spring; flat areas for tenting.

Rand's View: panoramic view of the Taconic range you will follow for the next few days; great place for lunch on a good day, worth the 500-foot detour. Bring water up from Limestone Springs, and be a good guest. This is private property. No camping is allowed.

Conn. 41 (Undermountain Road): *Left 0.8m*—to the town of Salisbury.

♦ **SALISBURY, CONN.** (pop. 1,900): the quintessential New England town with everything in perfect order. *Services*—The Ragamont Inn: $60S $70-$100D $10EAP, some a/c and TV, no pets, restaurant, open May-Oct • Yesterday's Yankee B&B: $65-$75D (includes full breakfast) $20EAP, 4 max; a/c, use of refrigerator, washer/dryer, no pets (MC, Visa, AE) • The Sandwich Shop (in pharmacy) • LaBonne's Epicure Grocery: good for long-term resupply, deli with sandwiches and grinders to go; open Mon-Sat 7am-7pm, Sun 8am-2pm • Harris Foods: specialty foods • The Village Store: sporting goods • bank • pharmacy • doctor • hospital • veterinarian (in nearby Lime Rock) • Nearby community of Lakeville, two miles away on U.S. 44W, has laundromat, hardware store, doctor, dentist, and taxi service. Nearest cobbler is in Millerton, N.Y., six miles away. *PO-ZIP 06068:* Mon-Fri 8am-1pm and 2-5pm, Sat 8:30am-noon; 203-435-9485; LY-30+.

Riga Lean-to and campsite: shelter new in 1991, located beyond the old campsite on blue-blazed side trail, great view into the valley. Two tentsites available near old campsite. Water available from spring.

Bond Lean-to: water from small stream beyond the shelter on A.T.; level campsites beside the Trail.

Bear Mountain: the first 2,000-footer since Maryland; topped by a rock tower constructed more than a century ago, using no mortar. Good view from the top.

Sages Ravine: a beautiful area of trees and waterfalls. AMC-Connecticut Chapter caretaker is in residence from mid-June-Labor Day. Campsites were assigned by the caretaker; no fee in 1992.

Clubnote: The next 88 miles are maintained by AMC-Berkshire Chapter volunteers.

Wildlife: Red efts are the tiny red salamanders that you see on the Trail in abundance after a heavy rain. They are also known as the eastern newt. The newts lay eggs in water each spring, and the larvae remain aquatic until late summer, when they lose their gills and take to the land as efts. After a year or more on land, they become drab-green in color and return to the water for mating, never to leave.

Bear Rock Falls: with four tent platforms, privy, beautiful hemlock grove, and creek that plunges over the edge of a cliff. Sunrises can be awesome from the overlook. Overnight camping was free last year. So were the sunrises.

Race Mountain: a surprisingly beautiful, exposed section of cliffside Trail overlooking the valley below.

Mt. Everett: topped by a firetower that is unsafe to climb, so don't, even though you can get through the fence and climb around the missing steps. At the base of the mountain, 0.7 mile past the summit, is a picnic area with privies. Side trail leads from picnic area to Guilder Pond; swimming prohibited.

Glen Brook Shelter: Water source is the creek at the junction of the A.T. and shelter side trail. Water is also available at the shelter, if it isn't a dry season.

Jug End Road: Right 0.1m—to piped spring just off the road to the right. A bear was spotted near here two years ago.

Mass. 41: Left 1.2m—to the town of South Egremont.

Relocation: The Trail is being relocated off roads between South Egremont Road and Boardman Street. Watch signs and blazes closely.

♦ **South Egremont, Mass.** (pop. 1,300): *Services*—South Egremont Inn: $60-$90S, pool, tennis courts, meals • sandwich shop • convenience store • bakery • cheese shop • sporting goods store. *PO-ZIP 01258:* Mon-Fri 7:45am-5pm, Sat 7:45am-1pm; 413-528-1571; LY-30+.

U.S. 7: Right 0.4m—to Shea's Pine Tree Inn. *Right 2.8m*—to the town of Sheffield.

♦ **Shea's Pine Tree Inn:** restaurant owned by Joe and Barbara, who allow hikers to stay overnight (even on Tues, July 4th, and Labor Day, when the inn is closed). Hikers sleep on tables in the banquet pavilion behind the inn at no charge. Water is available from a spigot behind the restaurant, but toilets are only available inside. Remember to hang your food bag; curious skunks visit the pavilion at night. The restaurant (L/D, prime rib specials, seafood, chicken, burgers, sandwiches, salad bar) has excellent food, according to reports from several thru-hikers; open Wed-Mon 11:30am-2pm for lunch, 5-9pm for dinner. The bar is an Irish pub with Harp's on tap. No public telephone is available.

♦ **Sheffield, Mass.** (pop. 2,100): *Services*—The Shed Restaurant • Village Green Luncheonette: B/L, diner and take-out, American fare and Italian specialties; open Mon-Fri 6am-3pm, Sat 6am-11pm • Danto's Italian Take-out • Sheffield Market: small grocery store, deli-style sandwiches, barbecue chicken • bank • Gilligan Bros. hardware store •

doctor • dentist • Bonanza bus service • hikers may have UPS and FedEx packages delivered to the town hall (413-229-8752), but call ahead to confirm this service.

Tom Leonard Shelter: the showplace of the AMC-Berkshire Chapter and typical of the shelters it is now building in this section. The shelter has a picnic table, tent platform with a view into the valley, privy, and water from a cold spring at the bottom of Ice Gulch.

Mass 23: Left 4m—to the city of Great Barrington.

♦ **Great Barrington, Mass.** (pop. 5,500): *Services*—motel • restaurants • McDonald's • Burger King • Friendly's • Pizza House • Subway • supermarket: good for long-term resupply • grocery store • health food store: Lock, Stock, and Barrel • deli • bakery • laundromat • sporting goods store • cobbler • bank • Cirrus, NYCE, Yankee 24 • pharmacy • hardware store • department store • doctor • dentist • hospital • veterinarian • movie theatre • FedEx pick-up • local bus service • taxi service.

Benedict Pond: a beautiful glacial pond bordered by the A.T. Swimming just off the Trail, or take the blue-blazed Pond Loop Trail 0.5 mile to a sand-beach swimming area with picnic tables and a public telephone. Tentsites are available for $10, and canoes may be rented by the hour.

Mt. Wilcox South Lean-to: water from spring to the right of the trail just before climbing to the shelter turn-off; intermittent spring on side trail to the shelter.

Mt. Wilcox North Lean-to: 0.3 mile off the A.T.; water from small stream behind shelter, not dependable in dry seasons.

Tyringham relocation: The roadwalk down Jerusalem Road has been eliminated by a new relocation, which skirts the village of Tyringham. Where the Trail now crosses Jerusalem Road, a piped spring is 100 feet to the left.

Main Road: Left 0.9m—to the hamlet of Tyringham. Note: Main Road is the first paved road after you cross the wooden bridge across Hop Brook.

♦ **TYRINGHAM, MASS.** (pop. 335): an outside water faucet and public telephone are available for hiker use in front of the PO. The Golden Goose B&B does not take thruhikers, but Carolyn Canon (in the fourth white house to the right after the Golden Goose) caters to hikers. Room with bath $30S $60D, laundry $2 extra, no pets. Miss Canon serves no meals, but kitchen privileges and often a snack at night are provided. No camping is allowed in town. *PO-ZIP 01264:* Mon-Fri 8:30-11am and 4-5:30pm, Sat 8:30am-12:30pm; 413-243-1225; LY-47.

Upper Goose Pond Cabin: 0.5 mile to the left off the Trail after you've passed the pond. The enclosed cabin has bunk beds, gas stove and cooking utensils, outside privy, nearby swimming area, canoes, and a fireplace for cold nights. Volunteer caretakers are in residence from mid-June to mid-Sept, but only on weekends in early spring and autumn. $3 per night is accepted as a donation, $2 for tent platforms. Tavoli's Tavern and Restaurant is a 15 to 20-minute walk from the cabin, with Samuel Adams on tap.

U.S. 20: Left 0.3m—to Beldon Tavern, open for dinner and Sunday brunch only, fine country dining, international cuisine, steaks, seafood, pasta, Friday-night AYCE dinners and AYCE Sunday buffet brunch, open 7 days June-Sept 9. *Right 0.2m*—to Gaslight Motor Lodge, $35-$70S $40-$75D, 2 max; TV, use of refrigerator, no pets (MC, Visa); fishing lake, paddleboats, rowboats, and outside public telephone. *Left 5m*—to the city of Lee.

♦ **Lee, Mass.** (pop. 5,550): *Services*—motel • restaurant • KFC • Burger King • Friendly's • Pizza Hut • Subway • supermarket • laundromat • doctor • dentist • health clinic • veterinarian • UPS/FedEx pick-up • Greyhound bus service • taxi service.

October Mountain Lean-to: new in 1990, the same popular design as the Tom Leonard Shelter.

Pittsfield Road: Right 0.1m—to the home of the "Pittsfield Cookie Lady" Marilyn Wiley on the left, behind an abandoned house near the road. Marilyn and her husband have a blueberry farm (ripe berries from July to autumn) and are friends of hikers. They even had the outside water faucet next to the front steps installed for thru-hikers to use during the summer. When she's had time to cook them, delicious cookies are also offered. Note: The southernmost road shown as Pittsfield Road on the 1991 Trail maps is actually Washington Mountain Road. The *real* Pittsfield Road is three miles north, called Blotz Road and Pittsfield Road on the maps. *Right 5m*—to the town of Becket.

♦ **Becket, Mass.** (pop. 1,300): *Services*—motel • restaurant • grocery store • Western Union • doctor • veterinarian.

Kay Wood Lean-to: a prototype shelter named for a lovely lady and 1988 thru-hiker who lives in Dalton and helps maintain the Trail in this area (also contributes to this book). You may meet her. She often visits "her" shelter to chat with thru-hikers.

Notice: The route through Dalton can be a bit confusing. From Grange Hall Road, turn right onto South Street, go to the stoplight at Mass. 8/9, turn right, and go 0.2 mile, turn left on Park Avenue, passing Baker's Deli (sandwiches, soups and stews, salads, specialty items; open Mon-Sat 8am-6pm, sometimes on Sun), left again on Gulf Road, then look for the A.T. in the woods to the right. This route bypasses the business district.

Mass. 8/9: Right 0.5m—to "downtown" Dalton. *Left 1.5m*—to the large city of Pittsfield (pop. 51,974) with all services needed by thru-hikers. Bus service from Dalton to Pittsfield is available weekdays; flag down the bus anywhere on Mass. 8/9.

♦ **DALTON, MASS.** (pop. 7,928): *Services*—The Inn at Village Square: $55S $65D $5EAP, 4 max; a/c, TV, phone in room, pets outside, Jacob's Restaurant (food-and-spirits country pub) in motel (MC, Visa, AE, Dis) • Dalton House B&B: $48-$78D $10EAP, 3 max; a/c, cable, pool, no pets (MC, Visa, AE) • Dalton (Ozzie's) Restaurant: B/L/D, home-cooked meals reasonably priced, veal, clams; open Mon-Sat 5:30am-8pm, Sun 7am-noon • Dalton Pizza: open 7 days, 11am-11pm • Benny's Pizza & Grinders (on Depot Street) • Clarke's Market: good for short-term resupply, will fill water bottles; open Mon-Sat 8am-8pm, Sun 8am-5pm • Cumberland Farms:

24-hour convenience store, limited hiker supplies, open 7 days • The General Store: eclectic grocery store with limited hiker supplies, deli, fruit, pastries; open 7 days, 5:30am-7pm, located on Rt. 9 on far side of town • Bread Basket Bakery: "very good," according to Kay Wood • Depot St. Laundromat: FLW; open 7 days, located on Depot St. (where else?) • bank • pharmacy • Adams Hardware Store • doctor • dentist • local bus service (see above) • AMC's Dalton office (413-684-3900), located above Ozzie's • The Crane Currency Museum: operated by The Crane Company, Dalton's oldest manufacturer and maker of the unique paper used for all U.S. currency, open daily. *PO-ZIP 01226:* Mon-Fri 8am-5pm, Sat 8am-noon; 413-684-0364; LY-60.

The Cobbles: overlooking the town of Cheshire and valley below.

> Wildlife: *Porcupines crave salt and will eat your boots and sweaty items if you don't hang them out of reach. Years ago, one unfortunate hiker awoke to find only Vibram soles where he had left his boots on the ground the evening before. They also chew on shelters and privies. Porcupines feed at night and do much damage to trees by eating buds, twigs, and bark. They are large rodents with 30,000 barbed quills. When attacked, they turn their back and try to strike with their tail. Dogs never seem to learn that porkies are nasty business and will go for them every time they meet, usually with the same sad result for the dog. Porcupines can be encountered on the A.T. from New York to Maine.*

CHESHIRE, MASS. (pop. 3,500): a quiet residential community between the larger cities of Adams and Pittsfield. The Trail goes through the center of town, much to the pleasure of its residents. *Hostel*—St. Mary of the Assumption Catholic Church (Father Tom Begley, 413-743-2110) makes space available year-round for hikers, and more than 300 thru-hikers stayed overnight last year at no charge. When you arrive, check in at the church office. Father Tom, himself an avid hiker who has covered much of the A.T. in sections, will show you where to put your gear. Hikers sleep on the floor in the large parish hall, with restrooms adjacent. The restrooms have no showers and should not be used for bathing. Cooking must be done outside. Lights-out is at 10:30pm. Stay is limited to one night in July and August. Alcohol may not be used on the premises. Note: The town of Cheshire has a recycling law. Please help the church comply with this very beneficial statute. Cans and boxes for sorted garbage are provided in the parish hall. *Other lodging*—Beechwood Country B&B: $40S $65D includes full breakfast, common room with TV; in 200-year-old home with large porches. *Places to eat*—Donna Bella Restaurant: L/D, casual eat-in or take-out, pizza, grinders, pasta dishes, salads; open Tues-Thur 11am-9pm, Fri and Sat 11am-10pm, Sun noon-9pm, closed Mon • The Cedars Restaurant (left 0.4 mile on Rt. 8): B/L, American fare, closed Wed • Nejaime's Cheshire Market: Lebanese deli specialties, grinders; open Mon-Sat 6am-9pm, Sun 6am-6pm • Village Package & Variety: good subs and sandwiches; open Mon-Sat 6am-10pm, Sun 8am-8pm; located on a side street to the right as you come into town, before crossing the railroad tracks. *Groceries*—Nejaime's Cheshire Market: good for short-term resupply (see hours above) • Village Package & Variety: limited hiker supplies, ice cream, outside public telephone • convenience store (right on Rt. 8): snacks, ice cream, outside public telephone. *Stove fuel*—Coleman by the pint at Reynold's General Store, closed Sun. *Other services*—bank • hardware store • health clinic • veterinarian. *PO-ZIP 01225:* Mon-Fri 8am-1pm and 2-5pm, Sat 8am-noon;

413-743-3184; LY-200. *Nearby town*—Adams (four miles to the north, with hourly bus service for $1; catch bus at bench across from the Cheshire PO; no Sunday service).

♦ **Adams, Mass.** (pop. 10,772): *Services*—hotel • restaurants • McDonald's • supermarket: good for long-term resupply • convenience store • bakery • laundromat • bank • Yankee 24 • Western Union • pharmacy • hardware store • department store • doctor • dentist • veterinarian • FedEx pick-up.

Mt. Greylock: highest point in Massachusetts. The summit was the first in the nation to have a pay-for-observation tower, built on the spot now occupied by the distinctive War Memorial. Also on the summit is the state-owned, AMC-operated Bascom Lodge (P. O. Box 1652, Lanesboro, Mass. 01237; 413-743-1591), with bunkrooms, showers, meals, snack bar, picnic porch, Bullwinkle the Moose, lobby with sofas, inside public telephone, and nature tours. Bunkroom with shower is $20, dinner $9.50, breakfast $5, shower without stay $1.50 with towel and soap. Hikers can substitute $10 and two hours of work for lodging and meals. Weekends are always crowded, so it's best to call ahead for lodging and meal reservations (before noon for dinner). Moleskin, boot laces, and fruit are for sale in the lobby. No smoking or dogs are permitted inside. The lodge is open daily from mid-May until late October, managed and staffed by hikers who are totally tuned-in to the thru-hiking scene; may be used as a maildrop by addressing mail c/o Bascom Lodge at the above address (or UPS to: Greylock Visitor Center, Rockwell Road, Lanesboro, Mass. 01237). No camping or fires, including stoves, are allowed on top of Greylock. The pavilion in the parking area is for picnics only.

Wilbur Clearing Lean-to: water from a small stream 150 feet beyond the privy.

Mass. 2: Right 0.5m—to Price Chopper Supermarket: good for long-term resupply, deli and pharmacy inside, open 24-hrs except Sat night and Sun morning • Thrifty Bundle Laundromat: FLW, open 8am-9pm • Pizza Hut • Friendly's: B/L/D, family fare and ice cream; open 7 days, 6:30am-11pm • pharmacy. *Right 2.5m*—to the sprawling city of North Adams. *Left 2.6m*—to the town of Williamstown. Local buses run hourly between Williamstown and North Adams on Mass. 2. You can usually flag a bus down anywhere along the route.

♦ **NORTH ADAMS, MASS.** (pop. 18,063): *Services*—several motels • hotel • restaurants • McDonald's • Burger King • Dairy Queen • Subway • supermarket • convenience store • bakery • laundromat • sporting goods store • cobbler: Tony's Shoe & Leather Service • Western Union • Cirrus, Plus, Yankee 24 • pharmacy • hardware store • department store • doctor • dentist • hospital • veterinarian • movie theatre. *PO-ZIP 01247:* Mon-Fri 8:30am-4:30pm, Sat 10am-noon; 413-664-4554; LY-45.

♦ **WILLIAMSTOWN, MASS.** (pop. 6,285): *Services*—(located on near edge of town, 1.5 miles from Trail)—The Willows Motel: $38S $45-$49D $5EAP, 4 max; a/c, cable, phone in room, pool (MC, Visa, Dis) • Grand Union Supermarket; good for long-term resupply; open Mon-Sat 8am-11pm, Sun noon-7pm • pharmacy • restaurants. *Services* (in center of town)—Papa Charlie's Deli: celebrity sandwiches, frozen yogurt, open 7 days • Cobble Cafe: B/L/D, casual, American fare; open Mon-Sat 6:30am-3pm, Tues-Sat 6am-9:30pm, Sun 7am-3pm • Colonial Pizza: pizza, grinders, salads; open 7 days, 11am-midnight • Burger King • Slippery Banana (Eddie's on Cole St.): neighborhood market, good for short-term resupply, open Mon-Sat 9am-7pm • Clarksburg Bread Company: fresh bread, muffins, cookies, everything baked fresh daily, blueberry muffins come highly recommended, open Tues-Sat 8am-5:30pm • Water St. Laundromat: FLW; open 7 days, 24 hours • The Mountain Goat (413-458-8445): backpacking shop (Kelty, Gregory, Mountainsmith, Lowe, The North Face, Dana Designs, Sierra Designs, Eureka!, Asolo, Merrell, Vasque, MSR, Optimus/Svea, Caribou, Thermarest, Wigwam), Coleman by the pint, may allow you to camp in the back yard; open Mon-Sat 10am-6pm, Sun noon-5pm • bank • Yankee 24 • pharmacy • hardware store • doctor • dentist • health clinic • veterinarian • movie theatre • UPS/FedEx pick-up • local bus service (see above) • Greyhound bus service • Williams College. *PO-ZIP 01267:* Mon-Fri 8:30am-4:30pm, Sat 9:30am-12:30pm; 413-458-3707; LY-40+.

Sherman Brook: with several wading pools visible from the Trail. On a hot day, the cold water is mind-boggling.

Sherman Brook Campsite: wooden tent platforms, dependable spring, privy, and fireplaces. This is a designated campsite; avoid camping elsewhere in this section.

Vermont-New Hampshire

This chapter takes you from the Massachusetts-Vermont line to the New Hampshire-Maine line and corresponds to *Data Book* chapter two.

Long Trail: completed in 1931, extends north to the Vermont-Canada line. The nation's first long-distance trail, it was mostly completed by 1921 when the A.T. was proposed. The A.T. and the Long Trail share the same treadway for about 100 miles before the A.T. turns east, just north of Sherburne Pass, and heads for Maine. The Long Trail is managed by the Green Mountain Club. GMC caretakers are on duty during the summer months and a $3 overnight fee is charged from mid-May to mid-Oct at the following locations: Stratton Pond, Peru Peak Shelter, Griffith Lake area, Little Rock Pond area, and Lula Tye Shelter.

Clubnote: The next 122 miles of the A.T. are maintained by GMC trail crews and volunteers, in cooperation with the Green Mountain National Forest.

Seth Warner Shelter: water from a small stream, possibly overflow from a beaver pond (true of water at many shelters in Vermont).

Congdon Camp: an enclosed cabin with bunks, wood stove. Water is from a small stream that flows out of a beaver pond.

Harmon Hill: view overlooking Bennington. The monument and Bennington College can be seen in the distance.

Vt. 9: Left 5.1m—to the large city of Bennington.

♦ **Bennington, Vt.** (pop. 16,451): *Services*—Avalon Motel • Mountain View Motel • hotel • Martin's Restaurant • Alldays and Onions Restaurant: supposedly fantastic food • Panda West: good Chinese food • McDonald's • Burger King • Friendly's • Subway • Wendy's • supermarket: good for long-term resupply • bakery • laundromat • cobbler: King's Shoe Repair • sporting goods store • bank • Western Union • Cirrus • pharmacy • hardware store • department store • doctor • dentist • hospital • veterinarian • movie theatre • UPS/FedEx pickup • local bus service • taxi service • Bennington College. *PO-ZIP 05201*: Mon-Fri 8:30am-4:30pm, Sat 8:30am-noon; 802-442-2421; LY-27.

Melville Nauheim Shelter: water from stream behind shelter.

Goddard Shelter: on the site of the old Glastenbury Shelter (some guidebooks use the old name). This is a classy shelter with plenty of room, cold piped spring, and a great view south toward Greylock. Says Captain Noah of '90, "On a clear night, take in the sunset at the firetower on the summit. It's worth the climb."

Story Spring Shelter: last dependable spring until you reach the piped spring just before the summit of Stratton Mountain, although you will cross a stream.

Stratton Mountain: possibly the birthplace of the Appalachian Trail, since Benton MacKaye once said he thought about the desirability of an eastern continental trail while sitting in a tree on this summit. He said of the experience, "I felt as if atop the world, with a sort of planetary feeling." He later published his proposal for an A.T., and his ideas fired the imagination of many dedicated volunteers who created the Trail we all enjoy so much today. Recently, the A.T. was routed across the summit of Stratton, which has a firetower and cabin, usually with a ranger-naturalist in residence. No camping is allowed near the tower. A side trail to the right leads 0.8 mile to the top of the Stratton Ski Area, where you'll find the Starship XII gondola ride, which operates daily from late June to early October (11am-5pm, round-trip free for hikers). At the other end of the ride is Stratton Village with grocery store (limited hiker supplies), restaurants, and specialty shops geared toward the ski trade. Hikers can sleep overnight in the warming lodge or ski-patrol buildings on the summit. Both have electric lights and heat. Rusty hot and cold water is available at the nearby restrooms. Check in with the gondola operator, if one is on duty, as a matter of courtesy, and clean up before you leave.

Stratton Pond: Bigelow and Vondell shelters, both on left side of the pond, tent platform behind the farthest shelter, swimming area, camping areas on right side; busiest overnight use site on the Long Trail. A caretaker is on duty mid-May thru mid-Oct; $3 fee for overnight stay.

> Wildlife: *Hummingbirds are drawn to anything red. A hiker sleeping in a shelter at Stratton Pond was once awakened by the noise of a ruby-throated hummingbird checking a red cup hanging on his pack. The 3-inch-long ruby-throated is the only variety found in the eastern mountains. These tiny birds make frequent flights to fields and meadows where they feed on the nectar of wildflowers. Each year, hummingbirds fly to Florida, Mexico, and South America for the winter, an amazing distance (longer than a thru-hike) for such a tiny animal.*

William B. Douglas Shelter: located 0.5 mile to the left, but not, as many assume, named for the late Supreme Court Justice William O. Douglas, the eighteenth person to hike the entire A.T.

Prospect Rock: overlook with excellent view of Manchester Center area, to the left where the Trail leaves the forest road (Old Rootville Road) and heads into the woods.

Spruce Peak Shelter: an enclosed cabin with bunks, woodstove, sliding front door, and porch. The spring is possibly the coldest on the A.T., dependable except in driest years.

Vt. 11/30: Left 5.5m—to the town of Manchester Center.

♦ **MANCHESTER CENTER, VT.** (pop. 5,196): once described as a "yuppie Gatlinburg." This description is not too far off the mark, since the town's main industry is tourism. Most services needed by thru-hikers are available, although you will notice that prices reflect the influence of the two nearby ski resorts, Stratton and Bromley. You may want to pick up your mail before you head into the center of town (go left 3 blocks on Richville Road, across from Fleming Hardware), since the post office is on the edge of town, about 0.8 mile from the hostel. *Hostel*—Provided by the Zion Episcopal Church (802-362-1987, Rev. Jim Rains, pastor), open June 1-Labor Day. Hikers may sleep on the floor in the big room of the congregational hall. Hot shower is available (no towels or soap). The fully equipped kitchen can be used to cook group meals but must be cleaned thoroughly after use. A very comfortable sitting room with sofas, magazines, books, and cable television is adjacent to the congregational hall. No smoking is allowed in the building, and no alcohol is permitted on the premises. House rules are posted and should be observed to the letter. Donations are accepted and used for maintaining the hostel (donations purchased the shower). Stay is limited to two nights. Rev. Jim, an experienced hiker, has been a friend to many thru-hikers over the years. Directions to the hostel: At the intersection of Vt. 11 and U.S. 7 (main town intersection), turn right on U.S. 7, go three blocks to the church on the left. The congregational hall is next door. *Other lodging*—Sutton's Place: $20S $40D $10EAP, 3 max; TV, no pets inside, located on School Street (one block from main town intersection). *Places to eat*—Manchester Pancake House: breakfast all day, managed by Mom; open 7 days, 7am-3pm • Manchester Pizza House: L/D, eat in or take out, *Skiing* magazine's "best pizza in town," grinders, gyros, pasta dinners, salads, operated by Aris and Nancy Konstantinou; open Mon-Thur 11am-11pm, Fri and Sat until midnight, Sun noon-11pm • Sirloin Saloon: D, casual, fine dining, varied menu with prime rib, teriyaki steak, trout, salmon, salad bar with 30 items, apple crisp, mud pie (MC, Visa, AE, DC, CB); open Mon-Thur 5-10pm, Sat and Sun 5-11pm • Quality Restaurant: B/L/D, casual, American fare, steaks, seafood, burgers (MC, Visa, AE, DC CB); open 7 days, 6am-9pm • Friendly's: B/L/D, varied meals, ice cream, open 7 days • Mrs. Murphy's Donuts & Coffee Shop • Up for Breakfast: B/L, good food, but expensive • Zachary's Pizza (one block from hostel): pizza, pasta, calzones, grinders; open Sun-Thur 11am-10pm, Fri and Sat 11am-11pm • McDonald's • The Gourmet a Deli Cafe: L, outside patio and take-out, sandwiches, soups, salads; open 7 days, 11am-3:30pm • Vermont Bagel Works: all kinds of hot bagels (come in with your *Handbook*, and Jason will give you a discount!); open 7 days, 7am-5pm • Ben & Jerry's: ice-cream parlor with everything cold and creamy you could ever want, factory seconds for $1.75 a pint. (Ask for a "Blue Blaze," a special shake concocted only at this store for thru-hikers, created by "Salamander" of '91). *Groceries*—Price Chopper Supermarket: good for long-term resupply; open Mon-Sat 7am-10pm, Sun 8am-8pm • Grand Union Supermarket: good for long-term resupply, open 24 hrs • New Morning Natural Foods: open Mon-Sat 9am-6pm, Sun 11am-5pm. *Laundromat*—FLW, open 7 days, last load 9pm. *Outfitter/Stove fuel*—The Mountain Goat (802-362-5159): good assortment of backpacking gear (Kelty, Gregory, Mountainsmith, The North Face, Sierra Designs, Asolo, Vasque, One Sport, MSR, Optimus/Svea, Peak 1 parts, Trangia, Caribou, Marmot, Thermarest, ThorLo, Wigwam), Coleman by the pint, limited repair service for stoves and backpacks, friendly folks (MC, Visa, AE); open Mon-Sat 10am-6pm, Sun 11am-5pm. Also, factory outlets for Timberland Boots and Dunham Boots and the Sox Market (factory-second backpacking socks). *Other services*—cobbler • bank • Western Union • Cirrus, Plus, MAC, NYCE, Yankee 24 • pharmacy • hardware store • many specialty shops (you can say "hi" to Calvin, and Anne II!) • doctor • dentist • health clinic • veterinarian • Northshire Bookstore with huge selection • movie theatre (usually has recent movies) • UPS/FedEx pick-up • Greyhound bus service • taxi service. *PO-ZIP 05255*: Mon-Fri 8:30am-5pm, Sat 9am-1pm; 802-362-3070; LY-80.

Bromley Mountain: topped by warming lodge, observation tower, and picnic table, but no natural water (piped water may be available at lodge building in '92). Bromley chair lift at the summit is not in service during summer months, but you can follow it down to the Bromley Alpine Slide, an exhilarating ride; open 7 days, 9:30am-5pm in good weather only. Lower lift will take you to Bromley Base Lodge ($4.50 round trip, with lodge offering snacks). The Trail across the summit is a bit confusing. Directions going north: Stay on the A.T. as it follows the ski trail to the summit, continue past the short observation-tower side trail, then take a hard left on the summit, descending steeply on the A.T., which goes to the left of a small reddish building.

Mad Tom Shelter: Sliding doors make it an enclosed cabin. Great sunsets. Water source is a small boxed spring, not very dependable.

> Trail Fact: *The average thru-hiker loses 23 pounds in body weight and secretes more than 100 gallons of sweat on a hike from Georgia to Maine.*

Mad Tom Notch (USFS Road 21): water from pump with interesting mechanism . . . unless you can't figure it out. *Right 4.3m*—to the town of Peru.

♦ **Peru, Vt.** (pop. 324): *Services*—hotel • b&b • campground • restaurant • grocery store: good for short-term resupply • sporting goods store.

Peru Peak Shelter: shelter and tent platform. Water source is the creek unless you pick up water at one of the small springs along the Trail south of the shelter. Caretaker comes up from Griffith Lake to collect $3 fee for overnight stay, usually at dusk.

Griffith Lake: tent platforms, caretaker, and $3 overnight fee; caretaker tent located near the swimming area. GMC caretakers are usually very friendly and seem to enjoy having thru-hikers stop to chat.

Baker Peak: one of the finest views in Vermont.

Lost Pond Shelter: off the Trail a short distance to the left; creek is water source.

Big Branch Shelter: creek flows in front of shelter, plenty of swimming holes and usually warmish water. Maintainers wage a continuing battle against local porkies that seem to find the shelter floor tasty.

Danby-Landgrove Road (USFS Road 10): *Left 3.5m*—to the town of Danby.

♦ **Danby, Vt.** (pop. 1,193): home of the late Nobel Prize-winning author Pearl Buck. *Services*—motel • Danby Diner • two small grocery stores • hardware store • UPS/FedEx pick-up.

Lula Tye Shelter: $3 overnight fee, collected by caretaker from Little Rock Pond in the evening.

Little Rock Pond: excellent swimming, very good spring, tent platforms, and shelter; caretaker on duty mid-May thru mid-Oct, $3 overnight fee. Second busiest overnight site on Long Trail.

Homer Stone Brook Trail: leads west 2.5 miles to the town of South Wallingford.

◆ **South Wallingford, Vt.** (pop. 1,148): *Services*—Charlie's General Store: limited hiker supplies, coffee, pastries, Ben & Jerry's • Green Mountain Tea Room & Guest House.

Greenwall Shelter: water source marginal in dry years.

Vt. 140: Left 3.5m—to the town of Wallingford.

◆ **Wallingford, Vt.** (pop. 1,800): *Services*—restaurant • grocery stores • bakery • laundromat • bank • hardware store • dentist • Greyhound bus service.

Minerva Hinchey Shelter: to the right 300 feet, where the A.T. takes a sharp left. Water source is creek on blue-blazed trail in front of shelter.

Clarendon Gorge: spanned by the Mill River suspension bridge, dedicated to the memory of Robert Brugmann, a young hiker who drowned here during a flood in 1969. The gorge is a favorite swimming hole for area residents (Vt. 103 is just 0.1 mile north), with several delightful pools bordered by boulders. Diving from the rocks is dangerous, however. Camping is not allowed in the gorge area.

Vt. 103: Left 1m—to Clarendon General Store: good for short-term resupply, Ben & Jerry's ice cream and frozen yogurt, sodas, snacks, homemade cookies, candy, microwave foods, and outside public telephone; open 7 days, 7am-6pm. *Left 4.2m*—to the town of North Clarendon.

◆ **North Clarendon, Vt.** (pop. 2,500): *Services*—Country Squire Motel • several corner grocery stores • Clarendon Animal Clinic. Ray and Peggy Corey (802-775-0715) are friends of hikers if you need assistance in this area.

Clarendon Shelter: easily accessible from nearby road (the old A.T.), so be careful about leaving gear unguarded. Privy located about 200 feet in front of shelter.

Cold River: usually ankle deep, can be treacherous after several days of heavy rain, sometimes waist deep where the Trail crosses. The water level rises and subsides quickly.

Governor Clement Shelter: near dirt road, visited by partying neighbors on occasion. Water source is creek.

Killington Peak (4,235 feet): on a side trail to the right, 0.2 mile straight up. The summit, where the state was christened "Verd-mont" in 1763, offers panoramic views of Vermont, New Hampshire, New York, Massachusetts, Maine, and Canada on very clear days. A hundred yards beyond the summit is the Killington snack bar, with coffee, snacks, pastries, and fruit, all items priced to match the altitude; open 7 days, 9am-4pm through

Labor Day. You can take the chairlift down to the base lodge, 10am-4pm daily from early July-Labor Day and the last two weeks in Sept.

Cooper Lodge: an old stone structure with bunks, table, plastic over the windows to deter rain and wind, and very bold chipmunks. Water is available from a nearby spring, marginal in dry years.

Pico Camp: an enclosed cabin like Congdon Camp. Piped spring is located 100 feet north of the shelter on the A.T.

Sherburne Pass (U.S. 4): *On A.T.*—The Inn at Long Trail (see below). *Right 1.6m*—to the village of Killington. *Left 4m*—to T&M Brandy's Restaurant. *Left 10m*—to the city of Rutland.

♦ **KILLINGTON, VT.** (pop. 200): *Services*—motel • The Deli at Killington Corners: grocery store, good for short-term resupply, sandwiches to go, bagels; open 7 days, 6:30am-7pm • Bill's Country Store • bank • Plus • alpine clothing shop • public telephone. *PO-ZIP 05751:* Mon-Fri 8am-4:30pm, Sat 8am-noon; 802-775-4247; LY-42.

♦ T&M Brandy's Restaurant: D, casual, family-style dinners rated excellent by past thru-hikers; open 7 days, 5pm-9pm, closed end of Oct thru early Nov.

♦ Rutland, Vt. (pop. 18,230): large city with many motels and restaurants, supermarkets, laundromat, and Mountain Travelers Outdoor Shop (802-775-0814) with Camp Trails, Lowe, The North Face, Sierra Designs, Eureka!, Asolo, Merrell, MSR, Optimus/Svea, Caribou, Thermarest, Wigwam, Coleman by the pint (MC, Visa, AE); open Mon-Sat 10am-6pm (sometimes Sun noon-5pm).

The Inn at Long Trail: the first ski lodge in Vermont, built in 1939, operated by the McGrath family as an inn since 1977, open July 1 to late October. Rates, after 20% hiker discount and including breakfast, $35S $43D. Inn will hold UPS packages, but do not send packages by mail. No pets are allowed. The inn also has a bar, McGrath's Irish Pub (open 7 days, noon-midnight), featuring Guinness Stout served at the correct temperature, and Long Trail Ale, both on tap for $3.50 a pint. Sandwiches are available for lunch. *Skiing* magazine said of the bar, "one of the liveliest, coziest pubs this side of Dublin." Live music on weekends. Water is available at a spigot on the side of the building closest to the Trail, but please turn it off when you've finished.

Sherburne Pass to Hanover: GMC and DOC (Dartmouth Outing Club) have relocated most of the A.T. between Sherburne Pass and Hanover during the last few years. The new Trail route is more scenic and much improved, but the information in your pre-1992 guidebook may be out of date for this section. The actual Trail route has considerably more elevation change than indicated on the pre-1990 profile maps. The 1992 *Data Book* should reflect accurate mileage figures. The new Trail is well-marked, so follow the white blazes if you find contradictions with the printed materials.

Maine Junction: where the A.T. leaves the Long Trail and heads east for Katahdin, although GMC maintenance continues to Vt. 12. The GMC is raising money to buy a corridor to protect the Long Trail north of here. A 1990 thru-hiker, Robert "Dandelion" Burns, did a benefit hike to aid the effort. Let's wish them success in this important project.

Gifford Woods State Park: lean-to $12, tentsites $7.50, pay showers open to noncampers by paying $1.50 day-use fee (additional quarters required for shower), open Memorial Day-Columbus Day.

> Wildlife: *Toads do not cause warts and aren't poisonous to the touch. As tadpoles, they eat plants; as adults, insects. The latter trait is very important to the balance of nature. Toads grow to 5" in length, and you will see many that size in New England. Nevertheless, biologists worldwide have noticed a dramatic decline in the number of toads and are concerned. We should be, too.*

Mountain Meadows Lodge: on the A.T., to the right just before reaching the dam that creates Kent Pond (look for goose-shaped windsocks on the lawn), operated by the friendly Stevens family. A bed in the bunkroom (no linens), hot shower (no towel), and substantial breakfast is available for $20 per person, limited to four thru-hikers at one time. Dinner is available for $12, and the first hiker to ask can often substitute kitchen help as payment. Hikers can use the canoes and the swimming pool. No smoking, pets, or alcoholic beverages are permitted on the premises, and no reservations will be accepted for the hiker hostel. Stay is limited to one night. Not available to hikers during foliage season (usually late Sept thru mid-Oct). Stores are one mile away on U.S. 4 at Killington (see above). Ask at the desk for directions.

Notice: The A.T. no longer follows the road across the Kent Pond dam but takes a sharp right before the dam. This section is being relocated piecemeal, so watch carefully for new blazes.

Stony Brook Shelter: to the right on side trail immediately after crossing creek; easy to miss the sign if you are concentrating on crossing the stream.

The Lookout: a locked cabin with an observation platform on the roof. The cabin is private property, but a register box is provided on a tree for guests to sign. The cabin area has no water nearby.

Wintturi Shelter: off the Trail to the left, with red roof. Water source is a small spring in the rocks in front of the shelter. Flat areas for tenting are nearby.

Vt. 12: Right 3.1m—to the town of Woodstock.

♦ **Woodstock, Vt.** (pop. 1,178): *Services*—motel • b&b • restaurants • diner • Grand Union Supermarket • 18-Carrot Natural Food Store • bakery • laundromat • sporting goods store • bank • Plus • pharmacy • hardware store • department store • doctor • dentist • health clinic • veterinarian • movie theatre • UPS/FedEx pickup.

Clubnote: The next 75 miles are maintained by Dartmouth Outing Club C&T (Cabins and Trails) crews, student volunteers who are known on campus as "chubbers." Each chubber, in addition to a full academic load, works about 80 volunteer hours per year to build and maintain DOC trails in Vermont and New Hampshire.

"Tiger Paws": DOC now uses standard white blazes for the A.T., but you will still see the orange-black-orange blazes that were used for many years to mark the Trail route through DOC territory. These "tiger paws" are now used to designate winter ski trails, which criss-cross the A.T., so don't count on them to keep you on course. Follow the white blazes only.

Barnard Brook-Woodstock Stage Road: Right 1m—past Suicide Six to the crossroads community of South Pomfret.

◆ **South Pomfret, Vt.** (pop. 150): *Services*—Teago General Store: good for short-term resupply, deli section, fresh pasta salads daily, sandwiches, grinders, Ben & Jerry's, no public telephone, picnic tables on river for public use; open Mon-Sat 7am-6pm, Sun 8am-5pm. *PO-ZIP 05067:* Mon-Fri 8:30am-5:30pm, Sat 8:30am-12:30pm; 802-457-1147; LY-24.

Cloudland Shelter: now rerouted 0.5 mile off the A.T. on new side trail north of Cloudland Road, to the left. This shelter has the privy pictured in *National Geographic* magazine in 1987. Water source is the creek closest to the shelter.

White River (Vt. 14): The river attracts many area residents for swimming and tubing. Anyone foolish enough to disregard the prohibition against jumping from the bridge deserves the result.

West Hartford, Vt. (pop. 198): *Services*—West Hartford Country Store: limited hiker supplies, ice cream, sodas, snacks, deli, outside public telephone; open Mon-Sat 6am-9pm, Sun 8am-9pm. *PO-ZIP 05084:* Mon-Fri 7-11am and 1-5pm; Sat 7-10am; 802-295-6293; LY-21.

Happy Hill Cabin: oldest shelter on the A.T.; possibly leaky, but usable. Water source is small creek just before the cabin, but it isn't dependable in dry years. Used by neighbors for beer parties on occasion.

Norwich, Vt. (pop. 2,500): *Services*—Norwich Inn: $50-$99D $10EAP, 5 max; a/c, cable, phone in room, pets possible (MC, Visa, AE); restaurant in inn • The Jug Store: deli, sandwiches to go, snacks, sodas, public telephone nearby, and picnic table across parking area • Dan & Whit's General Store: where "seeing is believing." *PO-ZIP 05055:* Mon-Fri 8:30am-5pm, Sat 9am-noon; 802-649-1608; LY-20+.

Connecticut River Bridge: twelve states down, two to go. Don't get too excited, though. As a 1987 thru-hiker observed, "When you reach Hanover, you've done 80% of the miles, but you still have 50% of the work left." What do *you* say, southbounders?

HANOVER, N.H. (pop. 6,300): "the most sophisticated town on the Appalachian Trail" and home of Dartmouth College. Thru-hikers seem to love or hate this place. Some think it unfriendly and pretentious. Others relish the diversity and activity of an upscale college community. All major services needed by hikers are available in abundance, except inexpensive lodging. *Information*—Dartmouth Outing Club (603-646-2428): located in Robinson Hall on the Dartmouth Campus, a safe place to drop your pack when you get to town. Directions: Turn left at the stoplight, go to the second building on the left, look for

DOC sign out front. Maps and information about relos are available on bulletin boards in the lobby. The DOC is prevented by college rules from directing hikers to overnight lodging, but students in Room #13 generally know where thru-hikers are being put up and will pass along that information. The receptionist at the front desk has campus and town maps and can give you directions to the post office, laundromat, and places to eat. Don't forget to sign the thru-hiker register. Also, before you leave town, ask about the status of the "Atwell Hilton," located several days north of Hanover. *On-campus lodging*—Two coed "fraternity" houses, Alpha Theta and Tabard, have been taking in hikers for the past several years, either free or for a nominal overnight charge. This courtesy may or may not be extended in 1992, depending on how the members of each house vote at their spring meetings. Your best bet is to ask other thru-hikers who have stayed in Hanover about the status of these on-campus lodgings. If Alpha Theta and/or Tabard are open to hikers again this year, remember that you are a guest. If they want to stay up all night and party until dawn, that's their business. Be friendly with the students, but don't interfere with their activities. Try to avoid using showers and other facilities during busy times. Clean up the area designated for hikers, and obey the posted house rules. It also wouldn't hurt to tell the students how much thru-hikers appreciate the hospitality they provide. Donations to help with the extra expense would also be a nice gesture. Both houses are located a long block beyond DOC on N. Main Street, Alpha Theta on the right, Tabard to the left on Tuck Drive. Frats are usually closed during mid-term break from late Aug to mid-Sept. *Other lodging*—Occom Inn: $46S $52D $5.50EAP, 3max; a/c in some rooms, TV, washer/dryer, no pets (MC, Visa); reservations suggested • Hanover Inn: $154D (no, that isn't a misprint!), 4max; a/c, cable, phone in room, pool, washer/dryer, pets allowed (MC, Visa, AE, DC). *Places to eat*—Everything But Anchovies: B/L/D, student casual, pizza, inexpensive AYCE pasta special every evening (MC, Visa); open 7 days, 5am-2am; a thru-hiker favorite and EBA responds, "We love hikers!" • C&A Pizza • Lou's Restaurant & Bakery: B/L/D, 1950s-style food, ample country breakfasts, Mexican dinners, San Francisco-style superburrito, soda fountain with good milkshakes, pastries; open Mon and Wed-Sun 6am-3am, Tues 6am-midnight • Five Olde Nugget Alley: L/D, casual dining, varied menu (chicken, seafood, sirloin steak, salads, buffalo wings, BBQ ribs), pub with hundreds of beer cans on the wall and supposedly you get a free beer if you can name a brand not included in their collection (MC, Visa, AE, DC); open Mon-Sat 11:30-midnight, Sun 4:30-midnight • Peter Christian's: L/D, casual, hearty homemade soups, salads, sandwiches, fish chowder, roast beef, turkey, Mexican after 5pm on Sunday (MC, Visa, AE, Dis, DC, CB); open Mon-Sat 11:30am-12:30am, Sun 12:30pm-11:30pm • Cafe La Fraise: D, French restaurant in romantic setting, fine dining downstairs, country-casual upstairs, poached salmon a favorite (MC, Visa); open Mon-Sat 5:30-9:30pm • Deckelbaum's: L/D, casual eat-in or take-out, veggieburger, sandwiches (MC, Visa, AE, DC); open 7 days, 11am-10pm • Ben & Jerry's: the only B&J store on the A.T.; ask for a "White Blaze" • Thayer Hall: campus dining facility located behind the DOC building, a hiker favorite for breakfast. AYCE meals: breakfast 7:15-9:30am, $4.45; lunch 11:15am-2pm, $5.80; dinner 4:45-7pm, $8. Students who gain weight are kidded about putting on a "Thayer layer." *Groceries*—Hanover Consumer Co-op: considered by many thru-hikers to be the best supermarket on the Trail, good for long-term resupply, good natural-food selection; open Mon-Fri 8am-8pm, Sat until 6pm, closed Sun • Grand Union Supermarket: good for long-term resupply (MC, Visa); open 7 days, 8am-9pm • Stinson's Village Store: convenience store, good for short-term resupply, open 7 days until midnight. *Laundromat*—FLW, public telephone inside; open 7 days, 24 hrs. *Cobbler*—Hanover Luggage and

Cobbler Shop: no preferential service for thru-hikers (a very cooperative cobbler is reportedly available in nearby Lebanon). *Outfitter/Stove fuel*—The Dartmouth Co-op (603-643-3100): backpacking gear upstairs (JanSport, Kelty, Mountainsmith, Lowe, The North Face, Sierra Designs, Eureka!, Nike, Merrell, Vasque, Danner, MSR, Thermarest, ThorLo, Wigwam), Coleman by the pint, other fuels, repair parts (MC, Visa, AE); open Mon-Sat 9:30am-5:45pm, Sun 11am-4pm. *Other services*—bank • pharmacy • hardware store • department store • doctor • dentist • hospital • veterinarian • Dartmouth Bookstore: possibly the best on the A.T. • Nugget movie theatre • UPS/FedEx pick-up • Vermont Transit bus service • Amtrak (station in nearby White River Junction, Vt.) • in-town shuttle bus. *Special event*—Shriner's Parade: featuring clowns, bands, and motorized units representing "temples" from all over New England and Canada, usually held the second Sat in Aug each year. The two-hour parade is followed by a high-school football game at Dartmouth Stadium—Vermont All-Stars vs. New Hampshire All-Stars. Money raised by this event benefits children's burn hospitals and charities. *Points of interest*— Hood Museum of Art: free admission • Hopkins Center: full summer of activities, including theatrical productions, classical recitals, and rock concerts. *PO-ZIP 03755:* Mon-Fri 8:30am-5pm, Sat 8:30am-noon; 603-643-4544; LY-100+.

Velvet Rocks Shelter: marginal water source is 0.3 mile away on steep side trail. You may want to carry water from town. This shelter was first assembled on Boston Common as a DOC exhibit, then rebuilt here.

Etna-Hanover Center Road: Right 1.2m—to the village of **Etna** (pop. 200); with convenience store.

Moose Mountain Shelter: not 0.5 mile off the Trail as indicated in guides, more like 0.3 mile; limited tentsites in immediate vicinity.

Holts Ledge: a rookery for peregrine falcons, once on the A.T. but now on a short side trail. At latest count, New Hampshire had seven nesting pairs of this very endangered raptor, with one pair nesting here. Young falcons have been spotted taking their first flights from the ledges every year since 1988. They won't come back if humans intrude, however, so rejoice in the knowledge that the birds are back, and respect the signs posted on the fence above the ledge.

Trapper John Shelter: named for the "M.A.S.H." character, a fictional Dartmouth grad. Water source is creek, marginal in dry years.

Lyme-Dorchester Road: Left 4.2m—to the town of Lyme.

♦ **Lyme, N.H.** (pop. 178): *Services*—Loch Lyme Lodge and Cottages: $28S includes breakfast, numerous recreation possibilities (beach, swimming, tennis, boats, canoes, fishing, windsurfing), international college-age staff, probable ride back to Trail; operated by Paul and Judy Barker • restaurant • Lyme Country Store: limited hiker supplies, hot foods, open 7 days until 9pm • bank • hardware store • doctor • UPS/FedEx pickup • on the common, ATC regional office (603-795-4935) • shuttle-bus service to Hanover.

Smarts Mountain: topped by firetower, tent platform (the floor of the old Smarts Mountain Shelter), and old firewarden's cabin, which has a new roof and is water-tight on even the stormiest nights. Water is 200 feet down a blue-blazed trail to the Mike Murphy Spring; not dependable in dry years. If you have time, check out the Detroit-style privy at the tent platform, with one of the mountain's best views.

"McGee's Bridge": built in 1988 to provide safe passage over South Jacob's Brook. Don't drink the water straight. It comes from a beaver pond.

Hexacuba Shelter: with matching pentaprivy. Water source is the creek at the shelter turn-off sign on the A.T. This shelter was built in 1990 by a DOC cabins and trails crew. Led by physics major Jim DeCarlo, 20-30 chubbers participated in the construction. Peregrine falcons were seen on the ascent of Mt. Cube by "Weathercarrot" of '91.

N.H. 25A: Left 2m—to Mt. Cube Sugar House. *Right 2.2m*—to the community of Wentworth.

♦ Mt. Cube Sugar House: fruitstand, sodas, maple sugar delicacies, and a restaurant (breakfast only, Fri-Sun 8am-noon, July 4-Oct 15) run by a former first lady of New Hampshire, Gale Thomson, who became famous for her charity pancake breakfasts while her husband was governor. The Hiker Special (6 pancakes, 4 sausages, coffee-tea-or-milk, juice, butter, and maple syrup made from nearby trees, all for $5) is a favorite. Many feel the pancakes are the best on the Trail.
♦ Wentworth, N.H. (pop. 100): *Services*—Wentworth Inn & Gallery: $50S $60-$80D $15EAP, 4 max; cable, no pets (MC, Visa, AE, Dis, DC); possible shuttle back to A.T. • Mountain Laurel Inn: $65D ($50S for hikers Sun-Thur) $10EAP, 3 max; no pets (MC, Visa); shuttle back to A.T. • Hilltop Acres: $60D $75 (for cottage with kitchen) $10EAP, 4 max; cable, kitchen privileges, recreation room, no pets (MC, Visa); shuttle back to A.T. • Hobson House: $45S $55D $10EAP, 4max; cable, washer/dryer, possible shuttle back to Trail • Shawnee's General Store: good for short-term resupply, deli with sandwiches, some fresh produce and fruits; open Sun-Thur 6am-9pm, Fri and Sat 6am-10pm • swimming in nearby river.

N.H. 25C: Right 4m—to the little town of Warren.

♦ Warren, N.H. (pop. 450): *Services*—Moosilauke Restaurant: good food, reasonable prices • grocery store: good for short-term resupply • convenience store • laundromat • health clinic. While in town, check out the (not Samuel F. B.) Morse Museum and the incredible mystery missile (What's it doing here?).

Atwell Hill Road: Left 0.2m—*maybe*—to the "Atwell Hilton," a house that has served as summer residence for the DOC cabins and trails crew doing work in New Hampshire, but may be closed by NPS regulations this year. DOC crews are close knit and fun-loving, much like thru-hikers. A bunkroom has been reserved for thru-hikers; bunk $5 with shower (no towel), camping in a grassy area next to house $3 with shower. Meals are sometimes available with crew, $3 for breakfast, $5 for dinner. The house, if open at all, is closed from 10am-4pm while the crew is working; closes for season in late August. Water is available from a faucet on the right side of the house.

N.H. 25: Right 0.5m—to the hamlet of Glencliff. *Right 5m*—to Warren (see above). Note: Glencliff and Warren are the last convenient post offices for picking up cold-weather gear needed for going above treeline in the Whites.

♦ **GLENCLIFF, N.H.** (pop. 100): no services, except public telephone on old building adjacent to the PO driveway. *PO-ZIP 03238:* Mon-Fri 7-10am and 2-5pm, Sat 7am-1pm; 603-989-5858; LY-200+. Jack Hollinrake, who offered shuttles in past years, died last year while climbing Moosilauke.

♦ Roger's "House of Weather": the New England home of 2,000-miler Roger Brickner, the same Roger who hosted more than 1,700 thru-hikers at Roger's Appalachia Cottage in New York over the years. Now, Roger is living in a Federal-style house (circa 1810) east of Glencliff and, for the past two years, has operated a hostel in the loft of the barn attached to the house—open at no charge to thru-hikers. Mattresses are provided for sleeping, with a hot shower available in the main house. Roger prepares dinner, which is served after the MacNeil-Lehrer cocktail hour. After-dinner entertainment usually includes a briefing on the next day's weather (Roger is a weather observer and historian and wrote a fine book about the great hurricane of 1938). Downstairs in the barn is the A.T. hikers pub, surrounded by a 25-foot mural of the Trail that stood for so many years in the yard of the Appalachia Cottage. Samuel Adams faithfully stands guard over this masterpiece. You can usually get an invitation to the hostel by calling Roger (603-989-3167, 3-4pm only). He will run down and pick you up and return you the following morning after an early breakfast. The hostel will be open July 17 to Aug 25, but not at all on Wed and Sat, so don't call then. Of interest to alumni—Roger is establishing a Museum of American Weather, opening date set for July 4, 1993, and he promises a festive day, rain or shine.

Oliverian Brook: The bridge was washed away in a flood several years ago, and you may be, too, if the water is high. In that event, take the road around, going past the post office in Glencliff, then left on the first road, to the Trail.

Jeffers Brook Shelter: Water source is the creek; unusual privy takes you up, then down. Flat, straw-covered areas for tenting are near shelter.

DOC Cabin: to the left 300 feet off the Trail, just past the last paved road before you start up Moosilauke. Built by a DOC C&T crew in 1990. Do not plan to stay here, even on the porch; DOC rents the cabin. Water is available from a spring behind the cabin.

Mt. Moosilauke (4,802 feet): the first mountain on the A.T. above treeline as you head north. On a clear day, you can see five states, and the Franconia Ridge is laid out before you. A relocation between the summit and the Beaver Brook Trail is planned for 1992. Watch blazes carefully.

Alpine zone: The White Mountain National Forest is home to more than nine square miles of alpine areas (usually found above 4,000 feet), the largest alpine community in the eastern United States. These areas—many accessible from the A.T.—are some of the most delicate and easily damaged ecosystems you will encounter on your trek. Very slowly growing, alpine plants sometimes take up to 20 years to flower for the first time, and, although adapted to harsh natural conditions, they can be killed by a single boot imprint. Stay on the Trail or within "scree walls" at all times, especially above treeline.

Beaver Brook Trail: a steep descent, with some unique pinned steps on ledges, that will have your knees howling for a break. Don't let the pain dull your senses to the incredible beauty of this magnificent trail, which borders more than half a mile of cascading brook. The Dartmouth ski team reportedly runs *up* this trail as part of their training—without a pack, of course!

Beaver Brook Shelter: near a road, but no reports of problems last year. Water source is the creek. New shelter, to be built by DOC and the Appalachian Long Distance Hikers Association, will replace this one, in October 1992.

Kinsman Notch (N.H. 112): *Right 0.5m*—to Society for the Protection of New Hampshire Forests' Lost River Reservation, with visitors center and snack bar, $5 admission, open daily 9am-5:30pm, Memorial Day-Oct. *Right 5m*—to the town of North Woodstock (see Franconia Notch below for description).

Clubnote: The next 119 miles are maintained by AMC summer crews and volunteers and are managed in cooperation with ATC, USFS, the N.H. state parks agency, and others. Including the A.T., the AMC maintains more than 300 miles of trails in the Whites. Last year, three full-time crews, together with 500 volunteers and seven shelter caretakers, laid bog bridges, built steps, cleared brush, and did countless other chores to keep these trails in hikeable condition. The AMC trail programs are supported by monies generated by fees charged at other facilities, primarily huts.

White Mountains: The Whites offer some of the most majestic scenery to be seen anywhere in the world, and the days you spend here will be remembered as some of the finest of your thru-hike. You can make your transit through the Whites safer and more enjoyable by taking a few simple precautions:
• Adjust your mileage expectations downward, since the terrain is some of the most rugged to be encountered anywhere on the A.T. The notches are deep, the climbs are long, and the rocks and roots are many. Don't expect to maintain the same daily mileage that you have been doing with relative ease since Virginia.
• Pay attention to the blazes and cairns that mark the A.T. In many parts, especially above treeline, the Trail is nothing more than a slightly worn path through a field of rocks. The older regional trail names are used on signs, along with references to the A.T., so it helps to know these names and have Trail maps to help unravel any confusion at the dozens of trail junctions. Mileages on signs may be inaccurate.
• Don't underestimate the weather, because these mountains experience some of the worst in the lower 48 states. Temperatures can change rapidly, especially above treeline. Snow can occur any month of the year. Carry enough clothing to deal with severe changes in weather conditions. Remember that lightning is a real danger during summer storms, especially above treeline.
• Abide by the regulations on camping and fires, which are designed to protect the fragile alpine environment. Numerous areas in the Whites are designated "Restricted Use Area," which means that you cannot camp or build a fire above treeline or closer than 200 feet to any trail; closer than 0.25 mile to shelters, huts, and tentsites; or closer than 0.5 mile to a road. Above treeline, camping is permitted only at designated sites, and no fires are permitted. Stiff fines are handed out to violators.

• Realize that the Whites have been a heavy-use area since the 1800s, and plan to enjoy the mountains while sharing them with others (more than 1,200 miles of trails and 50 facilities attract thousands). Don't make others feel that they are intruding on your experience, and make sure that you don't intrude on theirs. Grin and bear it when DOC brings 800 freshmen on an orientation outing in early September.

AMC in the Whites: Many past thru-hikers claim that "AMC" is the abbreviation for "Appalachian Money Collectors," and there is a certain amount of truth to their wit. It is almost impossible for hikers of average ability to go through the Whites, staying on the A.T., without paying AMC camping fees of some sort (fees that go back into the AMC trails program). Two types of AMC-maintained facilities are available for use by thru-hikers: huts and campsites (both listed in the *Data Book*). If you use the hut system, the expense you incur will be considerably greater than if you use the campsites.

1) *AMC Campsites*—The AMC campsites, most with both shelters and tent platforms, are an attractive alternative to the hut system, especially in good weather, and allow you to go through the Whites with a minimum of expense. AMC has 13 A.T. sites; seven are free, but six high-use sites (15-20 people per night) have caretakers and charge $4 fees from mid-June to late September. Shelters are similar to those you have been using since the start of your trip. Tentsites usually have wooden platforms, with eyelets for tying off a tent (make sure you have enough cord); some are located adjacent to huts. In 1991, fees were charged at Liberty Spring tentsite, Garfield campsite, Guyot campsite, Nauman tentsite at Mizpah Hut, "The Dungeon" at Lakes of the Clouds Hut, and Imp campsite. Look for notices about 1992 fee locations. Shelters and tentsites are available on a first-come, first-served basis, with no reservations. Caretakers come around in the evening to sign you in and often to chat about thru-hiking and the Trail. They can also radio ahead to make reservations or check on the availability of work at huts (see below).

2) *AMC Huts*—The huts in the Whites are not the same as the huts in Shenandoah. AMC huts, some built in the 1800s, are similar to Bascom Lodge on Greylock, with lodging and meals available. Lodging consists of space in a bunkroom, with blankets (no sheets) and pillow provided. Huts have restrooms, but no showers. Breakfast and dinner (served promptly at 6pm) are available for overnight guests only. Snack foods (raisins, Hershey bars, peanut-butter cups) and drinks (hot chocolate, coffee, tea, lemonade) may be purchased by nonguests. No pets are allowed inside, and use of alcohol is discouraged. Each hut is run by a "croo," usually young collegians, and their friendliness to thru-hikers varies from hut to hut, depending on the personality of the crew and size of the hut. Also, crews, having answered 10,000 questions during the course of a summer, tend to get a little burned out at the end of the season. Reservations for overnight lodging and meals can be made as early as January (c/o Reservations, AMC Pinkham Notch Camp, P.O. Box 298Z, Gorham, N.H. 03581; 603-466-2727), but most thru-hikers who want to use huts wait until they reach Hanover or Gorham to call ahead for reservations, taking a chance there will be space available. Once in the Whites, you can also radio ahead from one hut to reserve space at another. Sometimes, if there have been cancellations, you can get space just by showing up, but don't get bent out of shape if you haven't made reservations and there is "no room at the inn." As a special courtesy, AMC offers member rates to A.T. thru-hikers for lodging and meals at huts.

• Full-service member rates: lodging, breakfast, and dinner, $47; lodging and dinner, $41; lodging and breakfast, $37; at least one meal must be taken with lodging. Credit cards and personal checks are accepted. All huts will operate full-service from May

30-Labor Day in 1992. Several huts operate full-service after Labor Day (check with AMC for exact information, 603-466-2727).

• Self-service member rates: $10 for bunk space, but guests must provide their own sleeping gear and food. In spring and fall, most huts will be open on a self-service, caretaker basis (dates for each hut vary; check with AMC for exact information).

• Work option: Thru-hikers can often exchange work for lodging and meals, at the discretion of the crew. If you want to try the work option, arrive before 5pm, and be prepared to leave late the next morning. A crew will often radio ahead to arrange work for you at the next hut, if you've done a good job at its hut. "Lentil Ben" of '91 observed, "The key to working your way through the huts is to recognize that, if you don't get a good deal at one hut, you may well get a good deal at the next one. Try to understand the point of view of the college-aged croo, and keep a sense of humor." Most huts can accomodate 1 or 2 thru-hikers a night.

AMC Shuttle: The AMC Hiker Shuttle operates from May 30 to Labor Day in 1992. Stops include Franconia Notch, Crawford Notch Visitor Center, Pinkham Notch Camp, and Gorham. Rates are $5-12, depending on where you are going. Call for schedule information and rates (603-466-2727).

Suggestions: AMC is seeking to improve its service to thru-hikers. You can share suggestions and complaints by writing to Reuben Rajala, AMC Trails Director, P.O. Box 298, Gorham, N.H. 03581. Reuben is a member of the ATC Board of Managers and is a long-time friend of thru-hikers. He can also tell you about ways to get involved in AMC's volunteer trails programs.

Kinsman Notch to Eliza Brook Shelter: a rugged little section that is at least a mile longer than any of the signs or guidebooks suggest. Allow extra time to cross this section.

Eliza Brook Shelter: located next to a bubbling brook with places to take a cold dip; privy located behind shelter; flat tenting area available. No fee.

Kinsman Mountain: the first real climb in quite a while, hand-over-hand scrambling, thoroughly enjoyed by most thru-hikers who climb it on a beautiful day (views from the top make all the effort worth it) but cursed by those who climb in the rain.

Kinsman Pond Campsite: shelter, tent platforms; no fee. Water from the pond should be purified. Believe me, you don't want to know why!

Lonesome Lake Hut: the first AMC hut for northbounders, and the first place you can radio ahead to make hut reservations. The lake has a dock for swimming and sunning. The view across the lake is one of the most scenic in the Whites.

Franconia Notch (U.S. 3): *Left 2.5m*—to Lafayette Campground. *Right 2m*—to The Whale's Tale. *Right 5.8m*—to the small tourist town of North Woodstock. *Right 4.5m*—on U.S. 3, then left two miles on U.S. 3A (first left past Clarke's Trading Post) to Lincoln. Note: North Woodstock and Lincoln are separated by only a mile, and thus function as one community.

♦ Lafayette Campground: tentsites $12 (2 people), pay showers, restrooms, and a small camp store with very limited supplies (bread, milk, cheese, sodas, ice cream, snacks).

♦ The Whale's Tale: water park with wave pool generating ocean-sized breakers, water slides, snack bar, and changing rooms with showers, $14 admission.

♦ **NORTH WOODSTOCK, N.H.** (pop. 1,167): *Lodging*—Cascade Lodge B&B: $18.50 per person includes a large breakfast, $16.50 without breakfast, pets outside, homey atmosphere, big front porch. The lodge is owned by friendly Betty and Bill Robinson, who have entertained hundreds of hikers since they moved from Massachusetts in 1983. Both know the hiking scene in the Whites extremely well and can plan a slackpack better than most thru-hikers. They sell Coleman by the pint and give rides to and from the Trail for $2 per person each way. AE cards honored *Other services*—IGA Foodliner: good for long-term resupply; open Mon-Sat 9am-9pm, Sun 10am-7pm • Wayne's Market & Deli: neighborhood store, good for long-term resupply, deli with grinders to go; open 7 days, 7am-10:30pm • Half-Baked: heat-and-eat food shop • The Chalet Restaurant: L/D, lobster, steaks, prime rib; open 7 days, 11:30am-9pm • Peg's Place: specializing in breakfast served all day; open 7 days, 5:30am-2:30pm • Landmark II Family Restaurant: B/L/D, specials every night • Truant's Taverne: L/D, casual, sandwiches and fine dinners; open 7 days after 11:30am • Govani's Italian Restaurant (on Rt. 112): D, northern-Italian specialties, open 4:30-9pm • Woodstock Station: B/L/D, casual dining on patio, fine dining inside • Hilliards Candyland & Ice Cream • Woodstock Wash Works: FLW, 24-hour laundromat • Davis Country Store (True Value Hardware) • UPS/FedEx pick-up • Concord Trailways bus service • stretch limousine service (Ride back to the A.T. in $tyle!) • concerts on the common, June-Aug. *PO-ZIP 03262*: Mon-Fri 8am-12:30pm and 1:30-5pm, Sat 8am-noon; 603-745-8134; LY-50.

♦ Lincoln, N.H. (pop. 950): *Services*—numerous motels and restaurants • McDonald's • Grand Union supermarket • Deke's Sport Shop: some hiking gear • North Face backpacking shop • Timberland Boots: factory outlet at the Depot • bank • Cirrus, MAC, Pocketbank • J&J Hardware • doctor • dentist • medical clinic • pharmacy • bookstore • movie theatre • Hobo Railroad: 15-mile scenic train ride along the Pemigewasset River, $6 round-trip.

Liberty Spring Tentsite: with tent platforms. Very cold spring at the tentsite is a welcome thirst-quencher after the climb; caretaker and $4 overnight fee. The summit of Liberty Mountain, 0.6 mile above the tentsite on a side trail, offers spectacular views and sunsets.

Franconia Range: mostly above treeline, which is at about 4,000 feet in the Whites. This range is considered by many to be the single most scenic section on the entire A.T. Some of the mountains crossed are Liberty (on side trail, 4,459 feet), Little Haystack (4,760 feet), Lincoln (5,089 feet), Lafayette (5,249 feet), Garfield (4,488 feet), South Twin (4,902 feet), and Guyot (4,560 feet). The distances between these peaks will fool you.

Garfield Ridge Campsite: shelter and tent platforms on 100-yard side trail. Water source is spring on A.T., so carry water in to save a few steps. Caretaker and $4 overnight fee.

Galehead Hut: one of the smallest and most isolated huts in the system. It usually has a very laid-back crew friendly to thru-hikers and is probably the easiest place to get bunk space and meals without reservations.

Wildlife: *Bald eagles are increasing in the Northeast, and you will have no trouble identifying this large bird should you see one. Its white head will be unmistakable, even from a distance. Bald eagles eat small mammals, waterfowl, and carrion, but they are not particularly good at catching fish, preferring to feed primarily on dead fish near the shores of lakes and rivers. The male has a high, clear "cac-cac-cac" call. Young bald eagles look like golden eagles.*

Guyot Campsite: Shelter and tent platforms, off A.T. about 0.7 mile on side trail, with cold spring and excellent sunrises. Caretaker and $4 overnight fee.

Zealand Falls Hut: located next to a beautiful, cascading stream. The falls are a great place for a lunch break.

Ethan Pond campsite: shelter and tent platforms. Best to treat the water, since testing has been inconclusive. Moose were spotted in the lake on numerous occasions last year. Tamarack (Eastern larch) trees line the shore. No fee last year.

Crawford Notch (U.S. 302): *Left 1m*—to Willey House. *Left 3.7m*—to Shapleigh Hostel. *Right 1.5m*—to Dry River Campground.

♦ Willey House: snack bar (coffee, donuts, ice cream, hot dogs); open 7 days, 9am-5pm, mid-May thru mid-Oct. Outside public telephone.
♦ Shapleigh Hostel: open year-round with caretaker, bunks, showers, public telephone; $15 per night. Be prepared for a steep walk up from the Trail.
♦ Dry River Campground: tentsites for $12 (2 people) $6EAP, privy, no showers.

Presidential Range: The 25-mile section between Crawford Notch and Pinkham Notch is mostly above treeline. Some of the mountains are Mt. Webster (3,910 feet), Mt. Jackson (4,052 feet), Mt. Pierce (formerly Mt. Clinton, 4,310 feet), Mt. Eisenhower (4,761 feet), Mt. Franklin (5,004 feet), Mt. Washington (6,288 feet) and Mt. Madison (5,363 feet). The Presidentials are absolutely breathtaking on a sunny day, but use care when going across this section in bad weather. Don't be reluctant to leave the ridge for cover if the weather takes a sudden turn for the worse, especially if lightning is occurring nearby. By the way, I don't remember Presidents Webster or Franklin.

Webster Cliffs: outstanding views back to Crawford Notch, but tricky on windy, rainy days.

Mizpah Hut and Nauman Tentsite: one of the classiest AMC buildings in the Whites, with an experimental solar power system. AYCE soup for lunch is usually available here for $2, but not every day. Nauman tentsite with privy is nearby in the trees; $4 fee. From just beyond here to north of Mt. Madison, the Trail is always above treeline.

Lakes of the Clouds: called "Lakes of the Crowds" by those who frequent the Whites because of its large size (up to 90 guests) and easy access from the summit of Mt. Washington. A small room in the basement, called "The Dungeon," has bunk space for eight hikers, limited space for their gear. Thru-hikers can radio ahead and reserve a basement bunk space, but no sooner than 48 hours in advance. Cost is $6 per night. Staying in the basement has become a thru-hiker tradition. Dungeon-dwellers may use the facilities upstairs and mingle with other hut guests.

Mt. Washington (6,288 feet): the highest peak in New England and the mountain proposed by Benton MacKaye in 1921 as the northern terminus of the Appalachian Trail. The summit, mostly a New Hampshire state park, has a variety of buildings, including a weather station that once clocked the highest surface wind speed ever recorded on Earth (231 mph) and the Sherman Adams Summit House, open daily 8am-8pm (Memorial Day-Columbus Day), with a post office (Mt. Washington, N.H. 03589), snack bar, backpacker room, and museum. The post-office hours depend on access to the summit by the postmaster, but the ranger at the desk has a key and will let you retrieve mail even if the postmaster isn't on duty. The snack bar is open daily 9am-6pm, if weather permits workers to ride to the summit, and has a variety of pastries, sandwiches, bagels with cream cheese, and beverages. The backpacker room is for sorting and drying gear only, since absolutely no hiker is allowed to stay overnight on the summit. The museum is open daily, $5 admission. Public telephones and restrooms are available in the lobby. No pets or smoking are permitted in the building. Also on the summit are the ends of the Cog Railway (oldest such railway in the world; $25 one-way last year) and the Auto Road (for vehicles only, no hitchhiking, but one-way tickets on the Mt. Washington Stagecoach, a shuttle service, are available).

Tuckerman Ravine Trail: the very steep route from Washington's summit that lets you bypass the Gulfside/Osgood trails around the northern Presidentials. The blue-blazed trail descends to Pinkham Notch, passing a short side trail to Hermit Lake Campground, with shelters and tentsites, caretaker, and $6 fee.

Madison Loop: the name given to the section of Trail between the summits of Mt. Washington and Mt. Madison (look at your map and you'll see why). The entire section is above treeline and exposed to the elements. Magnificent on a sunny day, it could be dangerous in a thunderstorm or in snow. Should you need to find shelter below treeline for the night, several facilities operated by the Randolph Mountain Club are available. RMC's Gray Knob and Crag Camp are enclosed lodges similar to AMC huts but have a caretaker instead of a crew and serve no meals; cost for each is $7 per night. The Perch is a shelter; cost, $3 per night. All are located about one mile off the A.T. (take Gulfside Trail to the left) and are shown on your A.T. maps. AMC's Madison Springs Hut is also on this route.

Osgood Tentsite: USFS facility with tent platforms, water from spring. No fee.

Pinkham Notch (N.H. 16): *On A.T.*—Pinkham Notch Camp (see below). *Left 4m*—to Camp Dodge. *Left 12m*—to the town of Gorham (see U.S. 2 below). *Right 17m*—to the town of North Conway.

♦ Camp Dodge (603-466-9469): home for the AMC volunteer trail crews from May until September. Thru-hikers are invited to join a crew for a day of work (usually in camp) in exchange for lodging, hot shower, laundromat, and perhaps meals. But, call Camp Dodge in advance to make arrangements; don't just show up.
♦ North Conway, N.H. (pop. 4,000): *Services*—numerous motels and restaurants • Sunnyside Inn: $28S $40-$60D $15EAP, 4 max; cable, use of refrigerator, dryer (MC,

Visa); shuttle back to Trail • McDonald's • Burger King • Friendly's • Pizza Hut • supermarket: good for long-term resupply • laundromat • cobbler • L. L. Bean outlet store • Eastern Mountain Sports (603-356-5433): gear (JanSport, Kelty, Mountainsmith, Lowe, The North Face, Sierra Designs, Eureka!, Moss, Hi-Tec Sports, Asolo, Tecnica, Merrell, Vasque, MSR, Peak 1, Caribou, Thermarest, Katadyn, First-Need), Coleman by the quart, other fuels, repair services (MC, Visa, AE); open Mon-Sat 9am-9pm, Sun 9am-6pm • drugstore • hospital • International Mountain Equipment (603-356-7013) • Chuck Roast: clothing and packs. On the outskirts of town is the small community of Intervale, home of the Limmer Boot Shop (603-356-5378), makers of custom leather boots; also Ragged Mountain Equipment (603-356-3042).

Pinkham Notch Camp: AMC's headquarters in the Whites and a year-round full-service lodge with rooms, cafeteria, camp store, and showers. Dormitory-style rooms have four built-in bunk beds (you may have to share a room with strangers) and come with blankets, sheets, pillows, and towels. Showers and restrooms are located down the hall. Lodging must include one meal, either a buffet breakfast (served 6:45-8am) or family-style dinner (served promptly at 6pm). Rates for 1992 are: lodging, breakfast, and dinner, $38; lodging and dinner, $33; lodging and breakfast, $28. Meals can be purchased by nonguests: breakfast $5; dinner $10, reservations recommended. AYCE buffet lunches are usually available in the summer without reservations for $3.50. The camp store has snacks, hot coffee, tea, and some hiking items (socks, guidebooks, maps, *etc.*) on sale. Coin-operated hot showers are available for public use; towel and change available at the front desk in the main lodge building. Pets and smoking are prohibited in the buildings. Concord Trailways provides daily bus service to and from Boston. Note: Thru-hikers may be able to exchange work for meals and space in a platform tent (maximum 4 thru-hikers, preference given to those who call or write ahead). If no work is available, camping is permitted in the Notch outside the Cutler River drainage, 0.25 mile south of the camp, and 200 feet off the Trail.

Wildcat Mountain: steep climb with wonderful views of the Presidential range above and Pinkham Notch Camp below. Gondola ride to the summit open during the summer, daily from 10am-4pm; $3.50 one way, $7 round-trip.

> Wildlife: *Spruce grouse are also called "fool hens," and, when you encounter one, you will understand why. These gray, speckled, chicken-like birds show absolutely no fear of man. Not surprisingly, they are a protected species. Spruce grouse eat the needles and buds of ever-greens, which probably explains why they don't taste very good when cooked. They range from Vermont to Maine on the A.T.*

Carter Notch Hut: one of the oldest huts in the AMC system, situated near two beautiful ponds. Because of its remote location, this hut usually has a very mellow crew and hiking-oriented guests. Look for the signatures of Earl Shaffer and "Grandma" Gatewood in the 1948 and 1957 registers, although a vandal seems to have removed the signature of "Grandma" from the 1955 book.

Imp Campsite: shelter and tent platforms, privy; caretaker and $4 overnight fee.

Carter-Moriah Trail: a blue-blazed side trail that leads directly into the town of Gorham. No hiker reports in 1991.

Rattle River Shelter: near stream with several excellent pools for "swimming."

U.S. 2: Left 3.6m—to the town of Gorham.

♦ **GORHAM, N.H.** (pop. 3,322): a small, compact tourist town with most of the services needed by thru-hikers. *Hostel*—"The Barn," adjacent to the Gorham House Inn (55 Main St., Gorham, N.H. 03581; 603-466-2271), owned by Ron and Maggie Orso, who moved here from Boston and became innkeepers "to have a simpler life." They opened the barn to hikers in 1986 and have since had hundreds of thru-hikers as guests. Hikers stay in the upstairs loft of the barn, which has mattresses on the floor for sleeping, electric lights, refrigerator, soda machine, and kitchen privileges by arrangement, all for $7 per night. A shower with towel and soap is $3 extra. Ron and Maggie are very in tune with the thru-hiking scene and go out of their way to make hikers feel comfortable. In Maggie's words, "We enjoy the hikers very much. They are such a diverse group of people, and we respect the drive they all have to do the long trek they do." Nevertheless, remember that this is an inn first and foremost. Do not disturb the regular inn customers. Avoid congregating in front of the barn (a group of grubby thru-hikers, no matter how well-behaved, can scare off tourists looking for the charm of a New England b&b). Obey the few house rules, which are posted in the barn. Hikers are also invited to stay in the inn as regular guests: $35S $25DO, breakfast included. Shuttles to nearby trailheads are available by arrangement. On Saturday, hikers can catch a ride to Boston with Maggie for $15 one way. *Other lodging*—Berkshire Manor: $20S $30D $15EAP, 4 max; kitchen, television room, shared bath, pets outside, possible shuttle back to Trail, owned by Alice Turgeon • Tourist Village Motel: $35-$45S $45-$58D $5EAP, 4 max; a/c, cable, phone in room, pool, pets allowed (MC, Visa, AE, Dis, AE, DC). *Places to eat*—Salidino's Italian Restaurant: L/D, casual, fine dining, pasta dinners, stuffed shrimp, homemade breads (MC, Visa); open 11am-9pm, closed Sun • Ruel's Seafood Restaurant: L/D, casual, fine dining, seafood, steaks, chops, prime rib, lobster, sandwiches (MC, Visa); open 7 days, 11am-9pm • Fred & Betty's (on Rt. 16 near Gorham House Inn): L/D, casual, eat-in or take-out, inexpensive home-cooked meals, seafood, subs, sandwiches; open Wed-Mon 11am-8pm, closed Tues • Wilfred's: B/L/D, turkey and dressing, steaks, seafood • Welsh's Restaurant: B/L/D, fresh donuts every morning, unbelievable cinnamon swirls on occasion, American fare (MC, Visa); open Sun-Mon 6:30am-2pm, Tues-Sat 5:30am-9pm • Mr. Pizza: L/D, casual, inexpensive Italian meals, seafood, pizza, subs (MC, Visa); open 7 days, 11am-11pm • The Cafe: L/D, casual, fine dining, maple baked pork chops, maple B-B-Q chicken (MC, Visa) • Yokohama Restaurant: fine oriental dining • McDonald's • Burger King • Subway. *Groceries*—Kelley's Supermarket: good for long-term resupply, deli; open 7 days • several convenience stores. *Laundromat*—Gorham Wash 'n Go: FLW, last load 9pm. *Outfitter/Stove fuel*—Gorham Hardware Store & Sports Center: some gear (JanSport, Camp Trails, Eureka!, Hi-Tec, MSR, Optimus/Svea, Thermarest, Wigwam), Coleman by the pint, repair service for MSR, maps and guidebooks. *Other services*—bank • pharmacy • doctor • dentist • health clinic • veterinarian • FedEx pick-up. *Points of interest*—Railroad Museum • Flea Market with good used clothing and wool sweaters. *Transportation*—Concord Trailways bus service available to and from Boston • AMC

Hiker Shuttle picks up in town. *PO-ZIP 03581:* Mon-Fri 8:30am-5pm, Sat 8am-noon; 603-466-2182; LY-340. *Nearby town*—Berlin (10 miles north on N.H. 16).

♦ **Berlin, N.H.** (pop. 13,084): *Services*—motels • hotel • restaurants • KFC • supermarket • bakery • laundromat • sporting goods store • cobbler (Moran Shoe Store on Main St.) • bank • Western Union • pharmacy • hardware store • department store • doctor • dentist • hospital • veterinarian • movie theatre.

Mahoosuc Trail: begins at the railroad trestle one mile north of Gorham, intersects A.T. (Centennial Trail junction) atop Mt. Hayes.

Trident Col Tentsite: tent pads only; no fee.

Gentian Pond Campsite: shelter and tent platforms, experimental solar privy nicknamed "The Throne." Get water from the small stream with log footbridge just before the shelter.

Maine

This chapter takes you from the New Hampshire-Maine line to Katahdin, and corresponds to *Data Book* chapter one.

Gorham to Stratton: the toughest section on the Trail. Low-teen days are in order through these mountains. If it's rainy, you'll be slowed down even more by boggy areas, wet roots, and slippery rocks. Despite the strenuous terrain, the miles ahead are considered by past thru-hikers to be some of the most enjoyable of the entire trip. The Maine woods will begin to work their magic as you head north.

Notice: The Trail in Maine crosses many bogs, some several feet deep. These alpine bogs are some of the most fragile habitat along the A.T. and easily deteriorate with abuse. For your own safety and for the protection of these unique areas, try to stay on the bog bridges, even when they are in poor shape. Bog bridges in Maine rot very quickly, and clubs have a hard time keeping them usable. AMC and the state of Maine recently installed hundreds of cedar walkways that should last longer.

Carlo Col Shelter: on 0.3-mile side trail to the left; water source is spring. No fee.

Goose Eye Mountain: side trail 0.1 mile left leads to the summit, with a panoramic view of the nearby mountains and the unbroken northern woods.

> Wildlife: *Red squirrels are smaller, reddish-colored versions of the gray squirrel. You will hear them before you see them. The harsh, strident call of this rodent has been likened to the opening of several rusty-hinged doors all at once. They inhabit coniferous forests at higher elevations and can be seen cutting cones from the tops of spruce and other evergreens to cache for winter. They also eat buds, sap, bird eggs, nestlings, and gorp, if you leave it unprotected.*

Full Goose Shelter: the site of many a horror story about "The Notch." Groups that have just gone through the notch delight in trying to scare the wits out of those poised to go through the next morning, and they usually succeed. No fee.

Mahoosuc Notch: You've been worrying about this magnificent jumble of rocks for days, and now you must go through it to get to Katahdin. Try to go through with a small group if you can. You'll have a much better time, and you'll have someone to take your picture when you're squirming under those house-sized boulders. Be careful on mossy or muddy patches. This isn't the place to have a bad fall. Toward the east end, when you hear the stream below, look for year-round ice in the lower crevices. A flat area for camping is located 0.2 mile north of the notch. If nothing else, take a break here before you climb up Mahoosuc Arm, which is steep.

Speck Pond Campsite: shelter and tent platforms. Beautiful, shallow alpine pond is the highest in Maine, has occasional moose visits. Caretaker and $4 overnight fee.

Grafton Notch (Maine 26): *On A.T.*—parking area with privy. *Right 12m*—to Bear River Grocery & Cabins (store has limited supplies; open Sun-Thur 6am-6pm, Fri and Sat 6am-7pm; cabins $45 per night). At intersection, 5 miles right on U.S. 2 to the town of Bethel.

◆ **Bethel, Maine** (pop. 1,225): *Services*—Chapman Inn (207-824-2657): hiker dorm with single and double beds, hot shower, private sauna, kitchen facilities, full breakfast, all for $16.50 per person; laundry privileges and shuttle to and from Trail are negotiable; Sandra and George Wight, innkeepers • Bethel Spa Motel: $28S $36-$38D $48(3 people) $52 (4 people); a/c, cable, phone in room (MC, Visa, AE) • Carmela's: B/L/D, casual, breakfast available anytime, pizza, subs, chicken and fish dinners, salads; open Mon-Thur 7am-10pm, Fri-Sun 7am-11pm • Skidder's Deli: take-out, sandwiches (Philly, Italian, Reuben, Chicken Parm, Steak Bomb, Baby Back Ribs, *etc.*), meats, cheese, breads; open Mon-Sat 10am-6pm, Sun 10am-3pm • ice-cream parlor • IGA Supermarket: good for long-term resupply; open Mon-Sat 8am-8pm, Sun 9am-6pm • bakery • laundromat • True North Adventurers: outfitter with clothing, some small backpacking accessories (no boots) • bank • Plus, Anytime Money • Prim's Pharmacy with Western Union • Brooks Bros. Hardware Store (hardware cloth suits?) • doctor • dentist • health clinic • veterinarian • UPS/FedEx pick-up. *PO-ZIP 04217:* Mon-Fri 9am-5pm, Sat 10am-12:30pm; LY-21.

Clubnote: The next 260 miles to Katahdin are maintained by Maine A.T. Club volunteers. These busy folks have relocated more than 190 miles of Trail and built nine new shelters in the past ten years, a monumental effort considering the terrain and the small size of the club. Thanks, MATC.

Grafton Notch Lean-to: off the A.T. to the left about 0.1 mile, next to waterfall and stream that serves as the water source. Excellent pools for taking a dip. Privy 200 feet in front of shelter.

Baldplate Mountain: interesting series of natural steps to reach the summit, can be ethereal on a foggy day. North of the summit is the "Ohthereitis ladder," one rung too short to be of much help to regular-sized northbounders. In fact, it can be dangerous. Best to lower your pack first, then scramble around through the bushes.

Frye Notch Lean-to: Water source is brook in front of shelter.

Dunn Notch Falls: beautiful waterfall spilling into a narrow canyon, great place for a lunch break. No camping is permitted in the area.

> Wildlife: *Snowshoe hares are similar to the eastern cottontail in appearance and size but have very large hind feet. In the winter, these feet develop huge fur pads that allow the animal to run on top of snow. Hares change color twice a year, in March to brown and in September to white. The process takes about three months, so you will probably see these rodents in mixed colors. Snowshoe hares range from North Carolina to Maine on the A.T.*

East B Hill Road: Right 8m—to the little community of Andover. A word of advice: You may have to wait for a ride, possibly an hour or more, but it sure beats walking into town.

♦ **ANDOVER, MAINE** (pop. 900): *Hostel/B&B*—"Wade's Loft," in the barn behind the Andover Arms Family-style B&B (Newton St.), Andover, Maine 04216; 207-392-4251), owned by ATC members Larry and Pat Wyman, who have been welcoming thru-hikers for the past four years. The barn is similar to the one at Gorham House Inn, with plenty of space to spread out. It has beds, sofa, writing table, rocking chairs, electric lights, and unlimited showers or baths with towel provided, all for $15 per night. No smoking or cooking is permitted in the barn, but kitchen privileges are included with all forms of stay. Camping in the yard, with bath, is $6.50. The b&b in the main house features private rooms with shared bath; $35S $25DO $15EAP; private bath $65D. Reservations are recommended, but no deposit is required of ATC members. Breakfast is available for $5. Laundry with soap is $2, dryer $1.50, or use the clothesline free. Larry has a small store with hiker items and Coleman by the pint. A VCR is available for those who wish to rent movies (Larry or Pat provides the popcorn). Other diversions: horseshoes, badminton, volleyball, lawn bowling, evening excursions to a local swimming hole on occasion, and target shooting. Well-behaved pets are welcome. Will hold mail or UPS packages for guests free of charge ($5 handling charge for nonguests). All facilities (shower, laundry, *etc.*) are for guests only. Shuttle back to Trail for a nominal fee; same for slackpacking. Credit cards (MC, Visa, Dis,) for b&b only. 10% discount for showing your ATC or AARP membership card. Thru-hikers can sometimes exchange work for lodging and meals. "Doc" of '90 said, "This was my favorite hostel. Pat and Larry know how to make anyone feel at home." *Other lodging*—Pine Ellis Lodging (Pine St., Andover, Maine 04216; 207-392-4161), owned by Paul and Ilene Trainor. Opened to hikers in 1990, this b&b features a family atmosphere with three upstairs rooms with shared baths (tubs and showers); $17.50 with hearty breakfast (discount rate for hikers willing to share room). Private rooms are available at slightly higher cost. Guests have full use of the house with VCR, books, smoking area downstairs, screened porch, and large yard. Kitchen privileges are included, and a BBQ grill is available for use by guests. Dinner is usually available, $5-8 depending on menu. Breakfast only $5. Shower only $2.50. Laundry is $1.50 wash, $1 dry, with clothesline free outside. Tentsites in yard $4 per person. Coleman available by the pint. Will hold mail and UPS packages. Ride back to Trail, $5. Shuttle to other points, including **Rumford** (with supermarket, bank, cobbler), by arrangement. Shuttle for slackpacking with two night's stay, $5 per person. The Trainors also have a campground on the Ellis River, three miles from their b&b. Hikers can rent a cabin for $25 per day, tentsites for $10. The rustic cabin sleeps several in the loft and has water and cooking facilities available. Price for both cabin and tentsites includes free shuttle to and from the b&b. "Kansas Kids" of '90 said, "Paul and Ilene were great hosts." *Places to eat*—The Andover Lunch Restaurant: B/L/D, known locally as "Addie's Place," the town's unofficial community center; open Mon-Sat 5am-4:30pm, closed Sun. Addie started the restaurant in 1964 and has been going strong since. As Addie says, "I have never taken a vacation, because I'm too happy doing what I'm doing." What she does very well is bake pies. Specialties include blueberry, banana cream, strawberry-rhubarb, cherry, and peanut-butter pies, $1 per slice. She also has big cheeseburgers, fries, and other diner-type foods. • Dave's General Store & Grill: "fresh dough" pizza, sandwiches, subs, fried chicken, burgers; open Mon-Sat 5am-11pm, Sun 6am-11pm • Aker's General Store: deli, sandwiches; open Mon-Sat 5:30am-9pm, Sun 8am-9pm. *Groceries*—Mills Market: groceries, meats, fruit, produce, toiletries, Ben & Jerry's, good hiker supplies, owned by friendly Roger Mills; open 7 days, 6am-10pm • Dave's General Store: limited groceries • Aker's General Store: limited groceries, some hardware items. Note: All stores together can be considered good for long-term resupply. *Other services*—Outside public telephone at Mills Market • UPS at Mills Market (will take packages 7 days a week) • Western Maine Transportation Service: bus to Rumford on Wed (catch in front of Elderwood Manor), $4 last year. *PO-ZIP 04216:* Mon-Fri 8:30am-1:30pm and 2-4:45pm, Sat 9am-12:45pm; 207-392-4571; LY-60+.

Surplus Pond: unofficial camping area on far side of pond, piped spring (not checked by MATC) 200 feet to the left on gravel road just past the pond. No fires.

Hall Mountain Lean-to: water from small spring south of shelter; privy north.

Moody Mountain: reroute over top of mountain removes arduous descent and ascent, affords some spectacular views.

South Arm Road: Right 9m—to Andover (see above). *Left 4.5m*—to South Arm Campground on Mooselookmeguntic Lake (now you know the answer to the question, "How do moose look?"). Stiff climb just ahead.

♦ South Arm Campground: tentsites $11-19 per family, campstore with limited supplies, showers for 25¢, laundromat, canoes, and boat rental, open May 15-Sept 22.

> Wildlife: *Lynx are among the shyest and most elusive creatures in the woods, and their range on the A.T. is limited to northern Maine. Consequently, very few hikers have seen one on the Trail. They look similar to the bobcat but are lighter, grayish-tan in color and have tufted ears. Lynx feed almost exclusively on snowshoe hares, and their numbers follow the 10-year cycle of the hare population up and down.*

Bemis Mountain Lean-to: water from a small spring to the left looking into the shelter. This fine shelter, new in 1989, is a good example of the type being built with increasing frequency by MATC. A red fox visited the shelter around dusk in 1991.

Bemis Stream: old bridge washed out years ago; unofficial campsites (fires prohibited) to the left of Trail on the north side of stream. Trail scheduled for relocation in 1992.

Maine 17: Left 13m—to the small lake-front community of Oquossoc.

♦ **Oquossoc, Maine** (pop. 350): *Lodging*—Horsefeather Inn B&B (P.O. Box 391, Oquossoc, Maine 04964; 207-864-5465), owned by Mac and Joann Macdonald. The inn offers home-style accommodations for $22.50 per person, which includes shared room with linens, blankets, hot shower or tub, detergent, fabric softener, use of charcoal grill, use of fishing gear, refrigerator, microwave, big breakfast, and ride back to the Trail (either Rt. 4 or Rt. 17) around 10am. Private rooms are available at slightly higher rate. MC, Visa cards accepted. Will hold UPS and mail packages. Coleman for sale by the pint. Shuttles to other locations by arrangement. Slackpacking shuttle between Rt. 17 and Rt. 4 available with two-night stay. Mac will pick hikers up in Rangeley (six miles east of

Oquossoc), free of charge with overnight stay. • *Other services*—restaurant • grocery store with limited hiker supplies • laundromat • public telephone.

Sabbath Day Pond Lean-to: scenic pond with resident moose that splashes around at night. Water source is the pond. This is always a good place to listen to loons if the moose doesn't scare them away. Swimming beach is 0.4 mile south on Long Pond.

> Wildlife: *Moose are considered ugly by many—"a horse designed by a committee," as the old joke goes—but they are truly majestic animals when seen in their natural habitat. They eat aquatic plants and are often seen browsing in the shallows of lakes and ponds. They also eat dry shoots and twigs. Moose are the largest member of the deer family, and big bulls can weigh 1,400-1,500 pounds. In case you haven't guessed, those neat little piles of brown nuggets you see along the Trail are moose droppings. A well-fed moose can create 100,000 nuggets a year. Moose sometimes wander as far south as Massachusetts but are usually seen only in upper New England on the A.T.*

Little Swift River Pond Campsite: popular with college outing groups, has water and privy. As many as seven moose have been seen in the shallows of this pond at one time. If you still haven't seen a moose, keep your eyes open. Several thousand are between you and Katahdin.

Maine 4: Left 9m—to the tourist town of Rangeley.

♦ **RANGELEY, MAINE** (pop. 1,400): once rated the 50th best vacation spot in America by Rand McNally. *Lodging*—Rangeley Inn: $52DO • Saddleback Motor Inn: $40S $48D $5EAP, 4 max; cable, refrigerator in some units, pets allowed (MC, Visa, AE) • Farmhouse Inn: $18S • Horsefeather Inn B&B: Mac Macdonald of nearby Oquossoc will pick up hikers in Rangeley at no charge (see above). *Places to eat*—Doc Grant's Restaurant: B/L/D, good pancake breakfast • Moosefeather's Restaurant: B/L/D, casual, B.B. pancakes, omelets, basil chicken sandwich, smoked turkey, seafood dinners, daily specials (MC, Visa); open 7 days, 8am-10pm (July and Aug), closed Tues-Wed other months • People's Choice Restaurant & Lounge: B/L/D, country-casual, varied menu (prime rib, seafood, chicken pot pie), dancing, live music on weekends (MC, Visa, AE); open 6am-9pm • Red Onion Restaurant: L/D, semi-Italian menu, pizza, pasta dishes, sandwiches, burgers, chili; open 7 days, 11am-9:30pm • Mike's Sports Pub: bar food • Rangeley Inn Restaurant: B/L/D, casual, fine dining • Pine Tree Frosty: ice cream. *Groceries*—Taylor's IGA: good for long-term resupply; open 7 days, 8am-9pm (July 1-Sept 1), 8am-6pm rest of year • Rangeley Foodland: good for long-term resupply, Ben & Jerry's; open 7 days, 7am-7pm (Memorial Day-Labor Day), 8am-6pm rest of year • bakery. *Other services*—laundromat: no change or detergent on premises • Alpine Garden Ski Shop: small items (stuff sacks, fuel bottles, repair kits, shoe goop, socks, gloves, tevas), clothing (MC, Visa, AE); open 7 days • Rangeley Sport Shop (207-864-5615): Coleman by the pint, butane canisters, socks, polypro underwear, water filters, and trail guides; open Mon-Fri 7am-5pm, Sat 6am-5pm, Sun 8am-1pm • bank • Plus • Western Union (at Mountain View ERA) • pharmacy • hardware store • doctor • dentist • swimming in Rangeley Lake at the community area near the Visitor Information Center • UPS pickup • airport •

Friendly Jim Spunt at Tack "N" Sew has repaired many a frayed pack. *PO-ZIP 04970:* Mon-Fri 8am-5pm, Sat 8am-noon; 207-864-2233; LY-180.

Piazza Rock Lean-to: one of the older shelters on the A.T., built by CCC workers in 1935. Water from stream. Privy, tentsites. Short side trail leads to Piazza Rock.

Eddy Pond: unofficial, fishermen's campsites and piped spring on north side of gravel road, to the right in small dip. No fires.

Saddleback Mountain: the site of a prolonged disagreement between developers and Trail-protection interests. The ski resort below to the north, now mostly out of sight, wants to extend its ski facilities up the side of the mountain. If this is done, much of the pristine beauty you see from the Trail will be marred. ATC and MATC are trying to protect the long-term interests of the A.T. and hikers. From the summit, Katahdin can be seen to the northeast, a small bump on the horizon more than 105 air miles away. Compass heading: 40° (remember to correct for Maine's 18° magnetic declination).

Poplar Ridge Lean-to: baseball-bat sleeping platform, water from stream, privy 300 feet south of shelter. Maintained lovingly by Dave Field, long-time volunteer and former MATC president, current ATC New England vice chair.

Orbeton Stream: treacherous after several days of heavy rain (streams in Maine usually subside very quickly, so wait it out if it's raging), but normally a great area for wading and splashing where the Trail crosses.

> Wildlife: *Martens are excellent tree climbers, and that is where you have your best chance of seeing one of these elusive animals. Chiefly nocturnal, they sometimes chase squirrels along tree limbs during the day. Martens are members of the weasel family, brown in color, with a large bushy tail. The fisher is similar to, but slightly larger than, the marten. Both are rarely seen south of northernmost New England.*

Mt. Abraham side trail: excellent views from extensive alpine zone, mostly above treeline.

Spaulding Mountain Lean-to: completed in 1988, one of the new MATC designs. Water from dependable spring; privy is on A.T., tentsites in front of shelter.

Commemorative plaque: located north of Spaulding Mountain and before the Sugarloaf Mountain side trail; honors the CCC workers who built the last section needed to make the A.T. continuous from Georgia to Maine in 1937. The plaque was dedicated by MATC during a ceremony on August 14, 1987, one of 24 celebrations that year to celebrate the 50th anniversary of the Trail's completion on that date. Can you spot the error on the plaque?

Sugarloaf side trail: Right 0.6m—to Sugarloaf Summit House (no water), passing small spring about halfway up.

♦ Sugarloaf Summit House: enclosed building with splendid views, electricity, woodstove, and telephone to the lodge below. Hikers are permitted to stay in summit building overnight, and personnel below sometimes offer to let you ride down on the chairlift for a run to a nearby grocery store (weekends only). On a clear day, it's possible to see from Mt. Washington to Katahdin—almost one-sixth of the Trail!

Carrabassett River: can be dangerous during high water. Campsites on north side of river formerly used heavily by groups, now off-limits to campers.

Crocker Cirque Campsite: tentsites and platform located 0.2 mile off the A.T. to the right, located in one of the finest glacial cirques (natural amphitheater-shaped hollows) in Maine.

Maine 27: Left 5m—to the small community of Stratton.

♦ **STRATTON, MAINE** (pop. 700): *Lodging*—Stratton Plaza Hotel: $30S $35D, $45 for the "penthouse" that sleeps three and has space to spread out • Cathy's: $10 per person; cable, pets allowed, rooms located above the restaurant • Stratton Motel & "The House": $25S $30D $5EAP, 4 max; cable, phone in room, pets outside (MC, Visa, AE); free shuttle back to Trail with overnight stay. "The House," a large efficiency unit with several bedrooms, living room, and kitchen, can accommodate a crowd comfortably; $75 (1-5 people) $8EAP, 8 max;. Can be used as maildrop if sent c/o Stratton Motel; also, $1 will be donated to ATC for each hiker who stays overnight in 1992. *Places to eat*—Stratton Diner: B/L/D, standard diner menu, steak sandwich, lobster roll, seafood (MC, Visa, AE); open 7 days, 6am-8:30pm • Cathy's Restaurant: L/D (breakfast on weekends), casual, 2-for-1 entree (prime rib, seafood, chicken, and wild game) for $15 on Tue and Wed. Entrees any night come with full salad, fresh bread, and cheese bar. Said a sated thru-hiker, "This food is worth walking 2,000 miles for!" *Groceries*—Fotter's Grocery: good for long-term resupply, fresh fruit, Coleman fuel by the pint; open Mon-Sat 8am-6pm, closed Sun • Northland Cash Supply: groceries (good for short-term resupply), hardware items, socks, clothing; open 7 days, 6am-10pm. *Laundromat*—located on first floor of Stratton Plaza, detergent and change available at front desk. *Point of interest*—The Widow's Walk, for many years a thru-hiker favorite, is no longer open during the summer. Alumni are invited to say hello to Mary and Jerry when in the neighborhood; that is, if you can catch them home. They are busy pursuing other interests. • Phil Pepin, a member of MATC, lives nearby. Call Phil (207-246-4663) if you need information about the local area or the Kennebec ferry. *PO-ZIP 04982:* Mon-Fri 8am-12:30pm and 1:45-5pm, Sat 8-11:45am; 207-246-6461; LY-50+.

Horns Pond Lean-tos: double shelters and tent platforms near an alpine pond. The privy is probably the best on the A.T., at least from an environmental standpoint. No odor. Take a minute to sit and read how it works. Yum! Yum!

Arnold's Folly: During the Revolutionary War, fully equipped colonial troops, under the leadership of Benedict Arnold, floated and marched past the Bigelow Mountains on their way to take Quebec City. They were exhausted by the time they arrived (wonder why?), and you know the rest of the story.

Myron H. Avery Lean-to: named for the third and longest tenured ATC chairman, who was the driving force that turned Benton MacKaye's vision into reality. A native of Maine, Avery was the first person to hike the entire A.T. (in sections), finishing the feat in 1936.

He wrote the first guidebooks, designed the first shelters, and selected the route for much of the Trail. A plaque on a nearby rock honors his memory. The water source for this shelter is a boxed spring 0.2 mile north on the A.T., and tent platforms and a locked cabin (MATC caretaker residence) are near the shelter. No fee.

Little Bigelow Lean-to: a well-designed and well-built shelter with good springhouse, "The Tubs," and plenty of flat space for camping all around—the pride of MATC. A fascinating and very entertaining video showing construction of this shelter is available from the club.

West Carry Pond Lean-to: drinking water from spring house and swimming in the pond, which is a few hundred feet in front of the shelter.

> Wildlife: *Loons are the very essence of the wilderness experience. They usually come in pairs, and you will often hear them calling to one another across lakes and ponds. They have four calls, but you will probably be able to distinguish only two, the plaintive yodel and the almost maniacal laugh. Loons are excellent swimmers and can swim long distances underwater but must run with their legs across the water to assist take-off. Once airborne, they are strong, swift flyers. Loons are usually seen on the A.T. only in New England, but one was heard on Fontana Lake in 1990.*

Pierce Pond Lean-to: numerous reports of moose in the area for the past two years. Water source is stream on blue-blazed trail at south end of dam. Tenting here is difficult, at best.

Harrison Camps: on side trail 0.4 mile north of lean-to on A.T. (or from lean-to via blue-blazed trail near south end of dam), owned by Tim and Fran Harrison. Hiker's pancake breakfast with 12 pancakes, sausage or eggs, juice-milk-or-coffee, all for about $5; rave reviews from many past thru-hikers. Tim requests that you make reservations and verify time for breakfast the night before. They can also call ahead to make special ferry arrangements for crossing the Kennebec. When you visit the camp, keep in mind that the Harrisons have a toddler, as well as a camp to run. Their hiker services are a special courtesy they extend when time allows.

Kennebec River: the last major obstacle before Katahdin (unless you count the wonderful hospitality of the Shaws in Monson) and a dangerous river to cross; usually ice-free Apr 1-Dec 1. Don't underestimate the power of this river. A strong hiker observed, "The ford took a lot more energy than I expected. I was tired the rest of the day." A less fortunate hiker drowned here in 1985. Since then, a ferry service has been in operation from mid-June to October. This year, the ferry will operate for two hours, 10am-noon, on the following dates: weekend of June 6-7, then daily from June 13-Oct 4. Northbounders and southbounders can catch the ferry where the Trail comes down to the river. The ATC and MATC pay for this ferry service, which is free to hikers during the hours listed above. If you want ferry service at hours other than those listed, you can make your own arrangements by calling the ferry service (look for telephone number posted at shelters before the river), usually $5 per person for a group. It is strongly recommended that you take the ferry, since the water level can rise at any time (the dam releases automatically when power is needed, not on a set schedule as incorrectly believed by many). However, should you decide to take the risk and ford the river instead, here is some advice:

- Do not ford where the Trail crosses the river. Go upstream about 0.2 mile to the gravel bars.
- Do not attempt to ford the river if you can't see substantial gravel bars. These gravel bars will create three distinct channels in the river when the water level is low (usually before 8am). The channel nearest the eastern bank is usually the deepest.
- Do not remove your boots. The bottom of the river is slippery and rocky. Boots will allow you to get better traction and prevent you from cutting or bruising your feet.
- Unbuckle your waistbelt. If you are swept downstream, you can more easily slip out of your pack.
- Use a strong pole to help you keep your balance (some folks use two). Discarded poles can usually be found along the shore.
- Wrap your valuables in a plastic bag, and move your sleeping bag to the top of your pack if it doesn't interfere with your balance.
- Follow the ripples. A few feet upstream from the place where the water begins to ripple is generally the highest point of the river bed below. You will usually be able to see the bottom where it is shallowest. Look up often to avoid vertigo caused by the water flowing past. If you feel unsteady, use your pole to form a tripod with your legs, facing upstream, and steady your nerves.
- Do not attempt to ford the river alone.

U.S. 201: Where A.T. heads north into the woods, go right 200 feet, then left 0.3 mile on a paved road to the town of **CARATUNK, MAINE** (pop. 100), with Caratunk General Store & Hostel (P.O. Box 34, Caratunk, Maine 04925; 207-672-5532), owned by Dan and Marie Beane; open 7 days, 7am-7pm. The store has good hiker-food selection (good for short-term resupply), snacks and sodas, Ben & Jerry's, and an outside public telephone. The hostel is over the store. Bunkroom has single and double beds, shower, kitchen for cooking, and television in 1992 (maybe). Cost is $10 per person. Marie is the postmaster for the PO, which is located in the store. *PO-ZIP 04925:* Mon-Fri 8am-2pm; Sat 7am-1pm; 207-672-5532; LY-150. *Left 1m*—to Trailside Cabins. *Left 2.5m*—to Northern Outdoors.

♦ Trailside Cabins: bunkhouse, hot shower, and kitchen, $7.50 per hiker; private cottage for $30 per group, 4 max; owned by Steve Longley.
♦ Northern Outdoors: cabins $20 per person, tentsites $8 per person, showers free with stay ($2 per person without stay), coin-operated laundry, whitewater rafting, hot tubs, restaurant.

Holly Brook relocation: completed in 1991, taking the Trail off a paved road and rerouting it through a more scenic area. The treadway was a little rough last year, but, like all new Trail, a few years of use will mature it into a smoother path.

Pleasant Pond Lean-to: now off the A.T. 0.1 mile to the right, with new roof and other improvements added in 1990. Also, an A.T. tradition continues uninterrupted: The "Cookie Lady" still leaves cookies in a tin for hungry thru-hikers. She's been doing so for years. Does anyone know who this lovely person is? Anyway, many thanks for your little treats, dear friend. Blue-blazed trail goes to a beach.

Pleasant Pond Mountain: excellent views reward the tired climber.

Baker Brook: at the south end of Moxie Pond. For several decades, a double-cable crossing, one cable for feet, the other for hands, has challenged the more daring. The A.T. actually crosses several hundred feet downstream from the cable. For your safety, it is strongly recommended that you follow the official Trail across the rocks. The cable crossing is dangerous.

Joe's Hole Brook Lean-to: named for the little bay at the end of Moxie Pond, probably Joe's "fishing" hole. Another baseball-bat sleeping platform. Water is from small stream in front of shelter.

Moxie Bald Mountain: steep climb, but the views are magnificent. The blue-blazed foul-weather bypass might be a good idea in very bad weather.

Moxie Bald Mountain Lean-to: several streams located 0.5 mile south of shelter, or use pond in front of shelter for water. Baseball bats replaced by board floor in 1991.

West Branch of Piscataquis River: relo takes the Trail along the river for several scenic miles.

> Wildlife: *Beavers are in their element in Maine, and you will see much evidence of their activity. Tree trunks that look like they have been sharpened in giant pencil sharpeners are a sure sign. You will also see dams and lodges built on pond outlets. The beaver is an aquatic rodent, with four prominent front teeth and a large, hairless, paddle-like tail. No other animal has such an impact on the environment except man. Beaver ponds are an important habitat in the northern woods.*

Horseshoe Canyon Lean-to: completed in late 1991, to the left on blue-blazed side trail, not visible from the A.T. Water source is the river.

Logging road (gravel and dirt): *Right 0.3m*—on blue-blazed logging road to Pleasant Road, then turn left, and follow the road past the old quarry to the town of Monson.

Maine 15 (paved highway): *Right 3m*—to the town of Monson.

♦ **MONSON, MAINE** (pop. 500): The last true Trail town for northbounders, and a welcome relief for southbounders just getting underway. *Lodging*—Shaw's Boarding Home (Pleasant St., Monson, Maine 04464; 207-997-3597): owned by Keith and Pat Shaw and Keith, Jr., who have hosted more than 12,000 hikers since opening in 1978. In fact, it would be safe to say that the Shaws have probably met more 2,000-Milers than anyone else, and the hospitality they provide ("Simply the best stop on the entire Trail," said one thru-hiker) reflects their kinship with the Trail community. Hikers have a choice of bunkroom or private room. Bunkroom with linens, hot shower, and towel is $15. Private room with shower, towel, cable TV: $25S $35D $45 (3 persons). Tenting in yard: $4S $8D. Meals are extra: regular breakfast $4.50; AYCE family-style dinner $8. Laundry: washer with detergent $1.25; dryer $1.25. Shower with towel $3. The telephone is available for collect or credit-card calls (15-minute limit). Hiker supplies for sale include Coleman by the pint, butane fuels, Sno-seal, water-purification tablets, water bottles, socks, insect repellent, hip belts, pack straps, caps, T-shirts, *etc.* Keith offers taxi service for $1 per mile and shuttle service for $8 per hour by arrangement (rates for taxi and shuttle higher after 4pm). Cars may be parked in yard for 50¢ per day. No credit cards or credit. The Shaws will hold mail, UPS, and FedEx packages at no charge. No pets or smoking inside the house. Lounge area with sofa, chairs, television and refrigerator is available on the first floor for use by guests. A reminder to hikers: This is also the Shaws' home, and they are a family that needs some time to themselves. Try not to make too many demands on them in the evening. If possible, buy your fuel, make phone calls, and do other chores that involve the Shaws before dinner. Perhaps Keith will then have some time to play horseshoes, his favorite pastime, but you "experts" should take it easy on him. *Places to eat*—Appalachian Station Restaurant: B/L/S, family-style meals, snacks, ice cream; open Mon-Fri 5:30am-2pm, Thur and Fri 5am-8pm; also full meals and pizza on Sat (6am-2pm) and Sun (8am-2pm) • Sal's Country Store & Diner: limited hiker supplies, Ben & Jerry's (last on the Trail for northbounders?); diner with pizza, sandwiches, burgers, fries, chicken and seafood dinners; open Mon-Thur 5am-9pm, Fri and Sat 5am-10pm, Sun 7am-8pm. *Groceries*—Monson General Store: good for short-term resupply, Ben & Jerry's (ditto above); open Mon-Fri 5:30am-9pm, Sat and Sun 8am-9pm • *Other services*—Monson Laundromat: no detergent or change. • Cobbler: none in Monson, but check with Keith Shaw • hardware store • health center: open Tues-Thur 1:30-4:30pm • outside public telephone near PO. *PO-ZIP 04464:* Mon-Fri 8-11:30am and 12:30-5pm, Sat 8am-noon; 207-997-3975; LY-250. *Nearby town*—Dover-Foxcroft with full-service supermarket (good for long-term resupply) and bank.

The Wilderness: a 100-mile section through some of the most remote mountains and forest traversed by the A.T. Signs suggest that you carry a ten-day supply of food. Many thru-hikers make it through in less time, but consider taking your time. This is the climax of your odyssey, and a relaxed pace will help you enjoy it to the fullest.

Leeman Brook Lean-to: Creek 100 feet before shelter is the water source.

Little Wilson Falls: dramatic waterfall in slate gorge, great spot for a mid-morning rest break. Be careful: The rocks are very slippery.

Slugundy Gorge: featuring a cascading stream with many beautiful pools and sunbathed rocks.

Long Pond Stream Lean-to: new in 1990 and located within sight of the A.T. on a side trail 0.7 mile after you ford Long Pond stream. Water source is a small spring to the right of the shelter.

Barren Mountain: good view from the rock slide, 100 feet off the Trail to the right. Firetower a must on a clear day, but be careful.

> Wildlife: *Canada (gray) jays will astonish you with their boldness. These cousins of the raucous blue jay will steal food right out of your hand if you aren't careful, hence their more popular name, "camp robbers." They are found in coniferous forest at higher elevations. Lower down, the blue jay reigns supreme. Gray jays are seen on the A.T. only in upper New England.*

Cloud Pond Lean-to: located on spectacular pond that is often "in the clouds," as the name suggests. The small shelter has a dirt floor, but tentsites with a bed of pine needles can be found between the shelter and privy. New shelter may be in place for 1992 northbounders. Water source is the pond. A resident moose has been sighted for the past four years, usually feeding in the shallows in front of the shelter just after sunset.

Cloud Pond to Chairback Gap: This section is only eight miles long but can be a challenge when the rocks are wet and the weather is nasty. Take heed.

Chairback Gap Lean-to: Water source is spring 0.1 mile north of the shelter. Privy is south about 400 feet.

The Hermitage: spectacular white-pine trees, protected by The Nature Conservancy. Certain white pines (the biggest and best ones) were selected to be used for the masts of sailing ships and warships in colonial days and were considered the property of the crown. Settlers who poached one of these trees were hung. Ownership of these trees was a major factor in the rebellion of the New England colonists. Tea was secondary.

Gulf Hagas: billed as the "Grand Canyon of the East." A 1989 thru-hiker said, "It wasn't what I expected, the Grand Canyon and all that hype, but the detour was very much worth it. This is a spectacular area, like nothing else on the Trail."

Carl Newhall Lean-to: with resident moose that has been entertaining thru-hikers for several years. Best opportunity to see her is at dusk on the stream below the shelter, which is also the water source.

Sidney Tappan Campsite: water available from small spring (the second spring to the right, about 200 feet down the side trail). Watch for hornet nests in the brush. The A.T. north beyond the clearing follows the old road to the right. Don't leave without a look at the privy.

White Cap Mountain: exposed rocky summit; blazing sometimes hard to follow, so be especially alert. Great view of Katahdin as you begin the descent.

Logan Brook Lean-to: Water source is nearby creek. Few tentsites in area, none good.

Mountain View Pond: beautiful place, but pond infested with leeches. Where are you when we need you, Rosie Sayer?

Cooper Brook Falls Lean-to: baseball-bat sleeping platform, but the swimming hole out front is the best on the A.T. near a shelter. Water source is small brook about 0.2 mile north on A.T.

Antlers Camp: site of an old hunting lodge, the type that once dotted the Maine wilderness. On the shore of Lower Jo-Mary Lake, it now has a beautiful developed camping area with outstanding "Fort Relief" privy and, at least once a year, "manna from heaven." The cat's got my tongue, so only a fortunate few will learn what this means.

Potaywadjo Spring Lean-to: 15-foot-diameter spring, very cold.

Nahmakanta Lake: sand beach and unofficial camping area on south end; spring two miles north, off to the right on another sand beach.

Wildlife: *Timber wolves no longer inhabit the forests of Maine, although you will still hear "wolf stories" from oldtimers and hunters. Now and then hikers swear that they have seen a timber wolf (probably a coyote, now common in the area), but they haven't. The nearest wolfpack is more than 500 miles to the north in remote sections of Canada. There, the gray wolf roams free, at least for now.*

Wadleigh Stream Lean-to: water from stream flowing out of beaver pond in front of shelter; privy in Canada. Clam shells around shelter testify to the bounty in the nearby lake.

Nesuntabunt Mountain: not pointless at all. Spectacular view of Katahdin from overlook at summit, 100 feet off the A.T. to the right at the register box.

Rainbow Stream Lean-to: the shelter pictured in the 1987 *National Geographic* magazine article about the Trail. Baseball bats and active mice. Privy has interesting drawing. Is it a self-portrait?

Rainbow Ledges: fourth-best view of Katahdin on the Trail.

Hurd Brook Lean-to: register crammed full of thoughts and reflections about the end of the trip, its meaning, and well-wishes for those who follow. There is usually one last shelter register at Daicey Pond, however.

Abol Bridge: third-best view of Katahdin (it just keeps getting better, doesn't it?). Cross bridge on special hiker walkway provided by paper company, a great observation deck for photos of the mountain. On north side of bridge is the Abol Bridge Campground & Campstore (open 7 days, 7am-7pm, May-Nov; no telephone on premises), managed by Art and Linda Belmont. Store has hiker groceries (good for short-term resupply; some Lipton dinners, mac and cheese, microwave food, donuts, hot coffee, beer, wine, sodas, candy) and a good supply of friendly faces. Campground has tentsites for $10 per person, hot showers (for campers only), and canoes for rent; closes end of September. A telephone is available about seven miles away, at another store on the paved road to Millinocket. Ask Art and Linda for directions. Also, ask about free campsites across the road that may be available to thru-hikers.

Baxter State Park: donated by the late Gov. Percival Baxter, with the stipulation that it be preserved as pristine wilderness forever. The park has no paved roads, no electricity, no showers, no stores, and no telephones. Campgrounds are undeveloped, except for cabins, shelters, and privies. Camping is allowed only at designated camping areas, and cabins and shelters are available by reservation only (except at Daicey Pond, see below). No pets are allowed in the park, including the pets of thru-hikers. The park closes officially on October 15. Thru-hikers may climb after that date if the mountain has not been closed for the year due to permanent hazardous conditions. That usually doesn't happen before late October or early November, but it has happened as early as September. The park headquarters building is located outside the park at 64 Balsam Dr., Millinocket, Maine 04462; 207-723-5140.

Daicey Pond Campground: Two shelters are set aside for the overnight use of thru-hikers only, on a first-come, first-served basis, no reservation required. A $4-per-night fee is charged, payable at the ranger station when you sign in; stay limited to two nights. The thru-hiker shelters are located in a small grove of trees away from the other campground facilities and provide a perfect setting to contemplate the morrow's climb with your fellow thru-hikers. A privy is nearby. When you reach Daicey Pond, check in at the ranger station to the right at the weather bulletin board. In your excitement, don't miss the view across the pond, the second-best view of Katahdin on the A.T. The library with woodstove is open for campground guests. Canoes are available, too, sometimes free to thru-hikers. If you want to stay at Katahdin Stream Campground instead, ask the rangers here to check for openings. The rangers at Daicey will hold packages for thru-hikers.

Katahdin Stream Campground: shelters $8, tentsites $4, but not usually available to thru-hikers unless the weather causes cancellations.

Katahdin: the most beautiful mountain on the Trail, even more so after you've walked 2,000 miles to climb it. The Indian name means "greatest mountain," and it will be the single biggest climb of your trip, almost 4,000 feet of elevation change. The ascent will take 2-3 hours, even longer in harsh weather, so try to start up no later than 8am. You can leave your spare gear on the enclosed porch at the Katahdin Stream ranger station. A sign-in board is located at the entrance to the parking lot, where you must record the time you start up and indicate the route you will follow. You must also sign out here when you come down, or at another campground if you don't return to Katahdin Stream. Rain or shine, you will finally see the best view of Katahdin—on the summit. I wish you Class I companions for your climb.

Coming down: On your way back down the mountain, a soaking in Katahdin Stream will quite possibly cure your feet of two-thousand-plus miles of abuse. A swim in the stream is for the truly insane. By the way, the stream contains more than a few thru-hiker tears.

Heading south: Unless you have family and friends meeting you, you'll have to hitch out of the park to Millinocket, about 20 miles away. Luckily, most of the people leaving the park will be going your way. Ask around at the parking areas for a ride. Few new 2,000-Milers have any trouble getting a hitch into town. Once in Millinocket, you must hitch to Medway, 10 miles east on Maine 157, to catch a bus, which is the only form of public transportation heading south from this part of Maine. Cyr Bus Line (207-827-2335) has one bus leaving daily from Medway at 9:40am, heading for Bangor; fare is $10.50. You can buy a ticket and catch the bus at Terry's Irving Gas Station & Restaurant (207-746-3411), located at the intersection of Maine 157 and I-95. Once in Bangor, you can make bus or plane connections to your home.

♦ **Millinocket, Maine** (pop. 6,742): a good-sized pulp-and-paper community with everything but bus service. *Services near the PO* (in center of town)—Rooms: inexpensive rooms for $15 per person, in house owned by Joan Cogswell, 33 Penobscot Avenue ●

Terrace Restaurant: AYCE breakfast for $2.50 • hardware store • doctor • dentist • hospital. *Services on Maine 157* (a mile from the center of town)—Pamola Motel: $50S $55D $6EAP, 4 max; a/c, cable, phone in room, pool, Oriental restaurant, lounge, sauna and hot tub • Heritage Motor Inn: $60S $69D $5EAP, 5 max; a/c, cable, phone in room, no pets (MC, Visa, AE, Dis, DC); restaurant in motel • two supermarkets, both good for long-term resupply • McDonald's • pizzeria • large bookstore • Baxter State Park headquarters (near McDonald's). *PO-ZIP 04462:* Mon-Fri 8:15am-4:45pm, Sat 8:15-11:30am; 207-723-5921; LY-30.

♦ **Medway, Maine** (pop. 525): *Services*—Farley's Motel: $25S $30D (special rates for hikers only) $5EAP, 4 max; a/c, cable, phone in room, washer/dryer, pets allowed (MC, Visa, AE). The bus station is about one mile from Farley's, at Terry's Irving Gas Station & Restaurant, on Maine 157 at the I-95 interchange.

Life After the Trail

Congratulations! You've now completed your thru-hike of the Appalachian Trail and, for the first time in many months, you have no more miles to hike tomorrow. Your journey isn't over, however, since you must now make the transition from Trail life back to the real world. Some people have no problem, but, for most, this change involves a period of stress. I've questioned quite a few 2,000-milers about their adjustment to life after the Trail and pass along these suggestions that may help smooth the way for you:

Celebrate with loved ones as soon as you arrive home. Let them participate in your achievement, and allow them to treat you like a hero if they are so inclined. Try to tell them about your trip, but don't get discouraged if you have trouble finding words to express your feelings and if you find family and friends unable to relate to your Trail experience in depth. After all, you've had 2,000 miles of adventure. Many months will pass before you begin to sort it all out in your own mind and gain perspective.

Allow yourself time to adapt to your surroundings when you return home. Remember how uncertain you felt in the woods when you began your hike? You will feel just as disoriented when you leave the woods and come face to face with the complexities of modern society again. Try to enjoy a week of leisure before you begin to reestablish routine in your daily life. If your finances will permit, don't start back to work for a week or two, and, if possible, avoid making any important decisions until you have settled in a bit.

Expect a few days of mild depression a week or so after returning home. This is due partly to physiological changes that take place when you stop thru-hiking and partly to the emotional letdown that comes from being abruptly separated from friends and freedoms so enjoyed on the Trail. Try to stay physically active by taking long walks or day-hikes during this period, and don't be reluctant to call your Trail friends for encouragement. They will probably be going through the same post-hike blues. Most will welcome the chance to reminisce with you.

Pursue your hike to its logical conclusion by tying up all loose ends. Clean and store your gear, catalogue your slides or photos, write thank-you letters to folks who provided assistance and/or friendship during your hike (perhaps including a stamped, self-addressed envelope, which will usually get you a delightful reply), give an interview to your local newspaper about your hike and the Trail (ATC can help you with background information), offer to speak to local groups about your trip, and (very important!) send me your corrections, additions, and comments for next year's *Handbook* (preferably before November 1). Stay busy with Trail-related activities until your attention begins to turn elsewhere.

Plan to attend the annual Gathering of ALDHA (Appalachian Long Distance Hikers Association), which will be held this year on the weekend of October 9-11 at Dartmouth

College in Hanover, N.H. This event attracts several hundred hikers for a weekend of fun, hiking workshops, slide shows and information about other trails, folk concerts, contra dance, *etc.* Cost is $17 per person, $27 for couples. Many 1992 thru-hikers will attend, and the fellowship with other folks who understand the Trail experience will help you ease back into society. For more information, write to ALDHA, 197 Big Springs Road, S.E., Calhoun, Ga. 30701

Consider getting involved with the Trail on a long-term basis. The Appalachian Trail Conference and its affiliated maintaining clubs need a variety of volunteer talents. If you still aren't an ATC member, now is another good time to join. You will receive the *Appalachian Trailway News* magazine and be kept informed about ATC activities and opportunities for service to the Trail project. The next Conference meeting is scheduled for 1993, in Dahlonega, Ga. More than one thousand members will attend, and the traditional 2,000-Milers dinner will be held during Conference week. For information, write to ATC, P.O. Box 807, Harpers Ferry, W.Va. 25425-0807, or call 304-535-6331, Monday-Friday, 9am-5pm, Eastern Time.

Send a brief description of your hike, including starting and finishing dates, to ATC at the above address. Your name will be officially recorded in the archives as a 2,000-Miler and will be published in the *Appalachian Trailway News.* You will receive a free 2,000-Miler rocker for your A.T. patch and a personalized certificate of congratulations suitable for framing. The certificate is impressive and looks like a diploma, which, in many ways, it is!

Finally, let me once more congratulate you for completing the Trail. I know that your thru-hike has been one of the most satisfying things you have ever done, and I'm sure you feel you are a better person for having spent your summer in the mountains and woods among friends. Perhaps you will someday hike on the A.T. again, or perhaps you will go on to other adventures. Whichever the case, the lessons learned and friendships gained this summer will serve you well. I also know from my own experience that the Appalachian Trail will be a part of you forever, and that, come each spring, wherever you are, you will never be far from its enchantments.

—Wingfoot

How to Report Trail Problems

The A.T. is the world's finest long-distance recreational footpath. Its local maintaining clubs do an outstanding job of keeping it up to standards, but, as volunteers working primarily on weekends, they can't be everywhere at all times. You can be an important part of the Trail-maintenance process by being the eyes and ears of the maintaining clubs in their absence. As you hike along this year, note any Trail condition that causes you a problem, such as large blowdowns, weeds overrunning the footpath, loose privy seats, dangerous waterbars, leaky shelter roofs, missing signs or confusing blazes, guidebook and map errors, *etc.* Record the exact nature and location of the problem—it's easiest and most accurate to record the problem on your map's elevation profile. When you reach the next town, send the information to the appropriate ATC regional office listed below. The regional representative will pass your information along to the A.T. club assigned responsibility by ATC for maintaining that particular section and will periodically check back until the problem has been corrected. That's how the system works. With everyone participating, the Trail can be maintained in the best possible condition.

Springer Mountain, Georgia, to the Tennessee/Virginia border—
>   ATC Regional Office, Box 2750, Asheville, N.C. 28802
>   or call 704-254-3708

Tennessee/Virginia border to Rockfish Gap, Virginia—
>   ATC Regional Office, P.O. Box 10, Newport, Va. 24128
>   or call 703-544-7388

Rockfish Gap, Virginia, to the New York/Connecticut border—
>   ATC Regional Office, P.O. Box 381, Boiling Springs, Pa. 17007
>   or call 717-258-5771

New York/Connecticut border to Katahdin, Maine—
>   ATC Regional Office, P.O. Box 312, Lyme, N.H. 03768
>   or call 603-795-4935

Important Telephone Numbers

ATC Central Offices 304-535-6331
Mail-order Outfitters:
L. L. Bean 800-221-4221
Campmor 800-526-4784
REI 800-426-4840
Manufacturers/Distributors:
Asolo 800-421-8093
Camp Trails/Eureka! 800-572-8822
Caribou 800-824-4153
Dana Designs 406-587-4188
Danner 800-345-0430
Fabiano 617-268-5625
First-Need 800-441-8166
Gregory 800-477-3420
Hi-Tec Sports 800-521-1698
JanSport 800-426-9227
Katadyn 800-950-0808
Kelty 800-423-2320
Lowe 303-465-3706
Merrell 800-869-3348
Moss 800-341-1557
Mountainsmith 800-426-4075
MSR 206-624-8573
New Balance 617-783-4000
Nike 800-344-6453
The North Face 800-888-9991
Peak 1 800-835-3278
Raichle 914-279-5121
Rocky Boots 800-421-5151
Sierra Designs 800-423-6363
Tecnica 603-298-8032
ThorLo 800-438-0209
Timberland 603-926-1600
Timberline 303-494-4104
Trangia 800-522-2519
Vasque 612-388-8211
Walrus 415-526-8961

Note: *The above-listed brand names reflect the equipment most frequently used by thru-hikers on the A.T. Listing does not imply any endorsement or guarantee that such equipment will be suitable for your thru-hike.*

Post Office Information

Note: Post offices in this listing are the ones most frequently used as maildrops.

Suches, GA 30572—Mon-Fri 7:30-noon and 1-4:30, Sat 7:30-11:30; 404-747-2611
Franklin, NC 28734—Mon-Fri 8:30-5, closed Saturday; 704-524-3219
Fontana Dam, NC 28733—Mon-Fri 8:30-noon and 1-5, Sat 10-noon; 704-498-2315
Gatlinburg, TN 37738—Mon-Fri 9-5, closed Saturday; 615-436-5464
Hot Springs, NC 28743—Mon-Fri 8:30-11:30 and 12:30-4:15, Sat 8:45-11:45;
    704-622-3242
Erwin, TN 37650—Mon-Fri 8-5, closed Sat; anyone working will answer buzzer at rear of
    PO after hours; 615-743-4811
Elk Park, NC 28622—Mon-Fri 7:30-noon and 1:15-4:30, Sat 7:30-10:30; 704-733-5711
Roan Mountain, TN 37687—Mon-Fri 8-11:30 and 12:30-4:30, Sat 8-11; 615-772-3661
Damascus, VA 24236—Mon-Fri 8:30-12:30 and 1:30-4:30, Sat 8:30-11; 703-475-3411
Troutdale, VA 24378—Mon-Fri 8-noon and 1-5, Sat 8-11; 703-677-3221
Atkins, VA 24311—Mon-Fri 8-noon and 1-5, Sat 8-11; 703-783-5551
Bastian, VA 24314—Mon-Fri 8-noon and 12:30-4:30, Sat 8-10:30; 703-688-4631
Bland, VA 24315—Mon-Fri 7:30-4, closed Saturday; 703-688-3751
Pearisburg, VA 24134—Mon-Fri 8:30-5, Sat 8:30-noon; 703-921-1100
Catawba, VA 24070—Mon-Fri 8-noon and 1-5, Sat 8-10:30; 703-384-6011
Troutville, VA 24175—Mon-Fri 8:30-noon and 1-5, Sat 8:30-11:30; 703-992-1472
Cloverdale, VA 24077—Mon-Fri 8-noon and 1-5, Sat 9-noon; 703-992-2334
Big Island, VA 24526—Mon-Fri 8-12:30 and 1:30-5, Sat 8-11; 804-299-5072
Montebello. VA 24464—Mon-Fri 8-noon and 12:30-4:30, Sat 9-11:30; 703-377-9218
Tyro, VA 22976—Mon-Sat 9-2; 804-277-5731
Waynesboro, VA 22980—Mon-Fri 8:30-5, closed Saturday; 703-949-8129
Front Royal, VA 22630—Mon-Fri 8:30-5, Sat 8:30-2; 703-635-4540
Linden, VA 22642—Mon-Fri 8-noon and 1-5, Sat 8-noon; 703-636-9936
Harpers Ferry, WV 25425—Mon-Fri 8-12:30 and 1:30-4, closed Saturday; 304-535-2479
Boiling Springs, PA 17007—Mon-Fri 8-1 and 2-4:30, Sat 8-noon; 717-258-6668
Duncannon, PA 17020 Mon-Fri 8-4:30, Sat 8-noon; 717-834-3332
Port Clinton, PA 19549—Mon-Fri 7:30-12:30 and 2-5, closed Saturday; 215-562-3787
Palmerton, PA 18071—Mon-Fri 8:30-5, Sat 8:30-noon; 215-826-2286
Delaware Water Gap, PA 18327—Mon-Fri 8:30-12:15 and 1:30-5, Sat 8:30-11;
    717-476-0304
Unionville, NY 10988—Mon-Fri 8-1 and 2-5, Sat 8-noon; 914-726-3535
Vernon, NJ 07462—Mon-Fri 8:30-5, closed Saturday; 201-764-2920
Greenwood Lake, NY 10925—Mon-Fri 7-5, Sat 9:30-noon; 914-477-8005
Arden, NY 10910—7:30-noon and 2-5:15, Sat 7:30-noon; 914-351-5341
Bear Mountain, NY 10911—Mon-Fri 7:30-1 and 2:30-5, Sat 7:30-11:30; 914-786-3747
Fort Montgomery, NY 10922—Mon-Fri 8:30-5, Sat 8:30-noon; 914-446-2173;
    see note in text about accessibility from the Trail.

Pawling, NY 12564—Mon-Fri 8:30-5, Sat 9-noon; 914-855-1010
Kent, CT 06757—Mon-Fri 8-1 and 2-5, Sat 8-12:30; 203-927-3435
Cornwall Bridge, CT 06754—Mon-Fri 7:15-5, Sat 7:15-noon; 203-672-6710
Salisbury, CT 06068—Mon-Fri 8-1 and 2-5, Sat 8:30-noon; 203-435-9485
Tyringham, MA 01264—Mon-Fri 8:30-11 and 4-5:30, Sat 8:30-12:30; 413-243-1225
Dalton, MA 01226—Mon-Fri 8-5, Sat 8-noon; 413-684-0364
Cheshire, MA 01225—Mon-Fri 8-1 and 2-5, Sat 8-noon; 413-743-3184
North Adams, MA 01247—Mon-Fri 8:30-4:30, Sat 10-noon; 413-664-4554
Williamstown, MA 01267—Mon-Fri 8:30-4:30, Sat 9:30-12:30; 413-458-3707
Manchester Center, VT 05255—Mon-Fri 8:30-5, Sat 9-1; 802-362-3070
Killington, VT 05751—Mon-Fri 8-4:30, Sat 8-noon; 802-775-4247
Hanover, NH 03755—Mon-Fri 8:30-5, Sat 8:30-noon; 603-643-4544
Glencliff, NH 03238—Mon-Fri 7-10 and 2-5, Sat 7-1; 603-989-5858
North Woodstock, NH 03262—Mon-Fri 8-12:30 and 1:30-5, Sat 8-noon;
    603-745-8134
Mt. Washington, NH 03589—ranger at desk has key, 7 days, 8-8, Memorial Day thru
    Columbus Day; 603-846-5404
Gorham, NH 03581—Mon-Fri 8:30-5, Sat 8-noon; 603-466-2182
Andover, ME 04216—Mon-Fri 8:30-1:30 and 2-4:45, Sat 9-12:45; 207-392-4571
Rangeley, ME 04970—Mon-Fri 8-5, Sat 8-noon; 207-864-2233
Stratton, ME 04982—Mon-Fri 8-12:30 and 1:45-5, Sat 8-11:45; 207-246-6461
Caratunk, ME 04925—Mon-Fri 8-2, Sat 7-1; 207-672-5532
Monson, ME 04464—Mon-Fri 8-11:30 and 12:30-5, Sat 8-noon; 207-997-3975

IMPORTANT: Do not send UPS or FedEx packages to post offices, since, by law, they cannot accept them.

Commented one postmaster: "Most of us count it a real pleasure to meet, serve, and help every thru-hiker that comes thru our doors," but added that hikers should keep in mind that...

- *Personnel need time for closing out cash drawers and doing other lock-up chores. Don't wait until closing time to do your post-office business.*
- *Small post offices have very restrictive budgets. Don't take for granted that mailing materials (boxes, tape, etc.) are available free at every location, and don't ask personnel to call long distance to other post offices for you.*
- *Small post offices often keep minimum amounts of cash on hand. Call ahead to make arrangements if you expect to cash a large postal money order, and have I.D. ready.*
- *Customer areas should not be used for repacking if other users are inconvenienced. Avoid discarding foodstuffs in inside trash receptacles, and don't leave a mess.*
- *Change-of-address forms should be filed before you leave town or if you leave the Trail. State that you will pay postage for forwarding mail.*

Postal personnel also enjoy hearing that you made it. Drop them a post card when you finish your trip.

Glossary of Trail Terms

AYCE is the abbreviation for "all you can eat."

AYH is the abbreviation for American Youth Hostels.

Blazes are painted, 2-inch by 6-inch, vertical white rectangles that are placed at eye height on trees and other objects, in both directions, to mark the official route of the Trail. Side trails are marked with blue blazes.

Blowdown is a tree or shrub that has fallen across the Trail.

Blue-blazer is a hiker who substitutes a section of blue-blazed trail for a white-blazed section between two points on the A.T.

Cache is a supply of food and/or supplies hidden for later retrieval.

Cairn is a heap of stones, set up to look artificial, that serves to mark the Trail route in dense vegetation or above treeline.

Dodgeways are V-shaped stiles through fences, used where the Trail passes through livestock enclosures.

Double blaze refers to two blazes, one placed two inches above the other, at places requiring hiker alertness and usually just before a turn in the Trail. In some areas, the top blaze is offset in the direction of the turn.

End-to-ender is an alternative term for 2,000-Miler.

Flip-flopper is a thru-hiker who begins at one terminus of the Trail, hikes toward the other terminus, then jumps ahead to that other terminus, and hikes back toward the initial terminus.

Lean-to is another word for shelter, used primarily in New England.

Maintainer is a volunteer who participates in the organized Trail-maintenance programs of ATC and its member clubs.

NPS is the abbreviation for National Park Service.

National scenic trail is the official designation for one type of trail protected by the National Trails System Act of 1968.

Power hiker is a hiker who habitually chooses to cover very long distances each day, often hiking late into the evening.

Purist is a thru-hiker or section hiker who hikes past every blaze of the white-blazed (official) Trail.

Puncheon (also called a bog bridge) is a wooden walkway built to provide a stable, hardened treadway across bogs, mud flats, and marshy areas.

Section hiker is a person who is attempting to become a 2,000-Miler by doing a series of section hikes over a period of time.

Slackpacker is a person who is hiking a section of Trail without carrying a backpack.

Springer fever is the almost uncontrollable urge to be back on the Trail that hits thru-hikers of past years each spring.

Stile is a construction, usually wooden steps or a ladder, that allows easy passage over a fence.

Surge hiker is a thru-hiker who takes many days off in town, then power hikes to make up the lost time.

USFS is the abbreviation for United States Forest Service.

Thru-hiker is a person who is attempting to become a 2,000-Miler in a single, continuous journey.

Toxic socks is a whimsical term used to describe thru-hiker socks that are badly in need of a wash.

Trail magic is the term used to describe all the wonderful, unexpected things that happen to thru-hikers during their hike.

2,000-Miler is a person who has hiked the entire distance between termini of the A.T.

Volunteer is a person who works for the ATC or one of the local Trail clubs without pay.

Waterbar is a log or rock barrier that diverts water off the Trail to prevent erosion.

Yogi-ing is the good-natured art of causing food to be proffered cheerfully by strangers without asking them directly (If you ask, it's begging!).

Yo-yo-ing is the act of completing one A.T. thru-hike, then immediately turning around to begin another in the opposite direction.

Planning Information

Planning a 2,000-mile hike may seem an overwhelming task at first, requiring many decisions about things that are all too unclear. This section of planning information will give you general guidelines to help you begin making plans for your thru-hike, focusing your attention on those matters that should be considered first. Although not exhaustive, it will help you break your planning down into its logical parts. Once you get started, you will no doubt discover what many others before you have found: Planning an A.T. thru-hike can be almost as much fun as doing the hike itself.

Time: The amount of time you can make available is the most important factor in determining the type of thru-hike you will be able to plan. Assuming you have average hiking ability (average meaning that you can maintain a pace of about 14 miles per day), you will need at least five months to complete an end-to-end hike. If you can take six months, your hike will be even more enjoyable. Four months isn't enough time, unless you are an exceptionally strong hiker and want to do nothing but hike. Most thru-hikes take 160-190 days. Hikes of this duration require a steady daily hiking pace but allow ample time for smelling the roses as well.

Money: The amount of money you need will be determined by your personal style. If you plan a Spartan trip with few town days, you can budget more modestly. If you choose to visit many Trail towns, stay in motels occasionally, and eat often at restaurants, your expenses will be considerably greater. Most thru-hikers strike a happy medium. Assuming you already have your equipment, have purchased some of your food beforehand, and, not taking into account your travel expenses to and from the Trailheads, you will need about $2,000 (a dollar a mile) for a "normal" thru-hike.

Health: Good health is a definite requirement for doing a thru-hike, but health should not be confused with youth and athletic ability. People of all ages and abilities have hiked the entire Trail with no major problems. You should be in reasonably good physical condition before you begin your hike. Medical and dental checkups are advised. As for disease and disability, some otherwise healthy folks with such ailments as diabetes and epilepsy have made it all the way in good shape.

Experience: Lack of previous hiking experience by itself is not a major factor in an end-to-end hike. Many people do quite well on the A.T. without ever having hiked before. Your instincts, adaptability, and preparation will be as important as experience. Nevertheless, common sense says that, the more hiking experience you have, the better your chances of having a successful thru-hike.

Desire: The desire you have before your hike is a good way to predict whether you will finish it. A thru-hike is not an easy trip. Continuous hiking wears on you day after day and pushes you to your physical, mental, and emotional limits. If you don't have an overwhelming desire to hike the entire Trail when you start, you will probably fall short somewhere along the way. If you do have that desire, you are well on your way to a successful journey.

Goals: Establishing specific goals to be achieved on your thru-hike is very important. As goals occur to you during planning, write them down. These goals will give focus to your thru-hike and help you understand why you are hiking the Trail. Having specific goals in mind will also help you set priorities as you go through the planning process.

Publications: In addition to this handbook, you will need several other ATC publications to do your planning. The most important is the *Data Book*, which will acquaint you with the entire Trail and gives mileage between major points, such as shelters, roads, and towns. You will also find much useful information in the series of ten A.T. guidebooks and maps, which explain every portion of the Trail in great detail, including water sources. The maps, which include elevation profiles, are especially useful for helping you interpret the difficulty of Trail terrain. Several 1991 thru-hikers suggested, "Buy two copies of the *Handbook*, one to take with you and one to leave with the folks back home, so that they can read along as you hike."

Equipment

You will be tempted to take too much equipment on your hike, but, if you do, you will quickly learn that a light pack makes a happy hiker. How much should your loaded pack weigh? The average range seen on the A.T. is 25-35 pounds without food, perhaps a little heavier if you are young and/or strong. Partners can share some gear and proportion (not halve) total weight between them according to their body weights. Pack weight, with food, should never exceed one-third of body weight.

Backpack: Both internal-frame and external-frame packs are used successfully on the A.T., so the right type for you will depend on your personal preference. Internal-frame packs ride closer to the body and give more freedom of movement in rough terrain. They are also easier to handle when traveling by vehicle. External-frame packs are easier to load and balance, more convenient to use in shelters, and seem to be cooler in hot weather. With either type, fit is crucial. If you are using an internal-frame pack, make sure that it is sized to your torso and that the stays are bent to fit the contour of your back. If using an external-frame pack, make sure that the frame is the proper length for your height and is adjusted to your torso. With both types, make sure that the waist belt can be drawn tight and that it can be tightened more later, after you have lost 10-20 pounds. You may even want to buy a belt size slightly smaller than your pre-hike waist measurement. You should also purchase a pack raincover. No matter what claims are made by the manufacturer, no pack is waterproof in a driving rain without one. Be sure that the raincover is large enough to fit around your fully loaded pack. As for the pack volume required, that will depend on the bulkiness of your equipment and the amount of food you plan to carry. Most thru-hikers use a pack with a 3,000-5,000-cubic-inch capacity. Names frequently seen on the A.T. are: JanSport, Kelty, Camp Trails, REI, Gregory, Lowe, Dana Designs, and Mountainsmith.

Tent: The A.T. has an extensive shelter system, but you should still carry a tent or tarp for use in the event a shelter is full or in case of emergency. You will also find a tent useful for protection from insects on occasion, and having your own shelter will give you the freedom to camp between Trail shelters when you wish to have some privacy or make additional miles. The type of tent used by thru-hikers varies widely. A few use inexpensive tube tents, accepting the limitations and figuring that they will probably get wet a time or two. Others use expensive mountaineering models, often with many bells and whistles, and they stay dryer but suffer from the additional weight. Most hikers use something in between. When choosing a tent, try to keep the weight below five pounds per person. Check to see that it has enough room inside for you and any companions to sit up comfortably and pack gear during a driving rain. Make sure that it's easy to set up in the dark (practice this before you start your hike). Both free-standing and staked tents work well on the Trail. Whichever type you use, make sure that you seal the seams in accordance with the manufacturer's instructions. Also, check the stuff sack. Trying to put a wet tent into a tight-fitting stuff sack can be annoying, so you may want to substitute a slightly larger one. Names frequently seen on the A.T. are: Sierra Designs, Moss, Eureka!, and The North Face.

Sleeping bag: The problem with selecting a sleeping bag to use on an end-to-end hike is that the weather is usually cold on each end of the Trail and hot in the middle. The best solution is to have two sleeping bags and carry the bag appropriate for the type of weather you anticipate having. A good combination is to have one bag rated at 0-25°F. (the low temperature being determined by how early you start or how late you end your thru-hike) and another rated at 40-55°F. If you are limited to one bag, choose the bag for cold weather. You can always get out of it on hot nights, or use it unzipped as a blanket and sleep under it. Most thru-hikers use a mummy or modified-mummy-style bag. Try to stay under 4 pounds for a cold-weather bag, under 2 pounds for a summer bag. A down bag will weigh less for a given temperature rating but will cost more and be harder to wash on the Trail. Down is also useless as insulation when it gets wet, but this is not a problem on the A.T. unless you are careless. Whichever type bag you choose, synthetic or down, always carry it enclosed in a plastic garbage bag inside a stuff sack, the idea being to have a dry bag to slip into in an emergency. Be sure to get a bag that is long enough when you stretch out on your stomach. If you and a companion intend to zip bags together, make sure they mate. Names frequently seen on the A.T. are: REI, The North Face, Kelty, Caribou, Peak 1, and Slumberjack.

Sleeping pad: A pad under you while you sleep is a necessity, not only for cushioning, but to insulate you from cold and dampness. Even in warm weather, this is important. Two types of pads are seen on the Trail. The closed-cell Ensolite-type foam pad is lightweight and inexpensive. The self-inflating Thermarest pad is more expensive and heavier but considered more comfortable by most thru-hikers. Both types should be carried in a protective nylon sack. Weight can be saved by using the 3/4-length pad, but many thru-hikers appreciate a full-length pad because it cushions sore ankles and feet.

Groundcloth: A groundcloth should be carried for use under your tent. It can be made of inexpensive plastic sheeting, which will eventually puncture and may need to be replaced. In rainy weather, this item will often stay wet and dirty, so quite a few hikers carry a second groundcloth (often a small nylon tarp or space blanket) to use under their sleeping gear in shelters, which can be muddy in wet weather. If you have a second groundcloth, it can be used inside your tent to prevent wearing away the waterproof coating on your tent floor.

Sitting pad (optional): This item is useful when you take a break or stop for lunch, especially after you lose your body fat and it's bone against rock every time you sit down. A sitting pad can be made by cutting a 12-inch by 14-inch section from an old foam pad.

Stove: Few thru-hikers depend on campfires for cooking. If you've ever tried to start a fire with wet wood in pouring rain, you understand why. Many types of stoves are available, and your choice will be determined by your cooking requirements. If you plan to do a lot of cooking, you will need to look for high heat output and good fuel economy. You will also need a stove that simmers well. If you only plan to boil water once or twice a day, almost any type of stove will do. In either case, your stove should be easy to set up and should have good stability with your largest pot. Eating spilled food off the ground is no fun. You will have two main fuel choices, butane and Coleman-type white gas. Butane stoves burn clean, are easy to start and restart (they need no priming), and are generally lightweight. Butane fuel cartridges are relatively expensive, though, and hard to find in Trail towns, but some brands can be surface mailed (check with your post office). White-gas stoves often burn dirty and are heavier but put out a lot of heat and are the most fuel- efficient. Coleman-type fuel is available in most Trail towns by the pint (a fill-up costs about $1). Alcohol stoves are just beginning to appear on the Trail. They have the advantage of simplicity but are not as fuel-efficient. Wood-burning backpacking stoves are also beginning to appear more frequently. Whichever stove you choose, cook with it at home (outside, of course!), to make sure it works and to test its fuel consumption per meal. This will give you some idea of the size fuel bottle you need. Most hikers take a one-quart fuel bottle if they cook a lot, a one-pint bottle if they cook less. Alcohol requires an anodized aluminum bottle. A pour spout makes refilling your stove easier, safer, and less wasteful. Names frequently seen on the A.T. are: MSR, Svea/Optimus, Peak 1, Camping Gaz, Trangia, and Zzip.

Cookset: The pots and pans used by thru-hikers show more personality than any other equipment category. Some hikers use clever nesting sets made especially for backpacking. Others assemble odds and ends from their kitchen at home. Either way is fine. The important thing is to have enough cooking volume for your largest meal without having any unnecessary weight. If cooking for one person, you will need at least a one-quart pot and lid. A one-pint pot will also prove useful, but no lid is needed for the smaller pot. If you want to cook edible pancakes, include a nonstick frying pan. Good breads are possible with a BakePacker. A drinking cup with a liquid measurement scale is handy, especially if you are using freeze-dried foods, which require exact water quantities for proper reconstitution. A few Trail meals should be cooked at home to make sure your cookset is sufficient for the type of cooking you plan to do on your trip.

Utensils: A spoon is the only utensil carried by most thru-hikers. Some add a fork if they include a frying pan in their cookset. More exotic Trail cooks carry spatulas and whisks. Stay away from plastic utensils, which can melt and bend into interesting but unusable shapes.

Butane lighter (or matches): A lighter is easier to use and more dependable than matches, although it is wise to have a book of matches in a plastic bag as a back-up fire-starter.

Water bottles and water bag: The amount of water you carry while hiking will depend on your metabolism. Some hikers need large quantities. Others drink hardly any water as they hike along and only small quantities during breaks. If you don't know your requirement, start your hike with two water bottles (the wide-mouth types are easier to use with drink mixes), one each of the one-quart and one-pint sizes. This should be enough volume to hold you between water sources. A water bag is the best way to avoid extra hikes to the water source at shelters. It can also be used to carry water in your pack for short distances.

Water-purification gear: To be absolutely safe, you should boil or treat all water used for drinking, cooking, and cleaning. However, boiling is impractical as a purification method for the average thru-hiker because of the large amount of fuel and cooling time required. That leaves treating, which means using chemical purifiers or filters. Chemical methods usually involve chlorine (some hikers use household bleach) or iodine. Most of the more popular chemical purifiers use iodine, either in tablet or saturated-liquid form. They are fairly easy to use and very inexpensive per gallon purified. Some hikers don't like the "medicine" taste of chemical purifiers, and none are recommended for use day after day. Several types of filters are available. The prices and weights of these devices vary greatly. Make sure that any filter you consider removes the *giardia lamblia* cyst. Also pay attention to the volume that can be filtered before a replacement filter is needed (replacements on some models are expensive), and check the ease of cleaning both filter and pump. Names frequently seen on the A.T. are: Katadyn, First-Need, Timberline, Potable Aqua, and PolarPure.

Kits: The numerous small items needed on a thru-hike can be divided by function into kits. Components of each kit are best stored together in a stuff sack or Ziploc-type plastic bag for easy retrieval from your pack. You will need a first-aid kit and a grooming kit. You may also want to have a miscellaneous and repair kit for storing those odds and ends that are necessary to keep your equipment functioning on the Trail.

- *First-aid kit:* aspirin or equivalent, antibiotic ointment, fungicide, powder (for chafing), antacid tablets, lip balm, a few Band-aids, roll of 1-inch-wide gauze, 2 x 2-inch sterile pads, large sterile pad, surgical tape, 2-inch Ace bandage, and moleskin or equivalent. Optional items include allergy pills, cortisone cream, sunscreen, eye drops, toothache medicine, diarrhea medicine, Second Skin, scissors, tweezers, and snakebite kit. Many thru-hikers carry insect repellent, Muskol being the most frequently seen. Some also carry Avon Skin-So-Soft bath oil, which seems to repel no-see-ums.
- *Grooming kit:* toothbrush, toothpaste, floss, biodegradable soap, comb or brush, and nail clippers. Optional items include deodorant, razor, mirror, wash cloth, towel, and tampons. The new synthetic-chamois towel is considered a useful item by many thru-hikers.
- *Miscellaneous and repair kit:* spare parts for pack and stove, Thermarest repair kit, extra flashlight bulbs and batteries, boot glue, boot waterproofing, and sewing kit (include some big needles, top-stitching thread, and a thimble).

Knife: A knife is needed only for gear maintenance and food preparation, so these uses should determine the type of knife you select for your trip. Most thru-hikers take a Swiss Army-type knife with a variety of specialized blades and gizmos. You will need a good cutting blade and a can opener for food preparation, and a screwdriver and auger for doing maintenance on boots and pack. Some hikers swear by the scissors feature, and others are just as convinced that the corkscrew is a necessity.

Light sources: You will use a flashlight very little during most of your hike (it doesn't get dark until 9-9:30pm in midsummer), but your life may depend on it in an emergency, so choose a good one. The types most often used on the A.T. are waterproof and built to take abuse. A spare bulb and an extra set of batteries (which can be the ones in your radio if it uses the same size batteries) should be standard accessories. You should attach your flashlight to a loop of cord, so that it can be hung around your neck when you leave a shelter to "visit the woods" during the night. If you are the type that arrives late in camp, you may want to consider using a headlamp instead of a hand-held flashlight, so that your hands can be free to prepare supper after dark. If you plan to read or write in your journal after dark, include a candle lantern (or at least a candle) in your gear. This will conserve battery power and disturb other hikers less. Names frequently seen on the A.T. are: MagLite, TeknaLite, Panasonic, and Petzl.

Compass and whistle: You will probably never have to use either your compass or whistle. Nevertheless, you should have both with you at all times in the woods. The compass you choose can be basic but should be rugged and dependable. Equally important, you should know how to use it. If your compass doesn't come with instructions, check your library for a book on navigation. The whistle can be the inexpensive kind made of plastic. The reason for having a whistle is to allow you to call for help with a minimum of effort. You can blow a whistle a lot longer than you can yell, and it makes noise that carries farther.

Rope and cord: Rope isn't necessary on a thru-hike, but you will need light-weight nylon cord (1/8"-1/4" diameter is common) for hanging your food bag and for hanging clothes to dry. A 50-foot length should be more than sufficient, unless you are using a tarp for shelter. Melt the ends with a lighter to keep your cord from unraveling. New boot laces can be cut from this cord as needed.

Radio and cassette player (optional): Many thru-hikers consider these items out of place in the woods, but just as many wouldn't be without them. If you do decide to carry one or both, limit your listening to earphones. You will be able to get FM-stereo stations everywhere on the Trail. A radio is also a useful source of accurate weather information. As for listening while hiking, keep in mind that your best defense against a rattlesnake is the noise it makes.

Hiking stick (optional): A hiking stick is not a necessity for hiking the A.T., but many thru-hikers carry one because they find it so useful. Some even use two. On a rainy night in a shelter many years ago, a group of thru-hikers made a list of more than 200 ways in which a hiking stick could prove useful (for balance while hiking, for fending off dogs, for finding hidden stepping stones in muddy areas, for clearing weeds, for propping up a pack, for leaning on while talking to someone in the middle of the Trail, for hanging clothes during breaks, *etc.*). A number of companies make both wooden and metal models, some telescoping for easy travel. A ski pole makes an inexpensive hiking stick. Whatever you do, don't count on finding a good hiking stick in the woods. Few thru-hikers do. A name frequently seen on the A.T. is "Tracks" by Cascade Design.

Datapouch: Quite a bit of information must be carried along on an A.T. hike. The specifics will vary, but most thru-hikers carry the *Data Book*, this handbook, guidebooks and maps, a journal, an address book, hike schedule, postcards, nature guides or finders, and a pen or two. You should keep all of these items in a large Ziploc-type bag and/or a zippered nylon pouch for quick reference and for protection from the elements. You will also find it very useful to have all of this data, plus your wallet, together in one pouch when you are going to the post office, making telephone calls, and doing other chores in towns.

Using old equipment: Don't buy new equipment just to be fashionable on the Trail. It's true that some thru-hikers make much ado about having the very latest gear, but most don't. If you have old equipment in good condition, consider using it on your hike. It may be better than some of the newer stuff on the market.

Buying new equipment: You may be able to use some of your old equipment, but chances are you will have to purchase most of the gear needed for your hike. In selecting new gear, pay attention to weight, durability, and price, recognizing that few products will be superior in all three categories. Of the three, weight may at first seem the most important for a thru-hike. Total pack weight is the critical factor, however, not the weight of any single item, so you have some leeway. Put your spending emphasis on the major items (pack, boots, sleeping bag, stove). You can cut corners on the less important items.

Sources of equipment: You have two main sources, mail-order catalogues and local outfitters. The mail-order catalogues will have a larger variety and will probably be slightly less expensive, even after you pay shipping charges, but you'll have to wait a few weeks for delivery. Your local outfitter will usually have less inventory, but you can see equipment first-hand and make sure that it is exactly what you need. You also have the advantage of dealing face to face with a person. This is very important when you have problems with a piece of equipment out on the Trail. A good outfitter will then be able to deal with the manufacturer as an insider on your behalf, something difficult for you to do from a telephone booth at roadside.

Making equipment: If you have access to a sewing machine, you can make some of your simpler gear, such as stuff sacks. It's a lot of fun, the gear will be exactly the size you need, and you will often save money. Mail-order catalogues and many local outfitters still sell nylon cloth by the yard, and a wide range of accessories is available.

Back-up equipment: As you assemble the equipment for your trip, you will undoubtedly end up buying new gear to replace older items. These older items become useful back-up equipment you can send for as needed during your hike. The best way to do this is to pack all back-up items in plastic bags, one item per bag, and number them. Next, make a list of the numbers and the corresponding items. Take a copy of the list with you, and leave the numbered gear with the person who will be sending it to you. When you need an item, ask for it by number. This method doesn't require your helper back home to be an equipment expert and virtually eliminates mistakes.

Loading your pack: Once you have all of the equipment and clothing for your hike on hand, load your pack to see how everything fits together. Follow the weight-distribution instructions supplied by the pack manufacturer (heavy items on top, or whatever). Make sure that the pack is balanced from side to side. This is very important. Don't place a four-pound tent on one side unless you balance it with four pounds of something else on the other. Try to have everything packed inside the pack or inside a nylon sack strapped securely to the pack. Have a place for everything, and make sure that you have easy access to emergency items (first-aid kit, knife, flashlight, rainwear, *etc.*). With the pack fully loaded, check to make sure that it rides comfortably, and, if not, make adjustments until it does. Finally, verify that your raincover is large enough to cover your fully-loaded pack.

Boots

You should assume that you will need at least two pairs of boots during your thru-hike. This assumption doesn't mean that you must purchase two pairs before you start, but it does mean that you should be prepared to buy a second pair somewhere along the way.

Types of boots: Three main types of boots are seen on the A.T. The type you select will probably be determined by your wallet as much as anything else, but durability and weight are equally important on a thru-hike.
 • The light-weight fabric/leather boots usually weigh less than 2 pounds per pair. They are fairly flexible and thus give only moderate arch and ankle support, but allow good foot movement, which gives you a feel for the Trail. Few models are waterproof, unless they have a Gore-Tex liner. Fabric/leather boots aren't as durable as all-leather boots, but thru-hikers have been getting 500-800, sometimes 1,000 miles per pair.
 • The light-weight all-leather boots weigh 3-4 pounds per pair. They aren't as flexible as the fabric/leathers but give more arch and ankle support and are somewhat more durable. The all-leather construction offers more protection from water, even without a Gore-Tex liner. Thru-hikers have been regularly getting 1,200-1,600 miles per pair, occasionally going all the way in them.
 • The heavy-weight all-leather boots often weigh 6-7 pounds per pair. They are solidly built and almost indestructible. You won't wear out a pair of these boots with normal Trail use, even on a thru-hike, but the extra weight will slow you down and cause leg weariness, unless you have very strong legs.

Buying boots: If you've never bought hiking boots before, you will probably be better off buying them from a local outfitter. Most good outfitters can help you determine your requirements, can fit you properly, and will allow you to take boots home on trial. If your boots wear out, buying new boots from the Trail is not a major problem. Leave buying information with your helper back home, or find an outfitter near the Trail. You may even want to prearrange with your local outfitter for having a pair of boots sent later. What if your boots fail during your hike? Boots usually fail gradually, not all at once, so you should have at least a week or so of warning. When you buy your boots, you should ask your dealer about procedures for replacing boots should they fail (not wear out) on the Trail. If they say that you must return the defective boots to the manufacturer or a dealer for inspection before replacement or repair, look for another brand of boot or another dealer. Good manufacturers and outfitters will realize that you can't sit around a Trail town for a week or two waiting for new boots. Names frequently seen on the A.T. are: Vasque, Hi-Tec Sports, Merrell, Asolo, Danner, Raichle, Limmer, Tecnica, New Balance, L.L. Bean.

Fitting boots: When shopping for boots, always try them on with the socks you plan to wear on your hike. If possible, walk around with a loaded pack to see how the boots feel under weighted conditions. Make sure your toes don't jam against the front of the boot when you lunge forward (as you will when going down a mountain). Also, make sure that the boot shape fits your arch and verify that the boots bend where your feet bend. Check the heel cup to ensure the shape fits your heel. If boots don't feel good in a store, they won't improve on the Trail, so don't buy them. Keep shopping until you find a perfect fit.

Breaking in boots: Begin breaking in boots immediately, even if the manufacturer claims no break-in time is needed. The secret to breaking in a pair of boots is to put them on and walk and walk and walk some more. The more you can wear your boots before your hike, the fewer foot problems you will have on the Trail. You also have more opportunity to discover boot defects and improper fit. If you develop blisters during the breaking-in process, remember that these are blisters you won't have on the Trail. During break-in, you can also test to see if softer insoles are needed.

Waterproofing boots: None of the popular waterproofing products will keep water out of your boots, but they will deter it. Leather boots should be treated often to keep them supple and to prevent cracking. Small amounts of waterproofing can be carried in a plastic film canister. Special treatments are available for fabric boots.

Socks: The health of your feet will depend in large part on the socks you choose. Socks for your trip should be designed specifically for hiking and have padding placed where your feet take the most abuse. Especially important are the areas under the ball of the foot and around the back of the heel. Synthetic and wool hiking socks are both widely used on the A.T. Most thru-hikers feel that synthetic socks are cooler during hot weather. If you use wool hiking socks, you may want to use a thin, synthetic sock liner. You should carry as many pairs of socks as you can on your thru-hike, or plan to wash a few pairs often. Clean socks have more loft and give better performance. Names frequently seen on the A.T. are: ThorLo, Wigwam, and Fox River.

Clothing

You should choose your clothing carefully, with function in mind, taking into account that on the A.T. it must keep you safe and comfortable in cold, heat, wind, rain, sun, sleet, and snow, and it must give you protection from rocks, limbs, briars, poison ivy, stinging nettles, and insects. In addition, Trail clothing must be durable, easy to clean, and lightweight.

Layering: Your selection of individual clothing items should be guided by the concept of layering, meaning the use of several thinner layers of clothing together to create thicker layers. Layering gives you the ability to adjust ventilation and insulation as your body heat increases or decreases. This is very important on a thru-hike. For example, when climbing a mountain and generating a lot of heat, you can strip down to a single layer. When sitting around camp and producing less body heat, or when hiking in cool, windy conditions, you can add layers for warmth. In very cold weather, you can add many layers to keep warm. Layering allows you to use a few well-chosen garments to keep comfortable in any weather at any level of activity.

Warm-weather clothing: Most of your trip will be hiked in sunny, warm weather with no rain (really, it will!). On such days, you will wear a shirt, shorts, socks, boots, and little else. The shirt and shorts you use should be lightweight and easily washed, made of quick-dry nylon or similar material, and they should be loose to allow freedom of movement. You should have at least two sets, perhaps more in hot weather. A long-sleeved shirt will feel good in camp and deter insects. Underpants are optional and unneeded for hiking if your shorts have a liner. A pair of cotton underpants makes a comfortable set of Trail pajamas and helps keep your sleeping bag clean. Most women hikers use a hiking bra, but some do not. You may want to have a pair of long pants to protect against sunburn early in the trip, and they are useful for protection from insects later. A lightweight jacket (windbreaker-type or equivalent) is needed to prevent chilling when you stop for breaks, except in the hottest weather, and a lightweight sweater feels good in camp on many evenings. During the hottest summer months, either the jacket or sweater can be sent home, but plan to have one of them with you at all times.

Cold-weather clothing: The time of year you start and end your hike, and the direction you choose for doing your hike, will determine how much cold-weather clothing you need. If you plan a normal start (mid-March to mid-April from Springer, late May or early June from Katahdin), you will have mostly cool-to-warm days, but days and evenings can drop below freezing occasionally, and you may have some snow and extended cold at the higher elevations. In addition to the warm-weather clothing items above, you will need to add light- or medium-weight thermal underwear (synthetic, not cotton). You may want to substitute a heavier sweater or equivalent garment for the lightweight sweater, and you may want to carry a parka instead of the lightweight jacket. A ski cap is a necessity (the first cold-weather item you should put on while hiking), and gloves feel good in cold, windy conditions. This combination of warm- and cold-weather clothing should be sufficient for any early-spring weather conditions you will encounter. In the rare event you get caught in more severe weather, you can always lay over in a shelter and stay in your sleeping bag until conditions improve. If you plan to start your hike earlier than the normal period mentioned above, you will need to get information about doing a winter hike, which is beyond the scope of this discussion.

Rainwear: You will need some type of rainwear for an A.T. thru-hike, not so much for keeping rain out as for keeping body heat in. Most thru-hikers use a rain jacket and pants, constructed either from a breathable fabric (such as Gore-Tex) or from coated nylon. They can then wear jacket, pants, or both as conditions require. A jacket with zippered underarms is very helpful in controlling body heat. A few people use chaps instead of rain pants to save weight, but chaps have to be tied to a belt or something to hold them up. Some use a poncho, which is not ideal rain protection in windy conditions and can't be easily adjusted to protect against wind-chill effects. Gaiters will help keep water out of your boots. Whichever type of rainwear you select, know that nothing will keep you dry from your own sweat when you are hiking up a steep mountain with a pack. In hot weather, you will probably choose to leave your rainwear in your pack when it rains.

Town clothes: Some thru-hikers carry a set of town clothes in addition to their Trail clothing. This is purely optional, depending on your dedication to fashion. Most thru-hikers consider sneakers or camp shoes worth the added weight. Sneakers are a welcome change from wet boots in town and feel equally good in camp. Many recent hikers have used aquasocks and/or sandals for camp and town wear.

Clothes bag: A stuff sack is needed for keeping your clean clothing together in your pack (and makes an excellent pillow at no additional weight). Your clothes bag should be wrapped in a plastic bag, and (very important) you should always have one set of dry clothes protected in plastic in case of emergency. Dirty clothing, which is often wet and sweaty, should be stored in a separate plastic bag.

Buying clothing: The two main sources for buying backpacking clothing are, again, mail-order catalogues and local outfitters. As was the case with equipment, each has advantages and disadvantages. Mail-order catalogues offer more variety but may not save much money. Many brand-name clothing items seem to be priced about the same no matter where you buy them. Your local outfitter will have fewer choices of clothing, but you will be able to try on items and make sure they fit. You will probably be better off buying major clothing items (rainwear, parka, *etc.*) from a local outfitter if you've never had experience with these items.

Back-up clothing: As the weather changes from spring to summer and then to autumn, you may need to change or add items to the clothing you are carrying. Back-up clothing should be packaged, numbered, and listed, as you did back-up equipment, so that it can be sent without error when you request it from home.

Food and supplies

Your choice of food will be determined by nutrition, ease of preparation, cooking time (fuel consumption), weight, taste appeal, and cost. Two types of food are most often seen in the food bags of thru-hikers. One is freeze-dried food, which is very lightweight and needs only hot water for reconstitution but is very expensive per meal. The other is dried (and some canned) food from off the shelves of grocery stores, which is slightly heavier than freeze-dried in weight per meal, takes slightly longer to cook, but costs considerably less. Most thru-hikers use foods found in grocery stores, whether they buy them before or during their hikes. A few folks dehydrate their own food, and this type of food seems to work quite well, depending on the experience of the preparer. Vegetarians can eat well on the Trail but should not count on finding an abundance of suitable items in smaller stores, especially in the southern Appalachians. Fresh foods can be carried for the first few days out of towns.

Methods of resupply: Typical thru-hikers eat 200-300 pounds of food during their hike. Since you obviously can't carry that much weight with you from the start of your hike, you will have to obtain food as you go along. There are several ways to do this on a thru-hike (and, it might be added, living off the land is not one of them):

   • *Grocery stores:* The simplest way of resupplying is to purchase everything you need from grocery stores near the Trail. Using this method, you won't have to plan meal menus before your hike (they are dictated *en route* by availability of items in stores), and you can easily vary your diet to suit changing food preferences over the course of the journey. You will have to be adaptable, though, since the items you prefer may not always be available in small stores or may not be available in the small quantities you need. Prices will often be considerably higher than you pay back home (unless you live in a major metropolitan area, in which case prices may actually be lower). On the other hand, you won't have to pay postage for mailing food packages or make arrangements for having them mailed.

• *Maildrops:* The surest way of resupplying is to mail food packages to yourself and pick them up at post offices near the Trail. Using this method, you are assured of having exactly the items you need in the quantities you need. Specialty items, which are often impossible to find in many Trail communities, are as easy to include as regular fare. The nutritional value of your meals can be controlled, but you will have to plan menus before your hike, of course, and you will have to guess at the quantities of food you will want once you develop a Trail appetite. The cost of postage for mailing packages can be offset somewhat by buying food in bulk.

• *Combination:* While both the resupply methods above have been used very successfully on end-to-end hikes, most thru-hikers prefer to use a combination of mailing food packages containing major items and supplementing them with grocery-store purchases along the way. This combination method allows great flexibility. For example, you can mail nutritious breakfast and supper items in your packages, and buy easy-to-find lunch and snack items from grocery stores to provide variety.

Breakfast: A nutritious breakfast is as much a necessity on the Trail as at home, but simplicity is equally important if you don't want to spend all morning in camp trying to cook it. Many thru-hikers limit breakfast cooking to boiling water, although a few eat cooked meals every morning. In warm weather, most eat a cold breakfast, which has just as much nutrition and energy. You should choose breakfast items that can be eaten either hot or cold during the summer months. Some of the frequently seen breakfast components are granola cereals and bars, regular cereals, instant breakfast mixes, instant oatmeal, instant grits, cream of wheat, pancakes, French toast, Pop-Tarts, powdered milk, honey, margarine (added to cereals or pancakes to taste), bagels and cream cheese, instant coffee, and Postum.

Lunch: A good lunch around midday and/or several smaller snacks during the day will be required to keep your energy level up. Few thru-hikers cook lunch unless the weather is very cold. In that case, they heat water for soup and beverages. Once the weather warms, virtually no one eats a hot lunch on the Trail. Some of the frequently seen lunch components are loaf bread, English muffins, bagels, hard cheese, cream cheese, crackers of all types, peanut butter, jelly, sardines, canned tuna, Vienna sausages, beef jerky, instant soups, cookies, junk foods of all types, dried fruit, gorp (usually peanuts, raisins, M&Ms), Kool-aid, Wyler's, Gatorade, and hot Jello (as a beverage).

Supper: A hot supper is preferred by most thru-hikers, as much for morale as for nourishment. In fact, the only thing that will keep you going on some of the rougher afternoons is the thought of a good supper at the end of your ordeal. Suppers should be easy to prepare, preferably needing only one pot for preparation, since often you will have to cook your evening meal when you are very tired and the shelter is full. Most thru-hikers eat several courses (*e.g.*, soup, glop, and dessert), cooking one item and eating it before cooking another. If you are typical, you will eat your supper early, around 5pm, then nibble on snacks for the rest of the evening. Hikers occasionally share components to cook group suppers at shelters. These occasions are socially rewarding, and the culinary results often tasty. Some of the frequently seen supper components are mac and cheese dinners,

Lipton Pasta and Sauce dinners, Lipton Rice and Sauce dinners, Minute Rice or instant potatoes with soup mixes, Ramen noodles, Stove-top Stuffing, canned tuna/chicken/ham, dried beef, Vienna sausages, beef jerky, hard cheese, Jello (chilled in spring or stream), instant pudding, cheesecake, dried fruit, cookies, gorp, powdered milk, and squeeze margarine or butter. Some of the military-type ready-to-eat meals are quite good, but they are fairly heavy for the calories they provide, and the quantities may be small for a hungry thru-hiker.

Calories and nutrition: How many calories will you need per day? Some thru-hikers eat like birds and seem to have no ill effects. Others eat as many as 7,000 calories a day and still want more. The average seems to be about 3,800 calories a day, and that will be a good figure for your planning. Remember, you can always buy more high-calorie food along the way if you need it. Equally important on an extended hike is nutrition. A one-a-day-type multivitamin and mineral supplement is good insurance. You should also try to maintain the following ratio in your basic diet: 10% protein, 60% carbohydrate, and 30% fat, based on the ratio recommended for high-stress athletes by the U.S. Olympic Committee. Your doctor, who knows your health, can give you specific advice on calories and nutritional balance.

Supplies: You can save money by sending supplies to yourself. A roll of toilet paper should be placed in every food package, along with garbage bags (for wrapping sleeping bag and clothing), a large Ziploc (for garbage), small Ziplocs (for repackaging food), film, notebooks (to continue your journal), and any other items you regularly use but need only in small quantities. Be careful with soaps or detergents packed in maildrops. Their smell can taint food items. Pack unscented detergent only.

Buying food and supplies: You can usually save money by buying food and supplies in bulk. Catalogue outfitters sell bulk quantities of freeze-dried food that you can repackage. Most large towns have a discount food warehouse or co-op. The savings can be substantial.

Buying food along the Trail: The grocery stores along the Trail vary widely in inventory and prices. In general, you will find smaller stores in Trail towns in the South, especially below middle Virginia, and in Maine. Just about everywhere else, you will be able to reach a large supermarket without too much trouble. Going into grocery stores of any size will be one of the real delights of your trip.

Scheduling

Many thru-hikers prefer to do no scheduling before their hike, doing their planning piecemeal as they go along the Trail. Others prefer to have a prehike schedule. If you so desire, you can begin drafting a daily prehike schedule for your entire trip as soon as you have decided where and when you will start your hike, selected a target date for finishing, and received your *Data Book* from ATC. Keep in mind it will be impossible to follow this prehike schedule exactly once you begin your hike. Nevertheless, it has great value as a planning tool—for familiarizing you with the details of the Trail, for selecting maildrops, for predicting with some accuracy the food and supplies that should be sent to each location, and for budgeting expenses during your hike. Work on your prehike schedule until you have one that shows reasonable mileage for each hiking day, includes maildrops and sufficient town breaks, and fits within your starting and finishing dates. While you are making scheduling adjustments, you may want to check your daily plans against the map profiles to ensure you haven't scheduled a high-mileage day in difficult terrain. There are several other adjustments you may want to include in your schedule:

• Schedule lower mileage days for the first week or two.

• Schedule a short hiking day into a town, stay overnight, and schedule a short hiking day out. This plan allows you a full 24 hours in town, which is normally more than enough time to get everything done and to rest as well.

• Schedule days of varying length, with longer days toward the end of a section (when your pack is lighter), and schedule some no-hiking days occasionally (*e.g.*, a typical section might be: short day out of town, average day, average day, long day, long day, short day into town, day off in town).

• Schedule some two-day breaks along the way, perhaps at Hot Springs, N.C.; Damascus, Va.; Delaware Water Gap, Pa.; Hanover, N.H.; and Monson, Maine. These long breaks will allow your body to rest and relax to a degree that is not possible on an overnight stop. Long stops are also good opportunities to repair equipment.

• Schedule somewhat shorter days through the rocks of Pennsylvania (Duncannon to Delaware Water Gap), the White Mountains of New Hampshire (Glencliff to Gorham), and the Mahoosucs of Maine (Gorham to Stratton). You will beat yourself to death if you try to maintain 20-mile days through these sections.

• Don't count on being able to use the AMC huts through the White Mountains. You may be able to get a reservation by calling ahead, or by working for room and board, but the AMC hut system is not geared for thru-hikers and is used by relatively few. For scheduling purposes, count on using the designated campsites and shelters through the Whites. You can always make different arrangements when you get to the AMC area and have access to more information.

• Schedule higher mileage through the Shenandoah National Park and Great Smoky Mountains National Park if you wish. The Trail through both is relatively easy, although it is a shame to rush through these beautiful parks. Camping, except at designated shelters or campsites, is restricted in both areas.

Direction/starting time

You can do your thru-hike either south-to-north (the most popular way) or north-to-south. If you start down South, you can begin earlier in the year. Most of the bitter winter weather is usually over in Georgia by mid-March. You may still encounter occasional days and nights with freezing temperatures, and possibly some snow at the higher elevations as late as May, but, for the most part, you will be following the progression of spring northward. You will also be in the main flow of thru-hikers, meaning businesses and facilities that cater to hikers will be open. On the northern end, you will miss the blackfly season (June-August) and catch the foliage season (late September) in New England. If you begin in Maine, you must wait until late May or early June to begin, and there may be snow on the ground in some places. Blackflies and bogs will be bad in Maine. Streams will be raging. Early vacation crowds will be overrunning the Whites. Water in springs will possibly be low from New York to Virginia, and late-summer growth will be rampant in the southern Appalachians. Ice and snow are almost certain in the Smokies. Finally, you end up in Georgia during the October-November hunting season. However, you can have a more solitary hike by going against the flow, and southbounders seem to enjoy their hikes to the same degree as northbounders.

Average daily mileage

It is important for planning purposes to know the average miles per day that you will need in order to complete your hike in the time you have available. Determine a tentative starting date and a target finishing date. From a calendar, calculate the total number of days available for doing your thru-hike. Use the number of available days in the formula below to figure the average miles per day. The formula takes into account the hiking time you lose while in towns, taking rest breaks on the Trail, *etc.* and will be of great help in drafting your daily schedule. However, keep in mind that it is, at best, an approximation. Use it as a planning tool, not a rule.

$$1.2 \times (2{,}142.9 \text{ miles} \div \text{number of available days}) = \underline{\quad\quad} \text{ miles per day}$$

Maildrops

The number of maildrops you plan to use for resupplying will be determined by the food weight you want to carry between town stops and the pace at which you do your hike. Obviously, the more food weight you can carry and the farther you can hike each day, the fewer maildrops you will need. Having a small number of maildrops is not of prime concern, however. A compromise between the number of maildrops and total pack weight is best. Most thru-hikers carry 5-10 days of food (weighing 10-25 pounds), which allows them to hike 75-150 miles without resupplying. Most use a total of 15-25 maildrops. Your plans will probably be within these ranges. The towns you select for picking up maildrops should be towns that are regularly used by thru-hikers. The post offices in these Trail towns will hold packages almost indefinitely, whereas other post offices may send your maildrop back home after 10 days. It is also good to pick towns that have other services, such as laundromat and grocery store. Maildrop packages should be mailed a minimum of 10 to 14 working days prior to your due date at the post office. Be sure to compensate for holidays and weekends when calculating the mailing dates. A copy of maildrop locations and due dates should be carried with you on your hike, or the information should be noted in your *Data Book* for quick reference on the Trail. **Important:** Do not send UPS/Federal Express packages to a post office. They will not accept them.

Maildrop packaging/labeling: The boxes discarded by beverage stores are very strong, to protect glass, and make excellent maildrop boxes. Avoid thin cardboard boxes. Use a 2-inch plastic wrapping tape (avoid duct tape), and wrap tape completely around each box in several directions. Use a self-adhesive label, printed or typed clearly as follows:

> Your Name
> c/o General Delivery
> City, State, ZIP Code

Place the phrase "Hold for A.T. hiker" in the lower corner of the box or label. You may want to write your last name, destination of the maildrop, and ZIP Code in pencil on the box (under the label), for insurance just in case the label detaches. The Postal Service rarely loses maildrop packages that are properly wrapped and addressed, so take the time necessary to do a good job.

Et cetera—

Getting mail: Communicating with family and friends from the Trail is not a problem. You can pick up a telephone or write a letter from a Trail town. For the ones back home, however, trying to figure how to write someone with a constantly changing address can be confusing. You can help them communicate with you by giving them the list of your town stops (with ZIP Codes and due dates) before you leave. You also need to explain the method of addressing general-delivery mail (shown above). Hikers who do this find that many folks will send encouraging notes, cookies, and other tokens of support.

Carrying money: Traveler's checks are the easiest and safest way to carry money on the Trail. All businesses near the Trail accept traveler's checks, but you should avoid large denominations (the latter is true for postal money orders as well). Bank cards can be used to obtain money in some locations, but not all, so you should obtain a list of locations before you leave. Credit cards are handy if you have to order equipment from the Trail, and they are accepted at many facilities for food and lodging.

Having family/friends join you: Family and friends will want to share in your adventure, but think twice about having them hike with you unless you are prepared to slow down to their pace. Several weeks after you begin your hike, you will be cranking out the miles with ease. Those who join you will not be toughened to the demands of the Trail, and trying to keep up with you will not be their idea of fun. Many thru-hikers have found that having family and friends join them in Trail towns for dinner and relaxation is a better visit for everyone concerned.

Taking pictures: Photography on the Trail is a bother, no matter what equipment you are using. A camera means extra weight in your pack, and you have to stop and remove your pack every time you want to record a scene. Even professional photographers have chafed under the demands of doing photography under Trail conditions. Still, most former thru-hikers will tell you that the photos or slides they took on their trip are now among their most treasured keepsakes and that the extra weight and effort was worth it. If you are not an experienced photographer, you will probably do better with one of the small, lightweight 35mm automatic (autofocus, autoflash) cameras. They are easy to use in difficult conditions and produce very good results for amateurs. The decision to use slide film or print film depends on how you plan to use your pictures after your hike. If you think you will be sharing your pictures with large groups, slides are the way to go. If you will be sharing them mainly with family and friends, prints are easier to use and more personal. Use either 100, 200, or 400 ASA film for best results. A small table-top tripod (Lite-Pod weighs less than 2 oz.) will allow you to include yourself in some of your shots if your camera has a self- timer or remote shutter control. You can protect your camera by keeping it in a Ziploc bag in your pack.

Keeping a journal: Writing down the details of your trip is like taking pictures. It is a nuisance but later proves valuable as a means of recalling the events of your hike. Most thru-hikers use a small ruled notebook for recording their thoughts. Spiral-type notebooks are inexpensive, lightweight, and easy to use in the shelters, where most journal entries are made. Few hikers write in their journal as they hike along during the day. You should keep your journal in a Ziploc-type bag for protection from moisture. Helpful hint: Each day, instead of writing a diary to yourself, pretend you are writing a letter to someone back home who knows nothing about the Trail. You'll be much more descriptive. You'll also have an easier time writing letters when you reach town — they'll already be written!

Studying nature: Time invested in the study of nature before your hike will greatly enrich your time on the A.T. Any library has wildlife books and guides that will provide the information you need to begin your appreciation of nature's creatures. In addition, you may want to learn more about trees, wildflowers, berries, and ferns as you hike. An excellent set of inexpensive, lightweight guide-finders is available from the Nature Study Guild, Box 972, Berkeley, Calif. 94701.

Suggested reading

• *ATC Member Handbook** (published by ATC). The official introduction to ATC, containing a brief history of the Trail project and presenting the programs and structure of the organization.

• *Walking with Spring,** by Earl V. Shaffer (published by ATC). The narrative of the historic first A.T. thru-hike in 1948, told in simple prose and poetry by the man who did it.

• *Hiking the Appalachian Trail,* edited by James R. Hare (Emmaus, Pa., Rodale Press, 1975, two vols.). The narratives of the first 46 people to hike the entire A.T. It is now out of print but available from many libraries and occasionally advertised in the *Appalachian Trailway News.*

• *Mountain Adventure: Exploring the Appalachian Trail,** by Ron Fisher (Washington, D.C., National Geographic Society, 1988). The story of the Appalachian Trail today, as interpreted by a writer and photographer Sam Abell of the National Geographic Society.

• *A.T. Fieldbook: A Self-Help Guide for Trail Maintainers,** by William Birchard, Jr., and Robert D. Proudman (published by ATC). A pocket-sized guide that is filled with the basic terms and practices of Trail maintenance.

• "*The Appalachian Trail: Main Street, USA,*" by Jim Chase (Backpacker, September 1987).

• "*The Appalachian Trail: A Tunnel Through Time,*" by Noel Grove (National Geographic, February 1987).

Suggested video

• *Five Million Steps,** by Lynne Wheldon, 90 E. Union St., Canton, Pa. 17724. Fourteen 1986 thru-hikers are interviewed and shown hiking, one per Trail state, plus many scenes of places on the Trail.

• *Trail Magic,** by Carol Moore, P.O. Box 960, Laguna Beach, Calif. 92652. The A.T. Class of '90 as seen through the eyes of an 1989 thru-hiker. Interviews, scenes, and sounds that capture the essence of the Trail experience.

• *How to Hike the Appalachian Trail*,* by Lynne Wheldon, 90 E. Union St., Canton, Pa. 17724. Twenty-two thru-hikers with 60,000 miles of A.T. hiking share their experience.

Suggested accessories

"*The Official A.T. Answer Shirt*," designed by Carol Moore, P.O. Box 960, Laguna Beach, Calif. 92652. T-Shirt with answers to the questions most frequently asked by nonhikers, displayed across the front. (Have you seen any bears? *etc.*) $10 plus postage.

(*) Items with an asterisk are sold by the Appalachian Trail Conference, P.O. Box 807, Harpers Ferry, W.Va. 25425; or call 304-535-6331.

1992

JANUARY						
S	M	T	W	T	F	S
			1	2	3	4
5	6	7	8	9	10	11
12	13	14	15	16	17	18
19	20	21	22	23	24	25
26	27	28	29	30	31	

FEBRUARY						
S	M	T	W	T	F	S
						1
2	3	4	5	6	7	8
9	10	11	12	13	14	15
16	17	18	19	20	21	22
23	24	25	26	27	28	29

MARCH						
S	M	T	W	T	F	S
1	2	3	4	5	6	7
8	9	10	11	12	13	14
15	16	17	18	19	20	21
22	23	24	25	26	27	28
29	30	31				

APRIL						
S	M	T	W	T	F	S
			1	2	3	4
5	6	7	8	9	10	11
12	13	14	15	16	17	18
19	20	21	22	23	24	25
26	27	28	29	30		

MAY						
S	M	T	W	T	F	S
					1	2
3	4	5	6	7	8	9
10	11	12	13	14	15	16
17	18	19	20	21	22	23
24/31	25	26	27	28	29	30

JUNE						
S	M	T	W	T	F	S
	1	2	3	4	5	6
7	8	9	10	11	12	13
14	15	16	17	18	19	20
21	22	23	24	25	26	27
28	29	30				

JULY						
S	M	T	W	T	F	S
			1	2	3	4
5	6	7	8	9	10	11
12	13	14	15	16	17	18
19	20	21	22	23	24	25
26	27	28	29	30	31	

AUGUST						
S	M	T	W	T	F	S
						1
2	3	4	5	6	7	8
9	10	11	12	13	14	15
16	17	18	19	20	21	22
23/30	24/31	25	26	27	28	29

SEPTEMBER						
S	M	T	W	T	F	S
		1	2	3	4	5
6	7	8	9	10	11	12
13	14	15	16	17	18	19
20	21	22	23	24	25	26
27	28	29	30			

OCTOBER						
S	M	T	W	T	F	S
				1	2	3
4	5	6	7	8	9	10
11	12	13	14	15	16	17
18	19	20	21	22	23	24
25	26	27	28	29	30	31

NOVEMBER						
S	M	T	W	T	F	S
1	2	3	4	5	6	7
8	9	10	11	12	13	14
15	16	17	18	19	20	21
22	23	24	25	26	27	28
29	30					

DECEMBER						
S	M	T	W	T	F	S
		1	2	3	4	5
6	7	8	9	10	11	12
13	14	15	16	17	18	19
20	21	22	23	24	25	26
27	28	29	30	31		

1993

JANUARY						
S	M	T	W	T	F	S
					1	2
3	4	5	6	7	8	9
10	11	12	13	14	15	16
17	18	19	20	21	22	23
24/31	25	26	27	28	29	30

FEBRUARY						
S	M	T	W	T	F	S
	1	2	3	4	5	6
7	8	9	10	11	12	13
14	15	16	17	18	19	20
21	22	23	24	25	26	27
28						

MARCH						
S	M	T	W	T	F	S
	1	2	3	4	5	6
7	8	9	10	11	12	13
14	15	16	17	18	19	20
21	22	23	24	25	26	27
28	29	30	31			

APRIL						
S	M	T	W	T	F	S
				1	2	3
4	5	6	7	8	9	10
11	12	13	14	15	16	17
18	19	20	21	22	23	24
25	26	27	28	29	30	

MAY						
S	M	T	W	T	F	S
						1
2	3	4	5	6	7	8
9	10	11	12	13	14	15
16	17	18	19	20	21	22
23/30	24/31	25	26	27	28	29

JUNE						
S	M	T	W	T	F	S
		1	2	3	4	5
6	7	8	9	10	11	12
13	14	15	16	17	18	19
20	21	22	23	24	25	26
27	28	29	30			

JULY						
S	M	T	W	T	F	S
				1	2	3
4	5	6	7	8	9	10
11	12	13	14	15	16	17
18	19	20	21	22	23	24
25	26	27	28	29	30	31

AUGUST						
S	M	T	W	T	F	S
1	2	3	4	5	6	7
8	9	10	11	12	13	14
15	16	17	18	19	20	21
22	23	24	25	26	27	28
29	30	31				

SEPTEMBER						
S	M	T	W	T	F	S
			1	2	3	4
5	6	7	8	9	10	11
12	13	14	15	16	17	18
19	20	21	22	23	24	25
26	27	28	29	30		

OCTOBER						
S	M	T	W	T	F	S
					1	2
3	4	5	6	7	8	9
10	11	12	13	14	15	16
17	18	19	20	21	22	23
24/31	25	26	27	28	29	30

NOVEMBER						
S	M	T	W	T	F	S
	1	2	3	4	5	6
7	8	9	10	11	12	13
14	15	16	17	18	19	20
21	22	23	24	25	26	27
28	29	30				

DECEMBER						
S	M	T	W	T	F	S
			1	2	3	4
5	6	7	8	9	10	11
12	13	14	15	16	17	18
19	20	21	22	23	24	25
26	27	28	29	30	31	

Contributors

The author wishes to thank the following people who contributed information and ideas for use in this publication:

Lawrence Auspos ("Lightning Larry"), Wilmington, Del. • Dr. William Babson ("Blades"), Plymouth, Mass. • Joe ("Grey Owl") and Lenna Barrett, Pryor, Okla. • John Bauer, Willingboro, N.J. • Dennis ("The Cuda") and Virginia ("The Hobo") Booher, San Antonio, Texas • Leslie Booher and Kenon Garcia ("The Dynamic Anglican Duo"), New Harmony, Ind. • Craig Carpenter, Gainesville, Ga. • John Clark, Ridgewood, N.J. • Jacqueline Corrieri, Elizabeth, N.J. • Ken Cruse, Jr. ("Night Stalker"), Franklin, N.C. • Mark D'Andrea ("Sojourner"), Pearl River, N.Y. • Robert Dandelion ("Dandelion"), Warren, Vt. • Miriam and Roger DiPeppe, Backing Ridge, N.J. • Richard Dreselly, Brunswick, Maine • Andrew Dunakin ("Sloth"), West Hartford, Conn. • K.V.A. Erickson ("Minnesota Slow Foot"), Minneapolis, Minn. • David Esposito ("Ringo"), Milford, Conn. • Jean Feldman ("Jeanie Appleseed"), Chapel Hill, N.C. • Charles Fisher, Manchester Center, Vt. • Robert Fletcher, Denton, Pa. • Bill and Laurel Foot ("The Happy Feet"), Lynchburg, Va. • Carl Freiberg ("Marathon Man"), Fairfax, Va. • Paul Gaitanis, Richmond, Va. • Dick George ("The Georgia Gypsy"), Macon, Ga. • Lory Gordon ("Dr. Strange"), Cleveland, Ohio. • Jonathan Haas ("Eagle Green"), Media, Pa. • Bryce Hammack ("Oregun"), Portland, Ore. • William Hanaway, Wayne, Pa. • William Heckman ("$2 Bill"), Fleetwood, Pa. • "Honey Bear," Staunton, Va. • David Hughes, Chamblee, Ga. • Richard Hughes, Chamblee, Ga. • Ben Jacks ("Lentil Ben"), Portland, Maine • Geoff ("Curious Geoff") and Jodie ("Rainbow-Jo") James, Rockport, Maine • Phyllis Jobes ("Wildflower"), Cortland, Ohio. • Michael and Helen Jones ("Smiles in Our Hearts"), Newagen, Maine • Frank Krajcovic ("The Merry Slav"), Clifton, Va. • Tony Lagana ("Morning Dew"), Waynesboro, Va. • Louis LeBlanc ("Vagabond Lou"), Woonsocket, R.I. • Holly Leeds ("Doc"), Showlow, Ariz. • Al Lemire ("Keys"), Worcester, Mass. • Bill and Tim Leslie, Gettysburg, Pa. • Jack and Jennifer Long ("The Happy Hoofers"), Lutherville, Mo. • Gail Lowe ("One of the Chosen Wheeew"), Detroit, Mich. • Ronald McCowen ("Less miles, more smiles"), New Port Richey, Fla. • Jim Martin ("Jimmy No Stop"), New Bern, N.C. • Dorothy Mauldin ("Ankle Express"), Marietta, Ga. • Katherine Moore ("Marmot"), Escondido, Calif. • Noel O'Brien, Wilmington, Del. • Bill O'Brien ("Sprained Rice"), Meriden, Conn. • Vince Pernice ("Vagabond Vinny"), Colonia, N.J. • Laurie Potteiger ("Mountain Laurel"), Harpers Ferry, W.Va. • Aaron Rosenbloom ("Vegemite") and Carol Fleischman ("Dr. Marmot"), Philadelphia, Pa. • Paul Sanford, Meadowbrook, Pa. • Bunny Schneider ("Mountain Marching Mamas"), Bradenton, Fl. • Loren and Betty Schroeder ("The Kansas Kids"), Maple Hill, Kans. • Brian Shirley, Waynesboro, Va. • George Shollenberg, Bethel, Pa. • Chris Siegfried ("Sore Feet"), Naples, Fla. • Mary Sturtevant ("Possum"), Londonderry, N.H. • Capt. James Tidd, USNR (Ret.), Odessa, Fla. • Richard Tobias, Rohrerstown, Pa. • Tom Tomicki ("Zee"), North Franklin, Conn. • Pete Van Why ("The Cheshire Cat"), Norfolk, Conn. • George and Helen Verhey, Conyers, Ga. • Sam Waddle,

Chuckey, Tenn. • Greg Walter ("Weathercarrot"), Yardley, Pa. • Mort and Jean Weiser, Reading, Pa. • Jarrod West ("Rastabear"), Hot Springs, N.C. • Kay Wood ("Grandma Kay"), Dalton, Mass. • Dave Zimmerman ("Six Toes"), Wilmington, Del.

A special thanks is extended to the hundreds of hostels, businesses, and public facilities that responded to questionnaires about their services, and to ATC staffers (especially Brian King, Kay Bresee, Jean Cashin, and the regional reps—Morgan Sommerville, Mike Dawson, Karen Lutz, Kevin Peterson, and their staffs), A.T. club members, NPS and USFS personnel, and postmasters, who provided valuable information, too.